About the Author

Tony was born in Isleworth, west London and attended institutions of learning in that area, gaining a reputation for being a trouble-maker, upstart, delinquent and least likely to succeed amongst his three siblings. He surprised everyone, including himself, by forging a successful career in advertising as a copywriter, starting out at Saatchi and Saatchi in the early eighties. He wrote many famous adverts for blue chip companies, gaining him a leadership position as a creative director and agency founder. Tony has received multiple global awards for his creative writing. He lives in Richmond, Surrey and north Dordogne.

Château Shenanigans

Tony Malcolm

Château Shenanigans

Olympia Publishers
London

www.olympiapublishers.com
OLYMPIA PAPERBACK EDITION

A CIP catalogue record for this title is
available from the British Library.

ISBN: 978-1-80074-561-2

This is a work of creative nonfiction. The events are portrayed to the
best of the author's memory. While all the stories in this book are true,
some names and identifying details have been changed to protect the
privacy of the people involved.

First Published in 2023

Olympia Publishers
Tallis House
2 Tallis Street
London
EC4Y 0AB

Printed in Great Britain

Dedication

For Cosmo, my fifteen-year-old labradoodle who now resides permanently in the beautiful gardens of Château Gros Puy.

Acknowledgements

First and foremost, thank you to my wonderful wife Zakia. This has been her dream and she's worked like a titan to bring it all to life. She has been my biggest motivator and toughest critic in writing the book when enthusiasm was waning and pessimism set in during the pandemic. Thanks to my kids, Yazmin, Angus and Mackenzie whose legacy the château will be for all their help and love they've poured into this place. My son-in-law Tom has shared their amour for Gros Puy and takes real pride in this place. I'd like to thank all the dedicated and hardworking tradespeople who have put an incredible amount of effort into resurrecting this granite castle to former glories. I also want to thank my sister Elaine Bracken for always being there for me and my best mate Andy Chambers for keeping my spirits high with our shared sense of insane humour honed over fifty years of friendship and bonhomie, even through times of intense sadness and grief. I want to thank all family members and friends who've supported me as I've forged my way through this bizarre journey called life. My mum Eileen Newing, my dad Gordon Malcolm not forgetting the very important presence in my life, my grandad William (Mick) Newing. There are so many people who spring to mind I should like to thank, my beloved and dearly departed brother Dez, who left this mortal coil at the age of forty-three, leaving a hole so large, it nearly swallowed me up in a bottomless pit of depression and despair. His memory lives on in me and his spirit lives on in the lunacy of the writing in this book. Anyone who has contributed to Château Gros Puy with a paint brush, a hammer, a monkey wrench, a shovel, a strimmer, a bottle of red wine and a shoulder to cry on, I thank you. I want to pay tribute to the people I have worked with in my long career in advertising. Those who've nurtured and employed me, partnered up with me, taught me the craft of writing, kept me sane in distressing situations and given me a slap on the back when I mysteriously did something that was good, even when battling through immense self-doubt and dreadful bouts of anxiety. This book offers hope to those with mental health issues knowing that there is light at the end of that bleak, dark tunnel. I'd like to finish by remembering those who influenced me, including Zak's mum Kathleen, her extended family including her brother Art and her sister Safia. We've all been through a lot together. It would be remiss of me to not mention the permanent pillars in my life like Fulham FC and all their devoted fans. We will prevail. My faithful hound Cosmo who ran with me to escape that demon black dog and walked the back lanes and forest paths with me and died here in the Dordogne in my arms, you'll always be with us. I have to also mention other pets of course, Teddy and Coco the cats (RIP Teddy) and brief resident cat at the château, Loopy, who was a fine mouser. All the other characters you'll come across in the book, I thank you for making an impression that moved me to write words about you. I would like to sign off by thanking Olympia Publishing, who saw something in this book that they thought worthy of publishing. Let's hope it leads to Château Shenanigans 2, the documentary, the DIY show, the film, the merchandise and the blue plaque on the wall when I pop my clogs.

Prologue

As the coronavirus bites hard in the UK and I sit confined to my second floor Richmond flat, without a garden, I have been given plenty of time for reflection on the trials and tribulations of owning a French château in the Dordogne.

The fact I cannot get to the location where I have one and a half hectares of land and a vast property to be isolated in, only adds to my frustration of not being able to access this idyllic part of the world in the spring of 2020.

I could attempt to get there in my car with British number plates, but probably would be stopped by le gendarmerie at every juncture and junction on the eight-hour drive once through the Eurotunnel. Who knows, even owning a French residence with the relevant paperwork doesn't guarantee I won't be turned back at the border. Apparently, they've restricted journeys to one person per car and I don't fancy hiding under a blanket for the entire trip down there.

I've thought of going by ferry or flying, but with all flights and crossings postponed until further notice, I'm marooned here for the foreseeable future.

My eldest daughter Yazmin, who will one day inherit the historic pile and grounds, is so desperate to get out there, she's looked into chartering a private plane to transport us there at a cost of £7,000. Unfortunately, we don't have a landing strip on site or that sort of cash.

We thought she was joking, but she is having such

withdrawal symptoms from the charms of life at Gros Puy, the small hamlet outside of the village of Abjat-sur-Bandiat where the château is located, that desperation is creeping in.

This is the powerful draw of what we have purchased inside the Périgord Vert region of the Dordogne.

As I write, the grounds will be springing into life with a proliferation of flowers, herbs, fruits, berries, bushes, hedges and trees.

I have arrived there before in spring to see poppies in such abundance they could arouse suspicions that I'm running an opium farm on the premises.

The grass there will be reaching waist height by now and getting through it all will take hours of strimming and mowing.

So much needs to be done to lick the château into shape for the summer, panic levels start ramping up about the condition everything will be in by the time restrictions have lifted and we can get over there again.

Even the tradespeople we have been using for the last two years are in lockdown, so remote project management that my wife Zak has been in charge of, with her iron fist in a velvet glove, is to no avail. I think all of us sometimes wonder where the velvet glove has been hidden. When she wants something done and wants it done now, it's just iron fist sans any sort of softening outer coating.

As a copywriter of four decades working at many of the UK's most creative agencies, the only thing I can constructively do, other than binge watch Netflix, watch daytime TV or drive the downstairs people mental by pounding the Wii-Fit exercise board with my ever-burgeoning bulk in isolation, is write this book about our venture and adventures of the time we have already spent at Château Gros Puy.

I am now a freelancer whose last contract just ended in late March as Covid-19 tightened its grip on London and with budgets being put on ice during the crisis, not likely to get paying work for a while to come.

As that information about my career to date suggests, I am of an age where retirement isn't too far over the horizon.

The French residence has all been part of a grand plan that has been prompted by a love of France and the many glorious holidays we have spent as a family enjoying the abundance of natural attractions and culinary delights our Gallic neighbours have to offer.

We started our search for the ideal property long before 'Escape to the Chateau' reached its current level of popularity. Peter Mayle's 'A Year in Provence' also piqued interest in Brits about the challenges of living in France way before the Channel 4 programme found fame.

Peter was a copywriter like myself drawn to this part of the continent with all the fantastic produce reaped from the fat of the land and the laid-back attitude of those who are card and baguette-carrying natives. For those of a certain generation, Peter was famed for writing the slogan 'Nice one, Cyril' for the Wonderloaf bread company. Perhaps he repurposed it in France for a baguette company with the line 'Très jolie, Cyrille'.

His storytelling painted a vivid picture of the provincial or provençal lifestyle in those southern landscapes, but revealed warts and all the challenges of day-to-day living faced by an Englishman in a foreign land.

There are over 150,000 expats in many regions of France that moved from the UK and now live, work and thrive there. Something about large areas of France feels frozen in time, with tradition observed diligently and cultural norms followed to the letter to halt so-called progress in its tracks. I mean, in their lockdown, boulangeries and tabacs remained open as they exercised their fraternié, égaliterié and liberté to carry on eating bread and smoke like cheminées.

This stubbornness to join in with the world's insatiable appetite for progress has its appeal to many who are trying to escape the speed and constant change of modern-day life in a place where the sun shines brighter and hotter than it does in the land of Anglo Saxons. It probably accounts for why it is the most visited country on the planet with eighty-nine million tourists flooding in annually to enjoy the landscapes, wine and culinary delights on offer.

Not many of the expats I have met have regretted that decision to relocate, even though I have met the majority of them during the stunning summer months when we spend more time in Gros Puy before shutting up in the winter when everything slows to l'escargot pace.

I am a novice compared to the many of those who upped sticks and made the move permanently. I have a long way to go before I can consider myself a pillar of the local community or a French resident. I remain a rosbif in the land of chateaubriand.

My French is very limited but my desire to create a haven in the forests and fields of Dordogne knows no bounds. I've mastered the essentials like 'deux bière en pression s'il vous plaît mate' and 'd'accord' when repeating the round and when somebody tries to engage in conversation with me, I'll nod in violent agreement and retort 'oui monsieur' or 'madame'.

They could be saying anything like 'have you ever worn women's underwear while doing backstroke across the Channel shouting "up periscope"?'

Zak will often pull me up on this, asking 'so what were

they saying then?' to which I'll smile politely and use the first distraction technique that comes to mind… "oh look, a monkey on a bike," before turning on my heel and sprinting off in the opposite direction.

This book takes you on the initial stages of the journey my family and I are taking to forge a new life outside of everything familiar and routine in our lives.

Some have given us huge encouragement and support. Others have called us crazy and deranged.

They're probably right as the budget we set aside for the master plan was blown ages ago and Zak's eyes start doing that side to side motion whenever I ask for an actual figure causing her voice to go all high pitched as she tries to waffle her way out of trouble.

Bottomless pit is an overused metaphor of the financial situation we find ourselves in and it often strikes me that we may have bitten off more than we can chew.

Then I think, what have you worked so hard for all these years? My erstwhile grandfather who was a wily old sod with a philosophy for every occasion would say to me 'never be a slave to money, son, always make money a slave to you." Wise words Mick, even if you did fritter your own money away down the bookies.

Feel the fear and do it anyway is a book I've read and a philosophy I aspire to. Or my version is 'if you're bricking it, go and build something with that shit'.

Now the world has proven itself to be a very unpredictable and dangerous place, doubts creep in about how much of a financial commitment we've taken on and I don't think we are alone in feeling trepidation about what's happening in the future.

The flip side to that is realising life is short and we need to fill it with memories and experiences be they negative or positive. My family is ninety per cent creative and ten per cent adaptive. What we lack in knowledge we make up for in enthusiasm and fortitude.

We were all together in 2004 in Sri Lanka when the tsunami wiped out our hotel and we were lucky to survive. That gives you a different perspective on life that you never know when your time is up, so make the most of every second.

Zak was diagnosed with stage 3 cancer in 2015 and had to undergo a gruelling period of chemotherapy that changed her outlook on life. We all take our mortality for granted in our earlier years and things like cancer happen to other people. When it knocks on your door, however happy your home, it has a devastating effect on the whole family. Life doesn't look the same anymore and even when given the all clear, the spectre of it returning hangs over you like a dark cloud.

We were going to hold off until all the kids were financially independent and no longer at home, so It did act as a positive impetus to ramp up the efforts to stop dreaming and start doing. If we have anything to thank cancer for, it comes in the shape of a château and all the challenges that brings, adding much-needed optimism when pessimism had dominated our lives for so long.

I myself have had a series of knock-backs in business, having failed to conquer the US when I took a job in Chicago in 2014 and trusted the wrong person in setting up a company in Dubai in 2015 which failed to turn sand into gold.

I had been working at an agency called Leo Burnett in London for virtually ten years when I was to receive some devastating news. My younger brother Derek, or Dez as he preferred to be called, died suddenly after a prolonged battle with mental illness. He was forty-three with a young family. I received that fateful phone call while on a shoot for Crunchy Nut Cornflakes in Prague, with John Lloyd the director and Rob Brydon, the star of the campaign. Both of them were absolutely amazing in offering me their condolences and support.

Dez's death tore the heart out of me. He was eight years my junior, but age difference mattered not a jot and we were extremely close. We played and watched football together, shared a love of music, loved a party and I was best man at his wedding. I gave two speeches about my brother, one, which had people in hysterics at his wedding, and one that had people in tears at his funeral.

He was an extremely charming and funny man and his loss left a huge chasm in my life that I was struggling to fill with anything meaningful.

My sudden decision to leave Leo Burnett, just before my tenth anniversary there, was ill thought through. I just wanted to escape from everything in the UK that reminded me how fickle life can be to turn something brimming with joy into a black hole of negativity.

I'd been to Chicago with Leo Burnett on a couple of occasions and when their rival agency DDB came knocking to offer me the executive creative directorship of their part of the McDonald's account, I accepted without consulting anybody who knew the lie of the land in the land of the free.

In the states, McDonald's had been in free fall after many consecutive months of posting declining sales figures. The once booming appeal of fast food was now being rejected by millennials in favour of healthier options. This was a case of trying to turn around a vast, lumbering tanker with the agility of a speedboat. I had entered into a shark pool of competition between agencies, as even the senior management at Oak Brook were under intense scrutiny.

I arrived in Chicago to a hail of welcoming press. I was on the front page of the Chicago Tribune business section for two days on the trot. I ran into Rahm Emanuel, the mayor of Chicago at the time, in a renowned Italian deli called Denny's and I got my picture taken with him holding the Tribune front page, which he signed for me.

I was being treated like a Messiah coming to save one of their most prized institutions. It was like the clouds had parted and the sun was flooding through, even though it was in the middle of the polar vortex which had frozen Lake Michigan with several feet of pack ice. The coldest temperature of all time was recorded in the Windy City while we were residing there.

From a very promising start and a feeling we'd moved into a new chapter in a new land, making great new friends and a vibrant new social life, things started to unravel.

A new ball-buster of a marketing director came into McDonald's and cleared out all the top people I'd allied myself with, including the overall creative head who was responsible for bringing the 'I'm lovin' it' end line into existence. To this day, nobody has been able to kill that line after many assassination attempts.

Things became increasingly stickier after the McDonald's Congress where the world of burger flippers gather to admire new innovations in their markets, do a bit of networking and to celebrate their successes. This was held in Florida in a huge conference hall just outside Disney World and to give you a sense of the scale, they had hired Sting to be the star turn at the evening gathering. I wondered how he balanced that out with his ethics and got approval from his vegan wife Trudi, but then a noise went ker-ching in my head. Probably if Ronald McDonald had approached him, he might have well sung 'Don't Stand So Close to Me'.

I even got to meet Ronald McDonald in the flesh and greasepaint, which was a bit surreal and apparently there are seven people around the world who don the clown uniform and red wig to emerge through a *Stars in Their Eyes* mist to say 'Tonight, Matthew, I'm going to be Ronald'.

Usually ads from all over the world get screened at this event, but the mood was so low, only one was deemed acceptable. Thankfully it was one I was responsible for, featuring a promotional AR trick shot game on fries packets that celebrated the forthcoming soccer World Cup hosted in Brazil. It felt like a triumph at the time, but it was just a false sense of security.

Mrs Ball-buster got up on stage and gave everyone a bit of a dressing down to dampen the mood and demanded everybody raise their game. She had come from a large car company and was credited with having turned around their fortunes. Now she was here to kick ass in the world of fast food. This seemed a world away from fast cars, but hey, someone thought she was the right fit.

In the ensuing clean sweep where she got her big broom out, even the Global CEO fell victim, to be replaced with a Brit I'd worked with back in the UK head office of East Finchley. The old NIH (Not Invented Here) rule came into play and I was one of the casualties along with many more heads from the head office who had to wave goodbye to their McJobs. I had no idea the States was quite so cutthroat and corporate, but this was a steep learning curve for me.

I had been there ten months and moved my family across the pond. My daughter Mackenzie was at Ogden School and her next term was to be the beginning of her exam year. I had a decision to make and didn't have long to make it. In the words of the Clash, should I stay or should I go now?

My visa said I was an alien of exceptional talent, which made me sound like ET doing a juggling act and I had plenty of time left on it to find a new position in the US. But if that didn't come to fruition, what about Mackenzie? We couldn't gamble on her future.

We took the bold decision to move back to the UK and get her back into a British school and settle her in. I would be able to pick up a new job in London and we'd just put the whole American adventure down to a wonderful but weird experience. This we did, moving into a lovely cottage in St Margarets in West London but to be honest, what it had in abundance in charm it lacked in space. We moved all our belongings back including Cosmo, our labradoodle and two cats Teddy and Coco. They really didn't like this jet-set lifestyle. The two cats had become housebound in Chicago in case the huge rats that ran around in the alleyways ate them, or they ate the rat poison put out all over our part of town.

We also brought back our newly acquired 4x4 and massive sleigh bed, which you'll hear more about later. We had to remove a top floor window to get it into the cottage, as there was no way it could get in through the front door and up the narrow staircase.

I was in a vulnerable emotional state when a friend who had considerable experience of working with channel programming in the UAE, convinced me he had valuable high net worth contacts in the UAE who would all but guarantee us phenomenal success in the Middle East and beyond. Even when I got cold feet and attempted to pull out, pressure was brought to bear that made me feel like I was being disloyal by saying no. Zak rightfully pointed out what a soft touch I was being, but my faith in my own ability made me believe this could be the start of something amazing away from the grimness that haunted my every waking moment in the UK.

We started the agency in Dubai, but from the outset I realised my partner was not the right man for the MD job. He did indeed have very strong connections in the UAE, but they were all very old and all in disciplines that didn't lend themselves to growing an advertising agency.

I was soon to discover that business was done in a very different manner there, where someone not saying no, didn't mean they were saying yes. It is deemed extremely rude to say no in Arab circles, so you'd be chasing new business thinking you were on the cusp of landing it, only to find you'd been strung along.

The history of the UAE from the days of the Trucial States and foreign intervention had built a wall of distrust that was very difficult to overcome. Brits who'd once held favour there, were now way down the pecking order of preferred partners and we had to work twice as hard to even get an audience with people that were the decision makers. It still felt like it hadn't fully recovered from the big financial crash of 2008 when Brits fled to avoid insolvency, which is illegal in the UAE, abandoning their prestige cars at the airport in their hurry to beat a hasty retreat to the UK.

I did love Dubai, moving from the coldest place on the planet to the hottest. There's something to be said about waking up every day to the sun, warmth and cloudless skies and I loved the villa I had rented with its big air-conditioned rooms and pool in the back garden. The family would come and join me to stay during holidays and go on excursions into the desert for safaris and days out on the beaches, local attractions and the water park. The summer months, however, were unbearably hot and even on the short hop from your air-conditioned house to your air-conditioned car parked outside, you would get soaked through with perspiration.

Friends would come and stay in the cooler months and I was motoring to the airport on a regular basis ferrying people back and forth to the villa. It is true though, that everything is a facade and the treatment of migrant workers is nothing short of scandalous. Even expats in the region leave much to be desired in their behaviour, getting totally hammered at hotel brunches on Friday's, which is Dubai's Saturday because, as they constantly moan, there's nothing else to do.

Even when all my senses were telling me I was pushing water uphill, I soldiered on as my partner seemed to lapse deeper and deeper into denial. He brought his wife over and made her head of new business, even though she was totally out of her depth. The pair of them weren't converting any new business and at one stage, they even took a three-week holiday in Italy with their family, leaving me to man the fort alone. They did get us into the offices of some big hitters, but the responsibility to take full charge of converting business was falling more and more firmly on my shoulders.

It was during this time Zak phoned me and told me she'd been diagnosed with cancer. I was totally shell-shocked. I sought support from my partners, but they just became more and more obstructive, telling me how crucial it was, I stayed in Dubai to support the business. I returned to England to be with

Zak through some of her chemotherapy sessions, but in hindsight, I should have just gone home immediately and stayed there, no questions asked.

In the end, she came over to help me close down the villa and sell all the furniture online and extricate me from the situation under the cover of darkness.

The business was dissolved after much acrimony with the partners, but I was back in the UK and now life looked very different. We had sold our house to move to Chicago and were now living in a rental house that had more space than the cottage and a bedroom that could actually house the gigantic sleigh bed. Zak's treatment had come to an end, and now she was art director of a local magazine and working shifts as an autocue operator at the BBC.

I started picking up freelance work and slowly, we found a new normal, but we had been totally changed by our different experiences. Our family had ridden this particularly tumultuous wave with us and we were now just keen to be settled. Our son Angus came back from the Illinois Institute of Technology in Chicago after completing his Masters, Mackenzie successfully completed her exams in the UK, despite living through mental health problems while battling through her mother's cancer treatment and Yaz had her own flat with Tom in the gentrified enclaves of London Fields.

While I'd been in Dubai, Zak had taken on a project. With some of the proceeds of the house we sold pre-Chicago, to flip a two bedroom flat on Richmond Hill. She saved on rent, while undergoing treatment and unable to work, by living in it with Mackenzie for a year. When that eventually sold, the profit was used to buy the château.

The prospect of a quieter life in France now seemed like

the antidote to the turmoil we had lived through and the château has turned out to be the perfect panacea from pandemonium.

It focuses the mind, offers a beacon of hope when something unexpected like coronavirus turns your world upside down and hopefully will become an ongoing business venture that's far less cut throat than advertising.

Each member of the family now has a vested interest in the grand old place, which keeps us all together and galvanised.

Confrontation and conflict is never far from the surface end family, with strongly held opposing ideas often in evidence until order is restored and a consensus is reached after an appropriate period of sulking has run its course.

So strap yourselves in for a bumpy ride whether through the turbulence of air travel, pothole filled country roads or the unpredictable nature of owning a piece of history from the thirteenth century that likes to regularly throw spanners into the rusting old works.

I've called it Château Shenanigans, not just because of the alliteration, but because that perfectly describes what we've been through to date. This is more than a project, it is a labour of love to breathe new life into a building that has fallen into disrepair and much in need of TLC to bring it back to its former glory.

It has come into the possession of the Malcolm Clan and hopefully it will remain that way for generations to come.

Because an Englishman's home can be his French castle.

The Search

What better excuse to spend a long weekend just over the English Channel than to book in some viewings of French properties that are for sale.

This has taken us to several different regions to find that location that combines ease of travel with the right level of splendour and wow factor.

We have seen some outstanding places with palatial potential for renovation, with swimming pools, external barns and stables that could house small armies.

We started our adventure in Normandy travelling by car ferry. We chose this location because it was an hour outside Paris with a high-speed train stopping at a nearby station. This was to be one of our first forays into discovering how much bang we could get for our buck in terms of space and character. Or should I say how much Eureka we could get for our Euro with the exchange rate at that particular time.

In my memory, every time we ventured across Le Manche to view, the sun was shining brightly as though someone was trying to shine the best possible light on this idea. We even stayed in character properties in beautiful grounds with very accommodating hosts to set an example of what was possible if you set your mind to it.

The first property we viewed was a magnificent looking abode. It had an enviable position above the town set amongst fir trees and was every inch the quintessential property of genteel folk of yore. A central tower had a rounded exterior inside of which was a winding staircase. Stone steps with ornate balusters supporting heavy stone banisters dropped to the garden and converged with wider stairs descending into a front garden. The tower was the central core of the house with two wings spreading out with elegant uniformity. The architectural flourishes you'd expect from such a regal mansion introduced us to the grandeur to come. Stone carvings around the windows, Corinthian columns and ironwork supporting glass awnings were in evidence to inform the visitor the owner was, how you'd say in pre-revolutionary France, 'minted'. I was struck by how many windows there were, as the man who is often given the duty of running a shammy over the glazing at home.

We drove through ironwork gates and up a gravel driveway that encircled the mansion and pulled up outside the rear entrance. A cat sat on the marble doorstep as if the footman, ready to greet nobility and introduce us to the master and mistress of the house. An elderly French woman looked curiously out of the window like a startled ghost. Obviously, nobody had told her we were coming.

Thankfully, it wasn't long before the estate agent, a rather dandy looking chap with a waxed moustache, long flowing Llewellyn-Bowen type locks and winkle-picker shoes, turned up to take control. He had that sophisticated Franglais accent that added to the whole eccentric air he had obviously cultivated.

The elderly lady's daughter also turned up to join the entourage and monitor every reaction for genuine enthusiasm and we tiptoed past le chat like it was the guardian of an Egyptian tomb to enter the building. It was certainly beautiful with lots of wood panelling and period features in evidence and it had been divided up into about three different living spaces. On the ground floor, Maman had her own quarters to save her the trip up the winding staircase to visit La salle de bain. If they'd have fitted a stair lift, she'd just have got dizzy. We got lost going through door after door, floor after floor and then down into an enormous cave where a banqueting table could have fitted for entertaining guests amongst the racks of stored wine bottles. From this cavernous sous-sol, a set of steps leading up to double delivery doors opened up to emerge at the base of the tower beneath the front door. Throughout this rambling building, there were many rooms in a random order that suggested it had been divided up over the years into different apartments.

Eclectic, as a word, didn't do it justice with chosen colour schemes you can only describe as hideous and wallpaper designs that were enough to induce an epileptic fit, but we shuffled through oohing and ahhing, and nodding politely, poking our heads in at Maman as we voyeuristically peered into all her accommodations nooks and crannies. We felt as much under scrutiny as the mansion itself and probably over-egged the enthusiasm.

There were impressive elements like a split-level, boarded out loft room and a high-ceilinged ballroom with elongated windows where we could've danced all night. Alas! there was a huge crack that suggested advanced subsidence that stopped us coming back for more.

Emerging blinking back into the sunshine, we took a walk in the grounds, past a raised circular orangery to a swimming pool that nobody had swum in for some decades. The rainwater that had collected there wasn't something you'd want to practice your front crawl in unless you were doing an assault course in the army, but it had served as irrigation to a tree that had taken root in the deep end.

A tennis court with Medusa's hair net that her snakes had taken exception to strung between two posts, was enclosed in a metal chain fencing that resembled a moth-eaten string vest. The tarmac was strewn with cracks and hillocks to set balls flying off in all directions if they bounced off them. This wouldn't have passed muster with Wimbledon, unless of course we're referring to the banger-racing track.

Thrown into the bargain was an outhouse with the atypical hole in the ground that was abuzz with flies and filled with fossilised turds that could have dated from the renaissance period.

Somebody we didn't get to see and who probably wouldn't appreciate such noisy neighbours occupied a quaint little cottage near the entrance and the overall impression we left with was too much like hard work. I like tennis, swimming, dancing and drinking but not that much.

Of course, we knew these doubts would creep in nearly everywhere we looked, but I suppose we were beginning to define in our own minds what would be worth the effort and what would possibly bankrupt or kill us or both.

However, there was no denying this was a spectacular property that, for the right people, with the right vision, would make an epic place to live once Maman had departed either the property or this mortal coil, if she hadn't done so already and I, like the spooky kid in the film Sixth Sense, could actually see dead people that nobody else could.

It appears that French people are abandoning these character properties in their droves to live in more comfortable dwellings with all mod cons and less backbreaking work required to maintain. If you don't stay on top of maintaining such properties, they become run down, the grandeur quickly fades, things start crumbling around your ears and any dereliction of duty leads to a derelict pile of rubble.

If dilapidation isn't something that scares the living daylights out of you and you have the time, energy and financial resources to invest, there is a treasure trove of delightful Maisons out there waiting to be snapped up.

We knew this from visits to the French Property Show on a couple of occasions at Olympia, where we would salivate at an array of stands displaying available properties to gullible, sorry, I mean discerning Brits who were ready to make the leap.

The sale prices compared to the costs of a property of equivalent scale in the UK are mouth-wateringly affordable. You can buy a multi-storey, turreted château for the price of a one-bedroom flat in the suburbs of London.

After viewing another couple of run-down offerings, we squeezed in a trip to Paris where we headed to Versailles for a peruse of the home built for *The Sun King: Louis XIV*. This is something I would live to regret as looking over the splendid gardens with the carved marble fountains and immaculate, geographically concentric pathways, gave Zak ideas that I couldn't hope to emulate when the time came.

We had also been watching the Versailles series on TV and it painted a picture of flouncing about a staggeringly beautiful château in couture of flowing silks and velvet that looked the height of sophistication. I have since learnt there were a lack of toilets in the palace, so people would pee or poop where they stood, no doubt why Marie Antoinette favoured a large crinoline. Ironic, isn't it, that a woman in a crocheted bustle dress found favour as a toilet roll cover centuries later?

Unfortunate servants had to run around cleaning up after their masters and Versailles was renowned for a stench so bad, they brought orange trees inside to mask the whiff and it rightfully earned the reputation as being the filthiest palace in the world. Who says it was the peasants who were revolting in France, sounds like it was the aristocrats whose manners left much to be desired.

But back to the more hygienic days of May of 2017, where we made further appointments to see other suitable looking character properties a little more south in Normandy. The thrill of bombing down to Portsmouth to get a cross Channel ferry has always appealed to me. I suppose it dates back to the holidays we would take when I was a kid to go camping in Brittany with my mum, dad and three siblings, driving down to Dinard and Dinan where my parents had their honeymoon.

One property we went to view in Brittany held great promise and once again, we entered via a driveway that bordered a rather plain-looking field that was Le Jardin. We rolled into the grounds, which introduced us to a charming medieval homestead that was built in the formation of an L shape pivoting on the central turret.

The conical tiled roof with a weather vane was typical of classical French design. It didn't seem to be big enough to count as a château, but it had buckets of character and rustic charm. One wing of the home had an impressive archway which the car could easily fit through and you could imagine a horse-drawn carriage pulling to a halt beneath it for some grandiose guests to step out from before entering the building.

A millstone in the front courtyard now displayed a colourful floral display, bearing evidence to its former purpose, which was producing flour, not flowers. The ancient granite blocks of the main residence and outbuilding were covered in lichen and had escaped the French fondness of rendering that found favour as a fashion statement in centuries past, emulated by my parents in the 1970's by pebble-dashing our mid-terrace house to look like the top half of a FAB ice lolly dunked in hundreds and thousands.

We were welcomed by an extremely pleasant madame with a rural complexion and entered the home into a wonderful living room replete with a roaring fire and thick stucco walls. You could tell they were thick due to the windows being sunk deep into the granite stone, with sills you could quite easily curl up on in the sun's rays. The living room was tastefully furnished with period sofas and chairs and the large fire at the end had been lit to give the big room a cosy and homely feel.

We have sold enough properties to know all the tricks of the trade of flogging a property, like brewing coffee, baking cakes and getting a fire roaring in the hearth and even though past masters, we were falling hook line and sinker for this time-honoured tactic. It was a little chilly outside after all.

We ambled through to a very basic and small kitchen with a door that led through to the passageway between the main building and a disused outbuilding. Zak came up with a grand plan to open it up and fill the archways with huge sheets of curved glass to make a spectacular space complete with vaulted ceiling and exposed stone walls. As somebody who has studied glass and architecture at Saint Martins, I was confident she knew what she was talking about here and got very excited about the prospect.

Her work has been displayed at the V&A to add further confidence to my assumption. She probably was busking it, but I knew better than to question her. This would have made it into a spectacular cooking and entertaining space flooded with light. We walked up the steps inside the turret to the first floor and into a room that had a doorway to an exterior set of steps down to a well-stocked pond where we could see carp creating ripples on the surface. From this room we went up a few more steps and into a vast room with another fireplace inside it. Master bedroom, Zak muttered under her breath, quashing my immediate reaction of converting it into a man cave.

It was all falling into place and this was a real contender with an outbuilding that had been converted into a garage with a studio above where you could walk onto a balcony guarded by weathered gargoyles. Pros always come with cons and the price was more than we were willing to pay and although picturesque, the surrounding area was a little bland and uninspiring. When you come from Richmond, with a Royal Park on your doorstep, the bar has been set very high.

On this same trip we went to see other properties that we knew almost immediately weren't right. One was a long narrow building with a lot of land, its own carp filled lake and some very unusual features. In one bathroom the window was triangular and that unusual aesthetic continued throughout the building. I would describe it as Essex chic, which has its place in an Essex home owned by Joey Essex on The Only Way is Essex, but it shouldn't be the way in rural France.

The word potential was always in the forefront of our minds, but you have to feel it when you walk into a property. It's that intuition that guides you in these circumstances and you have to be able to see through cosmetic details and imperfections to envisage the wider picture. It was always when you added up the whole package that they would often fall short of perfection.

With a heavy heart, but a not too lightened bank balance, we marked that excursion down as a lovely break, but still were no closer to the French property we had set our hearts on.

Later that same year, with renewed enthusiasm and heightened optimism, Zak and I set off to mount another expedition to source that idyllic home from home, this time on a road trip that meandered ever further south.

There is an invisible line going through France above which, it is regarded as rainy and cold and below, warm and Mediterranean in climate. Zak's brother Art, who has already made the leap and bought a lovely mill building in the Pyrenees, convinced us that escaping Britain should also include leaving the grim weather behind.

Zak, whose heritage is half-Yorkshire, half-Indian, has definitely inherited the heat-loving side of that genetic equation and will always seek the sun, rejecting any voice in her head with a Sheffield accent saying, 'toughen up our lass, it ain't cold, you've just gone bloody soft'.

The majority of estate agents we met in France were Brits abroad, which helped with our rudimentary grasp of the French language. You would have to meet them somewhere like a car park or café, as they knew if they gave you the property address, you could cut out the middleman and go directly to the vendor.

We would follow them in their car to the mystery properties and they'd walk us through substantial living spaces with fireplaces you could stand up in and spectacular staircases you could imagine Marie Antoinette ascending maybe having a dump under her crinoline halfway down.

Acres of land were thrown into the bargain with outbuildings that could house entire families in their own right.

Aristocrats once inhabited these estates, before Madame Guillotine liberated their heads from their shoulders and here we were, mere peasants, being offered their palaces for a pittance.

Our third house hunting trip in October 2017 took us to an unpronounceable place called Richelieu in the Loire Valley to the first of the properties on our itinerary. We entered the town's inner sanctum through a single vehicle archway that emerged into a charming cobbled square.

Richelieu was the former hometown of Cardinal Richelieu who was immortalised in a villainous role in Alexandre Dumas's popular novel *The Three Musketeers*.

His residence was a huge, partly demolished castle, just outside the town's gates with acres of accompanying land now turned into a park. This was all very promising and looked like a perfectly picturesque place for us to start our quest.

We parked up la voiture and headed for a café in one corner of the square, which had the appearance of an abandoned railway station.

We ordered café au lait and watched the locals file in to enjoy refreshments ranging from crème de menthe to bière au pression. It also seemed to specialise in some sort of lotto with a booth dispensing tickets, and numbers appearing on an electronic board. Maybe the word Bingo is just a bit too, how you say, Angleterreish in France. Shouting out 'MAISON' when you've completed a line of numbers is too trashy for them, so they call it Lotto. Maybe they should combine the two words and call it Blotto, because that's what I'd have to be to get involved in a game like that.

This location was where we were to meet the delightful estate agents who turned out to be a married English couple who had moved here to flog domiciles.

They took us to a residence, a few miles out of town, which you entered through a small door within one side of bigger double doors that could open up to let a horse and carriage in, if the relatives came knocking. This took us into a big courtyard surrounded by a square of buildings connected by a main central annexe with loft space. This was above our heads as we walked in and we were informed that an owl lived in it. The droppings on the floor confirmed it spent some time here as a shitting tenant, undisturbed by humans who had abandoned this place some years previously. As a bird lover, this was a promising omen in my ornithological mind. French for owl is Hibou and Maison de Hibou struck me as a great name for the property.

Zak was *cooing* in that way I knew she was liking it. One thing, I had come to know through our years of house hunting is Zak likes her little runs through corridors and dark rooms. An explanation was given for this in a book her mum had about the Chinese horoscope. In the nicest possible way, Zak is a rat.

A rat isn't looked down upon as vermin in Chinese folklore, as it was the first animal that went to Buddha, so is revered for its resourcefulness. I, on the other hand, am an ox, which makes me a bit slow and ponderous and a lover of big open spaces. I also love nothing better than to be up to my gunnels in muck.

We meandered through the property that could easily be adapted, and knocked through to create delightful living spaces, albeit a little bit disjointed.

This part of the building was split level where the kitchen diner would have been installed and above, a studio cum sports room could have been reached up the wooden staircase.

The back garden was an orchard of trees, where to one side was a swimming pool. This piscine was surrounded by brambles and a little cracked around the edges, but nowhere near as decrepit as the pool with a tree sprouting out of it. The word piscine has always conjured up pictures of people pissing in the pool, which who knows, might have been the origin of the word's meaning.

Behind this were two more wooden beamed outbuildings, one that had been the shower room and changing rooms for the pool and another, a great big barn ready for renovation into a conservatory or workshop. All sorts of rusting garden equipment and a singular swing cane chair suspended from a main beam suggested it was a place where a reluctant gardener would have once hung out.

I could tell Zak was sold, hook line and sinker. Ox-boy wasn't feeling it so keenly, even though having a live-in owl appealed to me in a Harry Potteresque Hogwarts way. We did show enough interest to book a repeat viewing on our return trip to the UK, armed with a measuring tape, which no doubt got the agents' hopes up for a quick sell. It does appear that French properties can spend years on the books of the agent immobilier, hence the often-overzealous sales patter.

So back to Richelieu we went and into the town to a place that used to be a nursing home. It was built around a grand staircase with lots of width to the steps and spiralling banisters. It had a lovely townhouse feel to it over three floors and we were encouraged to look next door at a boutique hotel which was a similar building that demonstrated what you could achieve with a bit of imagination and a bulging wallet.

We walked through the big rooms, where no doubt the elderly residents lived out their last days with much of the paraphernalia to assist the infirm still in evidence. The lingering odour of stale urine still pervaded the entire building and probably would take some shifting.

Once again, the criteria for purchase were being narrowed, as we weren't impressed by the small garden and town living was something we were keen to avoid.

It was a shame that we hadn't stumbled across nirvana in this charming location, as we really liked the agents who would have made great company as we settled in and we had learnt how to say Richelieu correctly after having a competition to see who could pronounce it with the greatest authenticity in the car.

Ree-shirley-oo seemed to be the nearest we got to an accurate articulation.

Heading out of the Loire Valley, we drove two hours further south to a place called Luchapt, where we'd arranged to meet the estate agent called Clare near to the Mairie in a car park. We should have asked for an accurate physical appearance as we were walking up to any woman in the car park with furtive glances as if to say, 'Are you Clare?'

Maybe they thought we were British spies trying to meet up with our contact at a designated rendezvous. If we'd been wearing dark glasses and berets, twiddling flowers in the buttonholes of our lapels, which would have really aroused suspicions.

Clare did turn up, and we followed her to the next option on our list. A big house that overlooked the town on a gentle hill slope.

It was a substantial property with less renovation needed and wasn't without rustic charm, but there wasn't that little feeling you get in the pit of your stomach about it, where you try to conceal it from the owner with a poker face so you can barter on the price.

We forged further south to stay at a place outside Verteillac with a rather eccentric old fellah who had a big printed decal of his pug dog on a large electronic metal gate. I know us Brits are a nation of canine lovers, but this took the dog biscuit.

That evening, we ventured out for something to eat in the nearby town, but as we were in the winter months, not a single restaurant was open. We were passing a disused petrol station and spotted a mobile pizza truck with a plume of smoke billowing from a metallic chimney. Mobile pizza trucks are to be found doing their rounds all over France, and a Godsend when you've worked all day and don't fancy cooking in the evening. A quick leap into the car and a drive to a nearby car park, and you have that quintessentially Italian dish right here in the heart of France.

I have to say, as a global connoisseur of all things McDonald's, the golden arches serve up a far better experience in the home of gastronomy than elsewhere around the world, even offering up McBeer if you've got a thirst on.

On the road trips to and from the Dordogne, a stop off at Maccers was always factored into the journey, although the prices on their menu are far harder to swallow than those in the UK.

The Petrol Station Pizza turned out to be delicious and we made short work of them on our laps in the car before heading back to Monsieur Le Pug's place.

He also had a wife several generations his junior who, maybe unsurprisingly, heralded from Thailand. Did I say Thai bride? I wouldn't dream of being so assumptive.

We stayed in a wing of their house that had its own dining area, where she would come and serve us a breakfast that kept coming. No complaints from me of course, as it was a not too petit-déjeneur and kept us going all day long.

The only unnerving facet of the stay was when Monsieur would come into the dining area with his homemade wine and tell us all about his love life. I could sense Zak bristling as he spoke and thought any minute now she's going to projectile vomit all over him.

He seemed to know a lot about the property market in the area, and took us to meet a man who was renovating a place to a high standard just up the road. It wasn't our bag and it certainly wasn't in our price range, but the universal sign language of double thumbs up was enough to let them know we would get back to them if interested. We had got our sign language all wrong, mixing thumbs down with thumbs up, and to be honest the two-fingered salute made famous in Agincourt could have been used as we drove off.

The place we had actually travelled to view was just up the road, so we rolled out through pug-gates with our own electronic control we'd been supplied with and set off to see the next property.

It was the main reason we had driven this far, with Richelieu only a pit stop to fill our itinerary, as the pictures online looked ideal for our requirements. It didn't disappoint. The wooden door opened into a wonderful shaded courtyard with a spindly palm tree growing from the centre. The property flanked the yard on three sides with two floors, the top tier of which had beautiful stained-glass windows. It has a very ecclesiastical feel with an ornate cross carved into the wall outside.

It was owned by an English family who had closed it after the summer months, so it had that musty whiff that required a damn good airing. The family had good taste with some lovely furnishings that perfectly complemented the antiquated feel of the place. Inside one of the building's wings was an internal well. Of course this instigated the internationally recognised technique for gauging depth. Get a stone from outside, drop it down and wait for the splash.

Measuring the length of time the stone was hurtling through space, taking into consideration the size and velocity of the projectile, the gravitational pull of the earth and other factors we reached an accurate diagnosis.

Deep.

Venturing outside there were plenty of grounds in a mature garden of fruit trees, and a swimming pool beside a vast barn building that cantilevered to offer shade beside the pool. This created an ideal space at night to enjoy a barbeque beneath ambient lighting after a day of swimming, bombing and pissing about dans la piscine.

Boxes were being ticked left right and centre, but then a lorry passed on the road about 200 yards away. Another lorry roared past less than a minute later and all that good work went to waste. Living as we do under a flight path into Heathrow, traffic noise on a busy road nearby was a definite non-non. At this point, Zak was on the verge of tears as this was the place she had set her heart on, but she knew that traffic noise would shatter our peace in this otherwise tranquil location and that was an insurmountable problem.

So onward ever onward we drove, with Zak obviously hugely disappointed that her number one, odds on favourite had been flattened by a convoy of articulated lorries roaring past on a busy road.

We continued on our conquest to a beautiful little hamlet

called Sainte-Croix-de-Mareuil with a medieval church and grand château. The car only just squeezed through the narrow roads, and we parked up in the church car park.

The villa-style house was virtually next door, and we walked around the town to get a feel for the place while waiting for the agent. Bells rang out as we ambled around and this really had that *Jean de Florette* ambiance about it. We met with Dave, a bit of a wide boy who came from the barrow boy school of selling properties. 'Look I know I'm robbing myself, but I like your face and I tell you what, I'll throw in a barn for free and I can't say fairer than that."

With Dave giving a running commentary throughout, we walked into the villa that had a much more pristine feel about it over two floors with a wonderful terrace outside surrounded by stone balustrade. The inside had been finished to a high standard and Dave added 'You can move in tomorrow, no bother, it's a little gem this one, won't be around long before someone snaps it up, you mark my words."

I liked it, despite Dave buzzing in my left ear like an annoying gnat and it had a huge barn that could have doubled as an exhibition hall, set amongst beautiful grounds. Alas and alack, the price tag was as off-putting as Dave, and we needed something left in the budget to convert that mini Earls Court.

The last property of the day was a place that had its own big lake and a truffle orchard. 'Imagine that, your very own truffles, d'you know how much they go for at "arrods? Lovely jubbly, to you missus, fifty pound a pound."

We left Dave to prattle on to himself and spoke directly to the owners. They were an elderly couple who were charming and with his gravelly voice honed from years of smoking Gitanes, the husband kept talking to us about de truffe, which reminded me of Jack Nicholson in 'A Few Good Men' where he is in the dock at a military trial yelling 'you can't handle the truth'.

I, of course, have readapted that to put 'de truffe' at the end of the sentence in a French accent. Now, whenever I hear mention of truffles, 'You can't handle de truffe' is the standard reply, which Zak has learnt to tolerate along with my many other foibles, quirks and almost tourettes like outbursts.

They had a little dog that yapped like he'd also been smoking Gitane and I imagine he'd sniffed out more truffe than he could handle and was going off with the couple to retire in a new build somewhere.

One look at the property explained why they were abandoning ship. The place lacked any real charm, feeling more prefab than pretty fab and hadn't been touched since the '70s. Worse still was a road nearby which was too noisy for our liking and a deal breaker, no matter how Dave wrapped it up as something we'd learn to live with. 'We'll be in touch, Dave,' we said, knowing full well we never would be, and we bid our farewells, and headed back to our bed and board for one last night.

A disappointing end to a hard day's searching, but after a sound night's sleep and fortifying breakfast from Monsieur Pugs Thai Bride, sorry, beloved wife, we waved goodbye to our odd couple hosts and exited through the canine gates for the final time.

We headed to a town called Mussidan and a sprawling property that had its own stable area. It was obviously once part of a much larger estate with the main château just up a hill behind it that was now a luxury hotel with manicured grounds.

This property, with its large front courtyard, hadn't been

introduced to a lawnmower for some time. An opening of the door, and an ascent up the stairs informed you that the interior had been left to the elements as well.

You could see directly up into the sky where a roof had once been. The one bit of advice we had been given is don't get involved in places with dodgy or non-existent roofs, as they cost a fortune to fix.

Having said all that, there was a vast amount of living space with a separate apartment that had been maintained, but this would need an enormous amount of commitment to return it to former glories.

The stable area still had antiquated stalls for several horses, and a large vaulted room above them. Even though we had no plans to take on any chevaux, even as temporary guests, this was tempting us with its huge potential for renovation, but thankfully common sense prevailed, even if we could have driven a hard bargain on the price.

It was also undesirably close to a traffic roundabout, and having taken a little trip up a driveway to the hotel behind, had been met with a very snooty reception by the owners. We obviously weren't bourgeois enough for their exacting standards, so we roared off kicking up pebbles on their poncey drive like the proletariat scum we obviously are.

As I take you on this journey with us, using mere words to try and describe what we were absorbing with our senses, it's difficult to explain the visceral and mental impact these places were having on us.

Imagination runs wild, visions of grandeur are conjured, ambitions soar and that little voice inside your head urging caution, is drowned out by the screaming monster of avarice yelling 'buy it and be damned'.

Needless to say, we saw three more properties this day, all of which triggered emotional responses that spoke to that desire to own a staggering piece of French real estate that with a bit of spit and polish would become unbelievable places to live out the rest of your days in.

But with cons outweighing pros thus far, we were beginning to wonder whether we would ever stumble across a place that would supply us with that heavenly choir of angels singing from the cumulonimbus above conducted by the Archangel Gabriel.

So feeling a little deflated and beginning to doubt whether we would ever find something that would convince us to take the plunge, we headed to a rather nice-looking hotel in St Saud for a breather and a bevy. We bedded down for the night following an evening meal and dreamt of beautiful castles and stunning landscapes.

The following day, we had only two more properties to view, and then we would be heading back to port via Richelieu with the intention of maybe putting in an offer on Maison de Hibou. Expectations were running low, as the penultimate place to view was over our price range, but had been offered up by the estate agent on an electronic flyer as a property that had just come onto her books.

It came with flexibility on how much of the land we could buy with pasture land and a lake separate from the main dwelling and fenced off grounds.

The next morning we headed to a car park in a town called Abjat-sur-Bandiat. We drove in and parked amongst the horse chestnut trees. We were later to discover this car park was the venue for many events including, of all things, an international conker-fighting tournament.

There was a nearby boulangerie, and we walked over to grab ourselves a croissant and coffee, and settled down to wait for Jane in her Vauxhall Zafira.

Connection made, Jane drove out of town and we tailed her all the way to a tiny road that turned a corner where after half a kilometre or so, she drew to a halt. There, across the road from a large barn was Château Gros Puy. It looked magnificent, but get real, a bona fide château? You're having a laugh.

We entered through the door into a huge kitchen with a ceiling at least twenty feet high, a humongous mirror above a fireplace, and a door onto a terrace through the back that had a spectacular view overlooking a valley. The colour scheme was very peculiar, until we heard the owner had a love of Africa and in particular, Madagascar.

Gros Puy, we learnt, means Big Hill and this place sat majestically on top of it. Jane started showing us around, and we walked through a door to one side into a huge living room. The owner, Xavier, looked comparatively diminutive as he worked away at a desk in the corner and pleasantries were exchanged. Another grand mirror above a beautiful fireplace had a wood burner protruding from it to bring some warmth into the room. The aluminium flue trailing behind four feet from the fireplace itself was not exactly in keeping aesthetically with the surroundings, but as it was November, added a welcome cosiness to this aircraft hangar of a room.

The room was decorated with vintage paper with bucolic scenes depicting areas of old world Paris, and was yellowing like ancient parchment. The ceilings again were a good twenty feet high split right down the middle by a central boxed beam. I wasn't sure it would appeal to the rat aesthetic, but my ox heart was beginning to beat rapidly avec amour.

Back through the kitchen, we exited through a door into the thirteenth century turret's interior. Beneath us were about half a dozen granite stairs leading to a thick wooden door with huge iron hinges that opened with an ominous creak into the garden. Across the landing was a toilet, and then another door into the cave.

Above us were the steps, no doubt weighing a ton each, spiralling upwards in an anti-clockwork direction. Light flooded in through small windows sunk into the thick granite walls. Up we went to two further doors, one going into a huge games room where a table tennis table was set up, although I suspected a proper tennis court could have been fitted in there. A smaller wood surround fireplace was less spectacular, but still a grand addition to the room. A singular sink in the corner seemed a bit out of place, and a small room in the corner had a trap door in it that, once upon a time, would be where the grain was loaded.

Back into the turret, the door to the left took us into what is the west wing, with four bedrooms and a bathroom accessed from a central corridor. The bathroom had a shower and a straw toilet in it. Yes, a box with a bog seat on the top, so instead of flushing you pack down whatever you've done by putting straw on top. I'll leave that with you to contemplate for a while and imagine what emptying involved with the drawer beneath to facilitate what a flush would achieve in a modern-day lavatory, designed by Thomas Crapper, an English plumber and inventor, no doubt sick of straw-emptying duties.

All four rooms were of reasonable size connected by a hallway housing a cavernous great oak armoire. One bedroom had its own en-suite and walk-in cupboard. Feeding into the chimney from the fireplace below in the living room was a simpler fireplace, making four fireplaces in total.

The floor throughout sloped alarmingly and was made from huge planks of Limousin oak.

Further up the steps to the top of the turret was a landing stage and a door into the vast loft area where the bats hung out and wasps had a huge great nest. It was all supported by a network of wooden beams, holding up the huge roof and planks were laid over the rafters to help you navigate your way to seven shuttered windows. Above the door, you could peer through a gap into the conical turret roof, lit up by a single skylight. The engineering alone to construct this maze of wood that is seldom seen was breath-taking enough.

Back down to the ground floor, we went through a further big door from the turret into what had formerly been a chapel. This had been on the site since the thirteenth century, and the rest of the château had been constructed around it. The floor was a puzzle of square and oblong terracotta tiles, flanked by big granite stones. A utility room and storage room were behind two further doors with a grain loft above them both. The chapel had a fireplace so gigantic you could literally stand up in it and have enough room to barbeque an entire ox. No, not me thank you, but on that point, this was the property made for an ox-like me and ratty, it turned out, was pretty smitten with it too.

Eyes agog, we went out onto the terrace and took in the view. We could see across a valley to a lake surrounded by woodland and a field from where the owner's donkeys looked up at us curiously. The garden spilled down to their field over three terraces, packed with a variety of fruit trees, bushes laden with red currants, and down to a stream at the bottom, with its own bamboo forest.

The central garden was adjoined by two further gardens left and right packed with trees through which you could walk to a well spring and a lavoire where apparently the château staff, in bygone days, would go to wash their smalls.

Outbuildings included a chauvage where a massive state of the art wood burner had recently been installed to heat up this monster of a place and a little granite stone outbuilding where a board with two holes above a trough left you in no doubt what it was used for.

There was something about the place, its presence and atmosphere that left you in no doubt it was special.

Okay, our budget would have to stretch to afford it, but it had only just come onto the books of Beaux Villages having been with a previous agent who'd done very little to sell it, so it was basically fresh to market.

As we left and followed Jane to the next property about thirty minutes away, both Zak and I were speechless. Château Gros Puy had cast its spell on us, and we were powerless to resist. We did eventually muster up some words and tried to talk ourselves out of it, but the damage had been done and I can only tell you we cast a cursory eye over the next property and although a very nice townhouse, it just confirmed we'd been ensnared by something far, far grander and more intoxicating.

The Wedding

In May 2017, our daughter Yazmin was married to her long-term boyfriend Tom in a civil ceremony in Twickenham. As they had done this with only parents in attendance, they wanted to open up the celebrations to their friends and wider family in a ceremony held at a château just outside of Bordeaux. Château Saint-Étienne was their favoured location after they'd scoured a number of other venues that were large enough to accommodate a wedding, lunch, evening reception and enough room for the guests who could make the journey over.

As fiercely independent people, Yaz and Tom bore the majority of the financial burden themselves and only asked close family and dependable friends to help them with the arrangements. The château owner, Phillipe, was the kind of laid-back person we needed to leave us to it and not interfere too much. Rooms were made up; the grass was mowed and his dog's doo-dahs were cleared in the allotted fields so as not to be spiked by stiletto heels. We made dozens of trips to the supermarché for booze, food, ice and decorations. Madame Malcolm had spent months practising cake making, which put a real strain on the top button of my trouser waistline, having been designated as 'taster'.

The pièce de résistance this led to towered over four tiers into the stratosphere and was iced in a fetching colour of sky blue. This was all cooked in a nearby gite we had secured for a couple of weeks just up the road from Château Saint-Étienne.

The cake's construction involved thirty bags of Betty Crocker cake mix (because Zak couldn't understand the writing on French packaging) and she slaved for a week in the small kitchen leaving it looking like a frenzied cocaine party had taken place. Just as well the owners didn't drop by in the first week to see how we were getting on.

The cake was erected at the château around a central dowel that was under as much strain as my top trouser button had been from the sheer weight of baked cake and thick blue coloured icing. When I said towered earlier, I can only compare its magnificence to the one at Pisa, because it had a distinct slant to it that only added to the unconventional theme of the wedding itself. A vivid memory of the meal was all the guests emerging with blue tongues, leaving them looking like a pack of Chow dogs as they chowed down on the cake.

Tables and chairs were all moved into what was once a large derelict barn without a roof and shrubbery and trees inside it used to festoon lights and bunting. The only real outside help came in the form of a hog roast from a local farmer and the wedding dinner was a help yourself buffet of cassoulet, barbequed pork, stacks of salads and sauces and enough wine and beer on ice to sink the Titanic.

Château Saint-Étienne proved to be the ideal location with vows being exchanged in the cherry orchard to the rear of the property, with the celebrant being yours truly wearing full highland dress on a sweltering day. At least, I had sufficient ventilation blowing in under the Malcolm Tartan kilt and everything beneath it was getting a good airing as I addressed my flock and bumbled my way through the ceremony.

I had decided to put a bottle of Scotch whisky in my sporran to raise toasts throughout the ceremony like a man of the cloth who was too keen on the holy spirit, but every time I slugged straight from the bottle yelling 'sláinte', I was getting the evil eye from Mrs Malcolm who has perfected that stare over the years into a terrifying art form.

My pronunciation of the word sláinte was being corrected quite vociferously and repeatedly by the Irish contingent who obviously used that word a lot more than I ever did. So cheers to my new-found Gaelic friends.

I welcomed everyone, introduced the key members of the wedding party one after the other, the bridesmaids, the best men and of course the bride. There was somebody I had forgotten of course, which was the groom himself, no doubt due to one too many sláintes, so the bridesmaids shielded Yaz from Tom's gaze. I gave him a rapturous build-up and got him to the base of the cherry tree that was draped in ribbons and photographs of absent friends and dearly departed relatives before asking the bride to join us.

The congregation, who had already enjoyed a few libations, were in high spirits by now and did their own version of Felix Mendelssohn's Wedding March like a chanting football crowd.

Yaz and Tom had written their own vows, which I took them through point by point before they added their own personal messages at the end. Tom's loving words will always be remembered when he was distracted by a spider that had lowered from the tree onto Yaz's cleavage and he pointed it out as though part of his troth. This was greeted with howls of laughter from the congregation and wasn't even edited out by the videographer of the day and became affectionately known as the 'Spiderboob' incident.

Wedding rings slotted onto the allotted fingers, the party moved into the stunning courtyard, where roses were blooming in resplendent magnificence from climbers that had taken decades to grow in such abundance.

A few more drinks and photos were taken then everyone was ushered into the dining area to face the top table. Speeches followed that roused everyone into unbridled heckling, with some of the most heart-warming and sometimes least appropriate words I'd ever heard at a wedding ceremony.

Tom's best man and business partner to be, Hooper, donned a veil during his speech and weaved a tale of woe about how he'd always been besotted by Tom who had failed to notice his adoration. It was hilarious and cringe making in equal measure.

Everybody got a shout out from me who had made the effort to be there including a large contingent who had made the trip over from the States. This all gets pretty complex, but one of the guests was called Larry Lavin. He tells an amazing story of how he travelled from the US to a village in Ireland to try and trace his ancestry. He entered a hostelry and was talking about his quest to trace his Lavin lineage. The barman was elusive, as he wasn't sure whether this guy was a tax inspector or plain clothes Garda, but the barman spoke to the Lavin guy who lived next door to the pub, who happened to be his long lost relative.

Tom's mother is also a Lavin and the Irish connection was made and has been kept ever since. Larry lives in LA and before getting married, Tom and Yaz decided to boat-hop all around the world on an epic adventure starting in California. They stayed with Larry as they searched for yacht captains looking for crew.

That's not where the crazy link up stories end. When we moved to Chicago and I had a chance meeting and selfie with the mayor, Tom, my son-in-law to be, posted it on Facebook;

and Larry who is friends with David, Rahm Emanuel's, political adviser, saw it. Those with a global view on politics will know Rahm Emanuel was Barack Obama's White House chief of staff and was mayor of Chicago for nine years.

David and his partner Tom (American Tom) invited us to their apartment for dinner to say hello and we all became great friends. American Tom, David and Larry were all at the wedding and Larry even gave an impromptu speech in the middle of the ceremony after I asked him to rise and introduce himself.

So many more speeches were made with corks flying in all directions, it went well into the night before the disco started up and the bride and groom filed through an arch of sparklers to have their first dance on a large rug as a dance floor that now resides in the Château Gros Puy living room. Never has cutting a rug been more apt as everybody invaded the dance floor and threw some shapes. One gite in the Château Saint-Étiennes grounds had been renamed the Kaos Bar, after the bar in Southampton, where Tom and Yaz worked while studying at Solent University and those who could stay the pace moved inside as others staggered to their beds.

I, being a lightweight, headed to the land of nod as others headed towards the swimming pool area for some skinny-dipping, led, pied piper like, by a singular streaker who ran through the middle of the Kaos Bar. Thankfully Phillipe was hard of hearing as the after party became very raucous and ran long into the night and early morning.

It was an absolute triumph of an event, even though there were many sore heads the following day as we cleared up the total carnage the revellers had left in their wake.

Perhaps it was this that gave us a taste for château life. The backdrop that had created such a special moment in our lives had given us an appetite for what we could expect if we chose our own piece of rural French real estate.

I won't go into the finer details of the sale, but if you offer the asking price on the French property market, by law, that's the deal done. So that's precisely what we did when we got back home from the viewing on a Sunday morning, we emailed the offer through that afternoon. No messing about bartering, no playing mind games. We wanted it, so we leapt in with both feet and we got it.

Owners of a French château with a medieval turret and thirteenth century chapel, The Malcolm Family.

The end of one journey to find it and the start of a whole new one bringing it back to life.

The purchase of Château Gros Puy

Having made our offer, Xavier didn't accept it at first, saying a Dutch couple had already made a lower offer. Zak pressed home the point that if you offer the asking price, by law, the owners have to accept it, which they duly did. UK 1, Holland 0.

Unlike in England, the whole process is overseen by a notaire, without separate solicitors exchanging contracts. It strikes me as far fairer than all that gazumping nonsense that occurs regularly in the UK. First over the line wins the spoils, wham, bam, merci madame.

The first thing to be signed is the compromise de vente, which allows a ten-day cooling off period if something crops up in a survey or you suddenly wake up in a cold sweat screaming 'what the hell am I doing?'

Our vendors were called Xavier and Annette who had a son living with them called Jacques. We would have very cordial meetings, although communication was very disjointed with a lot of sign language and laughter at misinterpretations.

It turned out the property was inherited from Annette's family and apart from the eccentric colour scheme, everything had been done to a reasonably high standard. It was Annette's father who had prevented the château falling into disrepair which could have been irreversible, if he hadn't replaced the huge beams that kept it upright and installed electricity throughout.

It had been in their family for 200 years, but our suspicion was they'd run out of money and probably enthusiasm. After the sale Zak had asked Xavier how he liked his new house, to which he replied, with an enthusiastic response, 'FRESH!'.

There was still plenty to be done to get the château up to scratch and for just three people to rattle around in this place will have been a tough ask, especially with a straw toilet to contend with.

The toilet at the bottom of the turret was the only other working latrine in the whole of the building draining into a septic tank in need of replacement and the plumbing and electrics, or lack thereof, left a lot to be desired.

The heating was all in pretty good working order running from the massive wood burner and storage heater that was a recent acquisition that fed the radiators in the building, but the cost of getting it all installed was probably crippling for the family.

Jacques was the local lumberjack, so at least he was able to keep a steady supply of steres, which were measurements of wood pronounced stairs, stacked in and around the chauvage ready for burning. Filling the burner and getting it to light is a mammoth task in its own right, taking up to thirty logs at a time and requiring a bit of trial and error to get it to ignite. The wood has to be properly stacked and dried for a few months before being fed in, which is why everywhere you go in the Périgord Vert region logs of various sizes are stacked in huge piles and areas of forest have been cleared with little regard to the scarring left behind on the landscape. In time and probably not as much time as you'd think, nature greens it all up again with remarkable efficiency, no doubt explaining why the region the château is located in has the word vert in its title.

Limousin oak is the tree of choice in the area hacked into

different lengths of log in Jacques' neck of the woods, which he transports by tractor to be unloaded outside the chauvage door to be carried inside wearing gloves to avoid splinters on our soft townie hands. Xavier showed us how to feed the beast and ignite it, but needless to say, we forgot the technique immediately and only trial and error has enabled us to get the big red dragon breathing fire again.

Many have been the times we've had the chauvage looking like it is going up in smoke billowing black and white clouds out that always draws attention in the middle of a forest.

Any passers-by during this ritual would have thought we were announcing the failure of the inauguration of a new pope to the Vatican.

We now realise Xavier and Annette only seemed to occupy one room that was kept snug and warm, as keeping the whole place cosy in the depths of winter becomes a full time and very expensive job.

Perhaps our rose-tinted glasses prevented us from seeing the downsides of owning a gigantic ancient monolith, but we have just learnt to wear more clothes if we visit in the colder months, which we also tend to sleep in.

We also did a walk around the château with Xavier and Annette electing what to buy and what they could take with them. This is a French thing where they don't just take their stuff with them and leave what they don't want, you barter a price for the things you want to keep. Xavier was talking about £12k all in.

We agreed to offer him £4k for what we wanted to keep, which wasn't all that much. This included the large armoires I spoke about, along with a very tall and narrow grandfather clock and some huge dressers. Everything else was under fixtures and fittings, including the straw toilet unfortunately. They took the living room wood burner with them, but left the aluminium flue that went up the chimney stack.

The day came after the cooling off period, or the 'have you lost your marbles?' period, as I liked to call it, where we had to go and do all the formalities by French Civil Law under the auspices of the notaire.

This was quite a ceremony, with a portly but quite humorous chap behind a desk taking us through the formalities projected onto a screen on his wall, while ensuring we fully understood what we were signing up to on the 'acte de vente'.

This was quite a document to get through with Xavier, Annette, Zak and I with our estate agent and son Angus sat down like naughty school children about to be reprimanded by the headmaster. I know this to be true having experienced the real thing in my bad boy days at Hounslow Manor School.

Each page was read through with all four of us asked to acknowledge that we understood before signing each page electronically.

'What do you do for a living, Monsieur Malcolm?' he asked me.

'I am a writer,' I replied leaving the copy part off the beginning of that word.

'Oh, you have bought a very nice place to write in,' he remarked with a smile on his face that indicated he had creative leanings himself. An A4 piece of paper was stuck to his wall saying 'Je suis Charlie' to show his support for the Charlie Hebdo satirical magazine and the strongly held belief in free speech against tyranny from religious zealots looking to disrupt that most French of liberties.

It was either that or his name actually was Charlie.

His observation did evoke romantic connotations of sitting at a teak desk under a green desk light, tapping away on a keyboard while wistfully looking out of the window across the valley in search of inspiration. As the song from The King and I covered by Captain Sensible asks 'If you don't have a dream, how you gonna have a dream come true?' And guess what, that is precisely the set-up we currently have in the living room.

At the end of it all, hands were shaken, keys were exchanged, including the heavy cast iron one for the door to the turret, and I personally was a little bit unnerved about the look of sheer delight and relief on Xavier and Annette's faces.

The truth of the matter is that in the two years we've owned the place, they have already moved on from the 'FRESH' residence they subsequently bought and apparently their reckless selling of Gros Puy has prompted a bit of a family feud.

With the bureaucracy complete and keys exchanged, we went back to Gros Puy, getting hopelessly lost en route and when we eventually arrived, invited Xavier, Annette and Jacques to join us in a bottle of pink Champagne Zak and I had brought to commemorate this momentous occasion. The cork popped and we all toasted the successful exchange, apart from Angus who is teetotal and had been delegated cameraman for the ceremony to capture the moment on video for posterity. I have looked back at it since and like all footage you imagine will show you at your most magnificent, can only see how fat I was at that particular moment in time. Maybe in my eighties I will look at it again with my grandchildren and reminisce about how dashing I looked in my late fifties, but for now, I won't be searching it out in a hurry.

The empty bottle remains on the mantelpiece and will be

there for many years to come as a memento of the historic handover.

One thing I forgot to mention was the surrounding land. Xavier and Annette didn't relinquish all facets of Gros Puy. They retained the field to keep their six donkeys and the lake to the east of the château. They did believe that nobody would want to buy the château without the accompanying land, but we are more than happy with what we've got, as that's enough to contend with for the time being. The field is reached by a chemin, the ownership of which is hotly contested with the neighbour. He'll crop up a bit later on, suffice to say territories and borders are the bane of many a French property owner's life and they take it extremely seriously, no matter what it may say on your deeds.

What do I care? If you want a feud, I've got a castle with a turret. As my Scottish cousin Alasdair Malcolm has pointed out to me, the anti-clockwise twist of the staircase was totally intentional. In feudal times, everyone was right-handed (with lefties deemed the spawn of Satan) that allowed more sword swinging room for the defender descending the staircase where the steps are broadest, while the attacker had very little room to swing his sword, being constricted by the wall.

As I also discovered on night excursions to the only working toilet at the bottom of the turret, they also deliberately made the granite steps uneven so invaders found it very tricky to keep their footing. After a few sherbets and attempting to ascend the steps half cut, the same principle applies. Gros Puy has seen its fair share of fighting and Alasdair has reminded me of the auld alliance with Scotland and France, suggesting I fly the saltire from the turret roof, so if the worst comes to the worst, I'll just bring my Scottish ancestry up if a pack of torch-bearing villagers alight on my doorstep baying for blood of the English occupants.

We took over as proprietors of a medieval French castle in April of 2018 and with the previous owners dispatched, we looked around feeling content, if not a little nervous about the extent of what we had to do to bring this old place up to scratch. Madagascar is a great animated film, but as inspiration for a colour scheme? Errr, no. That'll have to go tout suite.

But not before we emptied all the furniture and fittings from the rental van parked up outside. We had travelled to get to the notaire in style in the clinking, clunking van all the way from Angleterre. Lord knows what would be awaiting us in the back when we opened it after a 600-mile journey over land and sea; A 100,000-piece jigsaw puzzle of what we had owned and purchased to fill our new home perhaps.

This was the first of many excursions back and forth with Zak's acquisitions from Lots Road Auction House and other weird and wonderful purchases, transported in a fleet of rental vans from the UK.

But that deserves another chapter in this book as well as in my life.

The Refurbing and Refilling of Gros Puy

The prospect of a château to fill with object d'art and things of wonderment and delightfulness sent Madame Chatelaine into a frenzy comparable to when the Warner Bros Tasmanian Devil goes into a tailspin, taking out everything in his path.

As a former antiques dealer and self-confessed hoarder, Zak has amassed a collection of exotic stuff that has filled garages and lockups the length and breadth of West London.

The sleigh bed from Chicago was so large, it filled up most of any bedroom we put it in after we decided to bring it back with us from the USA.

Suddenly, there was a place that would be a repository for these items where they wouldn't look out of place. In fact, it is so cavernous, it tends to swallow them up like that warehouse in Indiana Jones and The Temple of Doom, where they lose the Ark of the Covenant amongst the millions of crates that stretch off into the distance.

The sleigh bed looks relatively tiny in its new location in the master bedroom.

Obviously, everything that was to be transported to the Dordogne needed to be put into storage before the logistics started.

A storage facility tucked away on an industrial estate beside the Grand Union Canal in Brentford was sequestered for this military style operation. Getting the stuff into the first floor lock up required herculean effort and that's even before we'd set off.

Zak had become glued to the Lots Road Auction site and like an online gambling addict, was throwing money down with wild-eyed abandon. She even started going cold turkey when she was away from her computer for any length of time, becoming tremulous from the withdrawal symptoms.

She was, to her credit, securing some beautiful and eclectic pieces at surprisingly low prices. Two bergères with ornate fabric and carved golden wood that made them resemble thrones were delicately transferred to Brentford and into our storage space.

Jardinière, chandeliers, candelabra, mirrors, benches, cupboards and dressers, Corinthian columns, lamps, beds, tables, rugs galore and an Aladdin's cave of bric-a-brac were all crammed in until we could barely pull down the slatted door. We also were living in a rented property with a garage at the end of the garden that was filled to overflowing with gear destined for the château.

D-Day (Dordogne Day) dawned and the rental van was loaded up for the evening sailing to Caen with a reserved cabin.

We roped in some family muscle to load the van up and secure it to the sides so there were no breakages en route. Our labradoodle Cosmo was a little suspicious of what we were doing and in the past, when we had packed to go on holiday without him, had leapt into the boot of the car and sat on top of the suitcases. His eyes are very expressive and seemed to be pleading 'don't go without me'.

'Stone me', he must have been thinking at the amount we were struggling to force into the van, 'they must be going for the longest holiday to date'. We had bought Cosmo in 2005 in reaction to our near-death experience in Sri Lanka during the

Tsunami of Boxing Day 2004, after which we vowed never to go on holiday abroad ever again. We even bought a static caravan in North Cornwall as the kids grew up and for several years, stuck to our pledge enjoying many wet and grey holidays in Crackington Haven. The journey was almost as long haul as going to the Caribbean, taking hours to reach via the A303 and the obligatory traffic jam that always greeted us at Salisbury Plain, where the road narrowed beside Stonehenge.

Those deep psychological scars healed after a decade or so and what once excited the kids and Cosmo as adventurous in a Famous Five way of exploring rock pools and eating lashings of cream tea, suddenly became mind-numbingly boring, especially as getting wi-fi or any broadband down there was virtually impossible at the time.

Suddenly, holidays abroad were back on the agenda and Cosmo was left at home, staying with friends, family and dog walkers. This was no journey for him and he was soon replaced in the back of the van by a pouffe or a parasol.

He has joined us on one excursion to the château as an owner of a pet passport and lounged about the place with his trademark insouciance now he's a senior citizen in dog years. Taking dogs onto a ferry isn't much fun for them. You can leave them in the car overnight or get a dog friendly cabin. The longer the voyage, the more times you have to take them to the back deck to let them do what comes naturally to a dog.

I speculated on one of these walks to the back of the boat whether this explained why, in nautical terms, the poop deck is to the rear of the ship. I think the crew just hosed the poops into the sea into the wake of the propellers.

Poor old Cosmo has suffered many long journeys due to our wanderlust, even being tranquilised to spend time in the hull of a 747 to be relocated to Chicago and then back again.

On one holiday to France he came with us to Brittany where we stayed in Bayeux then onto a farmhouse for a week's holiday. This is where the now infamous story of 'cheesegate' occurred.

The very amiable hosts of the farm, who were caretaker, workaway people from South Africa, invited us and other guests from gites on the site, to a cheese and wine tasting event in the garden. All was very convivial as a woman who'd travelled from Sancerre with an array of soft cheeses and white wines, was spreading slices onto biscuits for our delectation and topping up our glasses on a regular basis.

I remember Zak was talking about Oscar Pretorius to the South Africans with her usual lack of diplomatic tact and nothing was to prepare us for what would happen next. Even Cosmo was given no pre-warning, as he lay prostrate next to Zak's chair.

Suddenly, in mid-sentence, like a bullet from Pretorius's gun, Zak turned to one side and let out an almighty stream of chunder all over Cosmo's back. It was like the scene from the Meaning of Life where Mister Creosote, after one last wafer-thin mint, jets vomit all over John Cleese playing the waiter.

The smell was horrendous, Cosmo leapt up in alarm yelping, silence descended the table and people politely said goodnight and beat a hasty retreat to their beds, probably trying to suppress their own dry heaves.

'Must have been the cheese,' Zak casually remarked as the evening came to an abrupt halt and everybody went their separate ways. Cosmo had to be doused with a hosepipe for ages but still reeked to high heaven. Labradoodles do not moult, so his fur was clogged with a potent combo of soft cheese and white wine for ages after.

To this day, Zak insists it was the woman transporting the cheese on a four hour journey in a hot car that prompted the dramatic hurl that came totally out of le bleu. Nothing to do with the several glasses of wine she'd necked back, obviously.

The following day it was all brushed under the carpet by the hosts, reacting as if this sort of thing happened every day. I bet they still tell the tale of the puking Brit woman with the unfortunate hairy dog. To add insult to injury, Cosmo had to be immunised against la rage once in France by a local vet, who no doubt wondered why le chien had a strange fromagey vin odour about him. Who'd be a dog eh?

Small surprise that Cosmo is less keen to travel with us these days and he always keeps a beady eye on his mistress if he decides to flake out next to her when she has a glass of vin blanc in her hand.

From home, the next loading stop was the lock up and this is where it turned into a comedy sketch by The Chuckle Brothers with a lift, trolleys with errant wheels, long narrow corridors and people who don't do removals for a living making a right hash of trying to look professional. To me, to you.

At one stage we lost Tom and heard his voice echoing at the back of the van before he clambered out like a Victorian kid emerging from a chimney. If only we'd recorded this on video, sped it up to comedic Benny Hill music and posted it on YouTube, we'd have gone viral for sure.

Van filled, we headed for the night crossing to Caen via Portsmouth and a cabin for a much-needed kip aboard a Brittany Ferry. We had worked out that a six-hour crossing to start travelling at dawn from Caen, knocked a few hours off the journey and got us there before darkness descended, which always slowed us down on those narrow winding roads in Dordogneshire.

There's no escaping the fact that you will be hitting many toll booths on the way that add up to a fair amount of cash along with the petrol money. The trip on Ryanair to Limoges Airport can come in under ten quid if you buy at the right time and can get you there after just one hour in the air.

I can say categorically that Stansted is my least favourite London airport because from Richmond, it is a nightmare of a journey to negotiate. We always try to go from Heathrow or Gatwick, but those BA flights are more expensive, so we bite the bullet and head from one side of London to the other.

That can involve a tube train to Liverpool Street then the Stansted Express, an overground to Stratford to connect with a coach, or get to Victoria Coach Station to board a magical mystery tour through east London before spilling out at the airport kissing the ground with relief that you've finally arrived.

Getting there is only half the trauma. At the height of the season, you are herded through security like cattle, zigzagging between cordoned off queues to security, where Zak is always pulled to one side due to the gold bracelets she can't remove from her wrist without a hacksaw or blowtorch.

Having been told to spread your legs and put your hands up above your head (ooh, you silver-tongued devil), you are then filtered into a holding pen after running the gauntlet of duty free. Emerging through the haze of sprayed fragrances and tempted to drink hard liquor, whatever the time of day, you join a game of musical chairs to find somewhere to sit amongst the sleepers taking up rows of seats because they've been delayed by French Air Traffic control strikes.

67

To get to this living hell on earth, you can risk a car journey into the maze of long-term car parks miles from the Stansted terminal, but that journey around the M25 and up the M6 feels like the reason Chris Rea wrote the song 'The Road to Hell'.

On this journey we were keeping wheels on the ground throughout and once the van was fully loaded, we set off down the A3 towards the south coast. Nothing keeps you more awake in transit than the rattling of all that eminently breakable stuff shifting around in the rear. Our son Angus had helped us with the loading and was attempting to find space in the cabin to put his legs up and find a decent sleeping position. Angus is a master at sleeping in the most uncomfortable of positions and somehow slept the majority of the journey with his mouth wide open, tempting Zak and I to a game of shooting hoops with sweets secreted in the glove compartment for sustenance.

The cabin space itself was taken up with our suitcases filling the passenger foot well and we just prayed that customs in Portsmouth wouldn't ask us to empty the back out for them to have a root around.

On one of the crossings we were directed down the stop and search channel, but thankfully they just shone a torch into the back and made us take our suitcases in to go through the x-ray machine. On a return home journey we were once again searched with the back empty, and asked if we'd stopped on the way to the port.

We had popped into a McDonald's in a shopping village outside of town, but thought nothing of it. Imagine our surprise when they found a refugee clinging to the bottom of the van, who was unceremoniously frog-marched away, no pun intended.

This being our first voyage over, everything we now take

for granted was a novelty for us. We joined the lorry drivers and holidaymakers in the bar for a quick nightcap. Some of the people crossing slept in the lounges, crawling into sleeping bags on the floor. Others settled down for a night of boozing watching the on-board entertainment that was usually an aspiring Jane McDonald caterwauling into a tinny microphone, battling feedback. Veteran lorry drivers took time to fill their lonely lives with a bit of company from fellow drivers playing cards.

After one drink, we headed for the cabin and worked out how to get the top bunk down from the roof that always became my bed, because it involved clambering up a ladder and often banging my head on the low ceiling above me. Zak and Angus took lower bunks and as the ferry clunked and rattled out to sea, the womb effect of the warm, rocking cabin sent us all to sleep quite quickly.

Something else I'd get used to is the god-awful alarm music they wake you up with, pumped through the speakers on these Brittany Ferry cross Channel crossings. At an unearthly hour in the morning, it drifts into your dream with the most surreal soundtrack, which sounds like someone on a lute plucking the first chords of Greensleeves. It is then joined by other acoustic instruments to urge you awake, but without being too violently insistent.

About 5.30am with around an hour left before we disembark, it goes off to allow you a snooze before coming back a bit louder and becoming a lot more intrusive. There is a shower room in the corner of the cabin if you need to freshen up before a long drive and pre-ordered coffee, croissants and orange juice are awaiting you in the dining area.

Cups and glasses drained and flaky crumbs brushed off of

your top from eating the croissant with crusty eyes still half closed, you are then invited to return to your vehicles and one by one, sent off over a ramp and back onto terra firma.

Once off the ferry at Caen we had the prospect of a six-hour drive trying to avoid every pothole in France and slow down to a crawl over every sleeping policeman. I wonder whether they call them qui dort gendarmerie once over La Manche. The toll roads are immaculately kept, so the going was smooth after the rocky crossing. I always have a good moan about how we should return the compliment and ask French visitors to chip in towards the upkeep of our roads, paid for by our road taxes, but then realise I sound like Jeremy Clarkson so immediately ferme mon bouche.

We were to learn this route like the back of our hands with a further trip with a van transporting a mini grand piano Zak managed to buy on eBay for the princely sum of 99p. The guy she bought it from was taking delivery of a new piano and just needed somebody to remove the other one so let it go for next to nowt. He wasn't too happy about the silly price, but time was against him holding out for a better price. That's eBay for you, if you get greedy waiting for a better price it can bite you full on the derriere.

Are we pianists? No. Zak can knock out a competent 'Chopsticks', but this Joanna was destined for the chapel where concerts are planned for future jazz evenings.

Oh the thinks you can think as Doctor Seuss once wrote and there was a lot of thinking going on about the overall vision for the château mostly thunk by Zak and Yaz and not always in total harmony with each other.

Yaz is an events coordinator and PR guru in her working life and has plans to make the chapel into a speakeasy. Sounds sacrilegious I know, but the space is perfect for a bit of entertaining and Yaz even has plans to produce Gros Puy Gin having taken a course on how to distil a bit of Vera Lynn and set up her own copper stills for small batch production.

She has also populated mood boards with colour swatches, architectural pieces and wonderful visual inspiration from magazines and websites. She has set out her plans for the whole place after being commandeered as interior designer by her mum, who often strays off-brief on her own tangent, leading to disagreements where I just duck for cover.

As that aforementioned ox, the garden is my domain and I am just required for lugging indoors, portering stuff up and down the turret steps that I have now got to know very well. My rock-hard calf muscles pay testament to my intimate knowledge of each step.

So, notaire admin done, champers necked and keys handed over, the van was emptied into the chapel space where it was to languish for months on end as the tradespeople did their hard graft in all the other rooms.

The chapel has a dark wooden ceiling that is permanently covered with cobwebs like a Scooby Doo haunted house scenario. It is reachable with a brush on the end of a stick kindly left by Xavier and Annette but that task is well down the list of priorities.

The walls are plastered with ancient waffle and daub that has that aged yellowing effect you associate with pub ceilings from the time when everybody smoked in the boozer. Once you have entered through the double doors, to your right is a sink sunk into the wall that drains out of a hole in the wall straight into a trough that snakes downhill around the château.

This trough also siphons away the overflow water from a

well that is covered by two big slabs of granite in the front garden.

Above the sink is a small porthole and a wooden shelving unit goes from floor to ceiling around it. I'm not sure whether this sink was once used for baptisms, but I am sure it isn't holy water that comes from the taps above it.

Just five feet in, the floor drops over two big granite steps that take you down into a pit where a large flagstone border surrounds a central area of old terracotta tiles. The seven-foot-high fireplace made of dark oak will have kept the congregation toasty as the clergyman looked down at them from his pulpit raised up on more granite steps rising to a window.

You can just imagine the dramatic effect of blinding light beaming out from behind him in a sacred halo. In front of the fireplace there are twelve stones that are different from the rest that I theorised were representative of the apostles. One is different in white granite, which in my ecclesiastical opinion represents Judas Iscariot.

As there is nobody around to make a counter-theory, that's exactly the tale I'll be spinning about them for time immemorial, hoping of course that I'm not being blasphemous to be cast into the flames of hell to burn for all eternity upon my passing.

Talking of flames, in the fireplace itself we have two large dogs. Not the canine type, but the iron variety for resting large burning logs on.

There is an all-pervasive atmosphere of calm in the chapel but it is the least used room in the château rammed with too much stuff to do any praying on bended knees. Opposite the fireplace is a wall that has two doors leading to different rooms.

One of the rooms is now the utility room and the other had

a staircase that led up to where the grain would have been poured in. This has since been dismantled and the ceiling above torn down to reveal windows set deep in the granite walls and exposing the beams from the small room above and increasing the head height. I remember on our first viewing where Zak asked Xavier whether he'd ever seen mice in the château, which he strenuously denied, only to open the door to this room to reveal two dead mice on the stairs. 'Ah, those? They're pets called Pierre and Gaston and they're just having an afternoon nap.' I put those words in Xavier's mouth of course as he promptly closed the door and moved on swiftly.

The piano was the cause for greatest concern in transferring from van to chapel, as the 99p price tag escalated to hundreds of pounds with the transport and brawn required to move it from Gloucestershire to London and into the lock up. These guys were no longer there to help us and it was me and Angus with Zak as foreman who needed to move this monstrosity of wood, strings and keys and three unscrewed legs as thick as your waistline into position.

This too was like a comedy sketch, or that vintage commercial for PG Tips with the chimps wrestling a piano down some stairs, the older one called Mister Shifter obviously portrayed by me. Being British workers, each stage of this operation had to be lubricated with copious amounts of tea. With straps and blankets and trolleys on wheels, the piano was manoeuvred onto the hydraulic lift, which creaked under its weight but didn't buckle. Thankfully, Angus didn't have to utter the immortal line from the ad, 'Dad, do you know the piano's on my foot?' but if he did, I was ready with the retort 'You hum it son, I'll play it."

Sliding it along the driveway, we managed to get it through

the double doors and into the chapel. We still had two granite steps to negotiate, but after going through the options, pontificating over more tea and then just laying it on the blankets, we dropped it down without trapping any fingers or toes or chipping off any wooden corners, much to our own amazement. It laid flat and legless on the floor, which is a situation I've found myself in on many an occasion.

We had to somehow raise this half tonne piano up into a position where we could quickly screw the legs in. This was a bridge too far for the three of us, so we left it until an opportunity arose where we could finish the job. This happened a few weeks later when a couple of strapping lads delivered a cooker we'd ordered from a French electrical store.

As they effortlessly lifted the range cooker into place in the kitchen, Zak kept nudging me and motioning with her gaze towards their muscular legs and lean glutes inside their tight-fitting shorts.

How blatant can you get, I thought, why not just wolf whistle, pant like a dog, say phwoar out loud and be done with it you hussy? It took a moment for the centime to drop, but Zak wasn't leering lustfully (well maybe just a bit), but seeing an opportunity to get the piano fully assembled.

It turned out they were two Rugby players and after Zak crossed their palms with some bière money, they lifted the hulking great thing like it was as light as a feather and we screwed the thick legs into the holes and lowered it into position.

That warranted a celebratory flourish of Chopsticks and one less job to worry about.

That piano, a noble instrument of fine tradition, has suffered the indignation of being used as a dumping ground for curtains, paint pots, rolls of wallpaper and a lean-to for the flat plan kitchen delivered by another group of less helpful delivery men. Liberace would be turning in his grave.

When the kitchen units turned up, the deliverymen were nowhere near as accommodating. They dumped pile upon pile of cardboard boxes outside the château, but pulled out the jobs-worth insurance excuse when asked to help us carry it all inside.

Zak, much to my chagrin, gave them a generous tip anyway and suddenly, insurance was no longer an issue as they helped me lug the kitchen parts into the chapel. Merci, mes amis. This was another valuable lesson learnt; Money talks and it speaks fluent French.

But I digress, as you will become familiar with as you progress through this book.

I am writing only in a rough chronological order and will go off-piste and after a few red Bordeaux wines, pissed, as I meander through this French saga.

Many colourful characters will drift in and out as I introduce you to them and the part they play in making these landmarks in our life so memorable.

With this being the first of many trips by road sea and air, I'll spare you the more boring details, suffice to say we have paid many trips to DIY stores, picked up hundreds of items for sale on the local network selling site and become regulars at the déchetterie, dumping rubble, unwanted fixtures and furnishings, bidets and of course a straw toilet.

This has been made so much easier after investing in a trailer and getting a tow bar on the back of our trusty 4x4. An all-wheel drive vehicle that we brought back with us from Chicago, is left hand drive and far easier to drive on French roads than on English ones. It was once a sparkling white brand-new BMW X3, but since being filled with all sorts of cement, rubble, stones, garden waste and château debris, it's become a knackered old workhorse rather than a prestige motor.

We have learnt in our short time in Gros Puy that life is work and work is life here. There is no such thing as a dull moment and on every to do list is another to do list. If this sounds like drudgery to you, then I assure you it is not.

Never have I been more worn out, but never have I been more satisfied than when a job is complete and you can stand back and admire your endeavours.

This includes the garden which has the disadvantage of growing like wildfire, so takes on the metaphorical equivalent of painting the Forth Bridge, especially when Madame Chatelaine has pretensions of replicating the gardens of Versailles. Oh yes, that trip I mentioned earlier to the former home of Louis XIV and all his courtiers was to become the subject of many a conversation about the back garden.

Or should I say the formal garden Zak has in her mind's-eye. I am hoping she doesn't envisage me carving the marble horses and manicuring the lawns with nail scissors, but the rambling rural grounds will have to undergo a transformation inspired by Louis himself, aka the Sun God.

Yaz also has plans to transform parts of the garden into a campsite with luxury yurts, where she can attract glampers with outdoor facilities to shower and self-cater. This will all be part of the push to make Gros Puy into a chambre d'hote with outdoor activities and cream tea afternoons.

Events are being planned for art holidays, yoga retreats, gin making breaks and music evenings to be updated regularly on the Gros Puy website and its social media channels.

Activities are planned and I will have to build a pétanque court for boules while archery sets and large targets have already been purchased, so I'll have to brush up on my Robin Hood skills and don my doublet and hose, although I don't want to frighten off potential customers.

Zak is honing her skills with even more cake making as well as scones and savouries. The coronavirus lockdown has freed up lots of time for experimentation and yet again, the old top trouser button is feeling the strain.

We have in the past made some amazing confiture from the mountains of berries picked from the bushes in le jardin. The next step will be to design the labels for our own range to be sold during the cream tea extravaganzas. But I'm getting ahead of myself here and how rude of me not to introduce you to some of the other people we've met in our formative years as château owners.

Getting to Know the Locals

You soon find in small French villages, that everybody knows each other and if they don't, they know all your business anyway.

In the land of vin and vineyards, the grapevine is very effective at letting you know what's happening in other people's lives and they know what's happening in yours.

The expat communities are a tight knit bunch and you'll find them gathering at local watering holes, planning events, having a chinwag and of course, drinking like poisson.

As we were newbies to the area, we joined Xavier and Annette for a drink or two at the local in Abjat. Here they introduced us to the Deputy Mayor Steve, a Brit from the Midlands as the interpreter between us with any pressing questions that came to mind.

Steve has that eccentric British air about him where his wardrobe is colourful and extravagant. He'll often be at an event wearing colourful beret, gaudy shirt and clashing trousers. We found him to be very open and helpful, although as with many people who take up a position of officialdom, he splits the jury in local popularity.

There are many rules and regulations to be observed and some just relating to etiquette. Should we get the mayor around to a ceremony to introduce ourselves to the villagers and throw a bit of a garden party?

The château had historically played a pivotal role in village life and an old bell is still attached to the turret that once called the locals to worship in the chapel. That has since been repurposed to be heard above the whir of the lawn mower so I can stop to hear my beloved's dulcet tones yelling 'TONE, FOR THE TENTH TIME, LUNCH IS READY.'

Other questions include at what time of year can we burn all the garden debris on a bonfire? Are there certain days where mowing lawns is frowned upon? What planning permission do we need if we want to install a swimming pool or build a conservatory and a thousand other queries. Spotter planes regularly patrol the skies overhead and any tell-tale plumes of smoke will have the local Pompiers, a brilliantly apt French name for Firemen, knocking on your door and dishing out hefty fines.

The French are fiercely protective of their land and forests and we were confident that the fields we had first refusal to buy from Xavier and Annette wouldn't suddenly be turned over to some developer who'd knock up a housing estate. Perhaps it's our towny ways that make us suspicious of councils, but we've had plenty of reason to not trust anyone in positions of authority with promises broken when big contractors start dishing out the back-handers.

Around our way, Richmond Ice Rink was demolished to make room for a luxury housing development with the pledge to rebuild a new one somewhere in the local area. Unless the River Thames freezes over, we have nowhere to strap our skates on and go full on Bolero, decades after that promise was made.

Town councils do seem to be more honourable in the Périgord Vert region and work hard to protect their residents from being bulldozed out of the way by unscrupulous land-grabbers.

We were quite thankful we hadn't bought the lake up front, as with new owners, that is subject to strict regulations on keeping it clean, when it should be drained and fish stocks taken into account. The many lakes of Dordogne are interlinked and you become part of a much wider responsibility, so bullet dodged there for the time being. Having said that I like the idea of adding a lake to things I never thought I'd own and have the possibility to add it to the list. Why lack a lac in your life when there's one at the bottom of your garden?

There were also many events in the area including the conker-fighting tournament that was organised by Steve himself back in 1990. It started as an event between British holidaymakers, watched by bemused French locals. By 1994, it had grown in size and attracted fifty competitors and was won by a Frenchman called Stephane Jally. Buoyed by his success and prowess with a horse chestnut skewered with a string with a knot at the end, he took a team to the 1995 World Conker Championship, held in Oundle in the UK, to represent France for the first time in front of 8,000 spectators.

Stephane won the championship in Abjat the following year, so to ensure this new-found enthusiasm for a quaint English tradition stayed in its French birthplace, Steve formed La Fédération Française de Conkers and the car park hosts this international annual event in early October every year. Such is its success it has been covered on British television by the BBC and ITV plus a host of other channels. Needless to say, the championship in the car park goes long into the evening with concerts and no doubt plenty of alcohol to fuel the celebrations.

This car park was the venue for many events from brocantes, vide-greniers, food festivals and a rock concert we attended where lots of booze was being consumed with some resultant head-banging, from people who should have known better. I was pretty sure some heads would have been banging the following morning.

We've spent many a pleasant day and evening there noshing on local grub, including oysters and quaffing 'Perigord Beers' craft IPA from the stall of a nearby brewery run by expats. Zak, who cannot pass a rug or garden furniture set without haggling over a price at the brocante, has landed a few bargains to grace Gros Puy.

The pub where we met Steve is called the Entente Cordiale and has a distinctly British feel about it with draft Guinness and real ales on tap and a big union flag on the wall. I spent one sweltering evening down there watching a World Cup 2018 England match on the big screen with my brother-in-law Art who also lives in France. I wish I'd been there when France lifted the trophy. I'm sure that would have generated almost as much excitement as the French Conker-fighting Championship.

A second bar cum restaurant in the village is called Le Cloche as it sits right beside the local church where bell ringers often do a bit of campanology. Zak had befriended the British waitress Trisha and we'd sit outside in the sun drinking the ruby Leffe bière and enjoying the seafood pasta, which was delicious. The real shame is La Cloche is now up for sale as the chef is moving on, so no more seafood pasta and no more draft ruby Leffe unless a new buyer picks up the reins.

On one Sunday afternoon visit, we were invited onto a table of several Brits mixing with their French counterparts. With the levels of laughter and competitive banter, it was pretty evident some libations had been consumed. Perhaps the number of glasses and bottles on the table was a further clue.

We were to discover there had been a pétanque tournament

in the local square and Abjat had emerged victorious against a neighbouring village and that typically British modesty in defeat was sorely lacking here.

This is where we first met our now good friends Ken, Suzy and Toby. Ken is an ex-journalist with a wicked sense of humour, not unlike my own puerile idea of fun, with Suzy his lovely wife and Toby a bon viveur who knows a thing or two about fine wine, having been a head steward on BA's first class.

Knowing that we had to open up our social circles, Zak immediately invited everybody for lunch. This happened outside on our terrace with a table groaning with local produce and a kitchen stocked with a few gallons of red, white and rosé wine.

We had bought a pretty basic BBQ from a nearby supermarché, and this had been used for all cooking as we were without a cooker at this stage. Everything from breakfast to lunch and dinner was grilled on it. Our morning croissants had a hint of charcoal about them. Saucisson became a big part of our diet apart from poor old Angus, who is vegetarian. I have spent years shouting out 'saucisson' in a faux French accent, which Yaz had just assumed meant 'lovely' because I'd yell it with such exuberance.

This misinterpretation led to a hilarious moment when she was boat-hopping with Tom as competent crew across the Pacific on their round the world trip. They were on a yacht with a family when the skipper called everyone on to deck to look at a spectacular sunset.

Yaz, with her usual enthusiasm, popped her head out of a hatch and on seeing the setting sun yelled out 'saucisson'. The dad looked at her quizzically and asked 'why are you shouting sausage?' Yaz, needless to say, went as glowing red as the sun itself. 'Thanks for making me look like a prize sausage, Dad'.

With the aroma of saucisson filling the air and the sun going roughly from east to west with the rear garden facing south, we started in the shade of the turret and as the afternoon wore on we were in the sun's full glare overhead. A huge parasol gave us cover and chilled water kept us hydrated. Which was just as well, because the wine was flowing and we were getting gloriously sozzled.

Ken was keeping everybody in hysterics with Suzy reprimanding him when the jokes became a little too bawdy and with us catching up on all the local gossip and scandal, lunch lasted into the evening and was the template for many other lunches to come.

Unbeknown to us, Tom's half-sister Lorraine lived less than twenty minutes away and as we had never met her over the many years of knowing Tom, she was invited over for a meal with her bonny wee son Rocco. We have spent many delightful lunches at home and in the nearby town of Brantôme as she and Tom got to know each other better.

He hadn't seen as much of her as she and her mother moved to France when she was young. Tom and Lorraine's dad David has also used the château as a rendezvous between father, daughter and grandchild and has become another huge fan of Gros Puy.

Brantôme is a nearby medieval town complete with abbey, grottes and a fast-flowing river, beside which are some wonderful restaurants where we could eat and drink as Rocco chased the local ducks around the garden.

We are extremely lucky to be a mere stone's throw from towns like Nontron, a charming fortified town on a hillside famed for its knife making since the 15th century. You haven't lived if you haven't visited the knife museum at Nontron.

St Saud, where we stayed before first clapping eyes on Gros Puy has a buzzing little centre and beautiful lakes to swim and canoe in. The biggest lake is at Saint Estèphe where you can go for a great swim if you can overcome the soft silt bottom squidging between your toes and brown brackish water. There are terrific events that happen here once a week in summer that are well worth a visit.

Ken and Suzy have invited us to their home and beautifully kept gardens overlooking a lake and Ken has given us useful tips about entertaining. He numbers his bottles from one to eight, or beyond, starting with the finest wine first, then going down the scale to the cheaper plonk when everyone is so hammered, their level of connoisseurship has been somewhat impaired.

Toby always turns up with number one wine and we have all become good mates, staying in touch both in France and at home. Toby has even ferried us back and forth to Limoges Airport when we haven't come by road, which is a proper result, because he drives a top of the range Mercedes.

Suzy is always the hostess with the mostess putting our BBQ'd offerings to shame and she introduced me to something I hadn't tried before, but now can't live without. French radishes are huge fat things like giant red and white thumbs, which she cuts the tips off for you to dip into sea salt.

Needless to say in this extremely fertile area, all fruit and veg is huge and tasty without the need for GM interference. Our garden gives us an abundance of produce with peaches galore, red and black currants, rhubarb, figs, tomatoes the size of your head and we have plans to create raised beds to re-introduce vegetable plots for growing beetroots, parsnips, garlic, swede, carrots and sprouts.

Annette was an avid veg gardener when she lived at the château but I've not been able to maintain her plots, due to things like uprooting bamboo forests. I'll birch myself in punishment with one of the thickest canes I can find.

We have had many subsequent long lunches on the terrace with friends and family coming over to visit and many more still to come. They will have to bring a paintbrush or sing for their supper, because all of this entertaining doesn't get the château refurbed. Our daughter Mackenzie has created a Monet-inspired mural of water lilies in our en-suite bathroom which our art teacher friend Vicky has helped complete and it is signed by both of them.

Zak to her credit enlisted on a French course in Richmond and befriended one of the students there who arrived at the château one evening through one of the worst storms I've seen here.

These are infrequent but very violent when they hit you. They are preceded by very dark and ominous skies that warn you of the impending armageddon that is about to be unleashed upon you. Time to go to the chapel to pray for your mortal souls.

From inside the living room, I could see hail and gale force winds blowing all sorts of debris around the garden. Windows rattled, hail crashed against the windowpanes like machine gun fire and the wind made it sound like the turret was taking off like a NASA space rocket. I even took a video of it, as outside of the Caribbean, I'd never seen a squall quite like it.

Zak's friend and her husband rang us shortly after the storm had passed and were trapped in their motorhome behind a tree that had fallen across the road. As Zak's brother Art was staying with us at the time, we ventured out, slaloming through branches and boughs littering the road to try and save them from their plight and arrived to see this was no sapling laying across the road, but a full-grown oak. Even with the 4x4 and some ropes in the back, we weren't going to be able to shift this. In the end, they had to back up the narrow road and drive several miles on an alternate route to get to us. One of our tradesmen has since told us he carries a chainsaw in the back of his van in case of such eventualities.

By the time they navigated their way back to Gros Puy, night had fallen and the only thing that seemed appropriate for the trauma they had suffered was to crack open a bottle or two of nerve settling Bordeaux.

We were often required to guide visitors in as the château is a little off the beaten track. We are on a small road, but as you'd suspect from the criteria set out earlier for selection, big roads were not for us. My dear friend and fellow copywriter Chris is a real Francophile, choosing to drive his string of exotic cars around the many spectacular roads in France.

He and his wife Carolyn were doing a grand tour through the Loire, Dordogne and beyond and we invited them to join us for lunch. The usual expat crew also joined the table set out for eight outside on the terrace and the table was on the verge of buckling under the weight of local produce and delicacies to be devoured with a modicum of rosé, white and red wines. Well when I say modicum, I might be underestimating the thirsts our guests usually arrive with.

We had to give coordinates for the sat nav and a bit of a visual guide for Chris to join us and unfortunately for him, he was drinking water as the designated driver. After a tour of the grounds and progress made, or lack thereof at that stage, we chowed down with gusto. The weather was in the words of Caroline Aherne as she imitated a Spanish weather reporter, 'Scorchio'.

Thankfully Ken was on top form and kept everyone amused with his anecdotes. Ken is a consummate jazz pianist and Chris knocks out a mean tune on his organ and had spent many years working on British Airways advertising and great stories between him and Toby about Concorde and one very famous actress who was a nymphomaniac were regaled, as I ferried the wine to the table with plenty of water for Chris.

I realised what sort of state the château must have looked at the time, as after a week of solid toil, we posted some pictures of the château on Facebook to which Chris commented 'Wow, you must have worked really hard since we were there.'

What we were doing was merely cosmetic, leaving the bigger jobs still to be tackled. The re-wiring, the plumbing, the bedroom reconfiguration, the kitchen fitted, the en-suites built and the walls and ceilings plastered.

Accomplished and capable tradespeople are a must and we have been blessed with the ones we secured as our devoted team. Thrown into the mix was the fact we needed to renew the septic tank (fosse septique) in the back garden so we don't need to keep going to the one working, look at the bottom of the turret or dare I even mention, crap on straw.

This alone took a week of dirty work involving an official called a Spanc woman, although I'm not referring to her figure-trimming underwear. She had to ensure we complied with all the rules and regulations before signing it all off after the French labourers had finished their tasks. Oh yes, it's no coincidence that bureaucracy is a French word.

How you find these professional and competent people is

another chapter, so I'll start a new one at this point and of course, take you through some of the tasks we have saved for ourselves. Just to warn those of a fragile disposition, some of the scenes I will be describing are distressing. Well they were for me anyway.

Tradespeople and Getting Your Hands and Everything Else Dirty

Finding tradespeople is a case of trial and error and word of mouth in the Dordogne. After years of project managing every home we'd bought in the UK, even running her own architectural drawing company and flipping flats from run-down ruins to contemporary modern residences, this was more Zak's wheelhouse than mine.

She knows exactly what she wants and any tradesperson who works with her for any length of time learns not to argue with her vision.

We are both Aries and if you know your astrological signs, we lock horns on a regular basis, but with interior design, I bow to her greater knowledge.

If there's one thing I hate, it's a tradesman who starts talking only to me when we are standing together and when Zak speaks, still refers back to me. I feel like Basil Fawlty when his hapless Irish builder O'Reilly speaks in a condescending tone to Sybil when she is berating him for his shoddy craftsmanship, insisting he loves a woman with a bit of spirit. Sybil, to Basil's horror, sets about O'Reilly with a brolly, leaving him cowering on the floor in terror.

Yes, that's what I can seriously imagine happening one day, so I keep any objects that can be swung in anger out of reach when tradespeople turn up to quote on a job.

Thankfully, the majority of tradespeople have been

excellent, apart from one that took part payment but didn't turn up to do the job. After a stiff email, the money was returned because that sort of behaviour earns you a bad rep in the area and if you don't want to work again, that's the way to ensure you won't.

When Johan turned up, Zak briefed him on the extent of the work that needed to be done and apparently, a look on his face informed Zak that this was a gargantuan task. Johan has been a stalwart of bringing Gros Puy back to life in its new guise and there was one period when he and I were both working at the same time through the hottest temperatures on record for France. The mercury was touching 49°C, which in the château where Johan was toiling away, was probably going well into the '50s.

I have fond memories of when I was at the château for five weeks where we would have croissants and coffee in the morning overlooking the valley and contemplate the day ahead in a moment of calm and tranquillity.

Johan has a great Belgian Malinois border collie cross called Bella, who was very wary of me at first as she's a rescue dog. Bit by bit I earned her trust and I was delighted when I saw Johan and his family at the rock concert and Bella leapt up at me with tail wagging enthusiastically.

Bella though would attract the St Bernard from up the road, christened Bruno by Zak, who would enter our garden and surrounding areas to have a mooch around with ill intent. I know they are mountain dogs but the only mountain associated with Bruno is what came out of his rear end.

I've had to scoop up, or should I say shovel up, his not so welcome deposits from Versailles and dispose of them responsibly. I often thought I should pile them up outside my neighbours' property where Bruno lives, but think that might not enhance Anglo-Français relations.

I wasn't sure about our next-door neighbour. He had already walked by with his fingers in his ears when I was mowing outside and had approached speaking about his ownership of le chemin despite what was on our deeds. His demeanour was far from endearing, with his mad, white, bird nest hair and dishevelled clothes made him look like a hostile castaway. There was a time he came marching up the road as we were outside talking to a passing couple. 'What now?' we thought.

Through his ramblings, we managed to decipher that he was telling us about the history of the place. He spoke of the Brun's, the family who had owned it and the castle at Montbrun and the link with the château at Châlus about twenty kilometres away. It was all a bit vague and rambling, but we nodded politely and pretended to understand, which we clearly didn't.

It did prompt us to dig a little deeper into the history of the venerable old place we had now taken possession of in an attempt to discover some of its dim and distant connections to the past.

Châlus was where Richard the Lionheart was mortally wounded by a bolt from a crossbow and it appeared the Lord of Gros Puy, a certain Pierre Brun had led a garrison to defend the castle there after King Richard and his men, on their way back from the Crusades, had plundered and razed the nearby towns of Nontron and Piégut.

Now history is a funny old thing and based very much on folklore and myth, but from the research of an author called Maurice Castellan and his son Sylvain, they claim in a book 'Chroniques d'un Périgordin Vert' that Richard had heard of buried treasure within the keep of Châlus and laid siege to the fortress walls, no doubt looking to fill the coffers of his war chest.

Richard was out taking a nonchalant evening walk around the castle walls, carelessly neglecting to don full armour and probably unaware of the latest developments in weaponry of the more accurate and powerful crossbow.

A bolt out of the blue, or should I say out of Châlus, struck him and went deep into his shoulder. He didn't die instantly but being an impetuous sort of king, he tried to pull the bolt out and only managed to snap it, leaving the pointy end still embedded deep in his shoulder.

Middle ages medical care was pretty basic back then and of course gangrene set in and poor old Dickie died three days later in the arms of his mum, Eleanor of Aquitaine, who'd rushed to be by his side.

Many times on our journey from Limoges Airport to Gros Puy, we had seen signposts plotting the route of Richard Coeur de Lion, which spans the 180km of fortified castles of the 11th century owned by the feuding Dukes of Aquitaine, whom Richard fought in his battles against Prince Philip of France.

We had seen pictures online of tours being conducted at Gros Puy with an historical society and Zak had contacted them for any information they could give us about the château.

It turned out our eccentric neighbour is Annette's brother, the aforementioned author Maurice Castellan who had written the book on the history of the area and what would have once been his family home. He's a bit of an academic and an authority on all things historical in the region. On closer scrutiny of the online post we had stumbled upon about Gros Puy, there is Maurice looking like the professor from Back to the Future, leading the group around the Gros Puy estate.

After our enquiries, the society had asked him to tell us more about the château and one day he turned up with his daughter who spoke perfect English and she gave Zak a potted history of our castle and handed over the book written by her father. Maurice, with his daughter as interpreter, related a story that there could be buried treasure somewhere in the turret walls of Château Gros Puy or sunk somewhere in the lake, which might explain why Xavier was so keen to retain it.

I for one feel I had misjudged our neighbour and can only imagine he was a bit miffed by these noisy Brits who had swung in and nabbed his family home from his misguided sister.

Perhaps our enquiry into its history made him realise our intentions are honourable and he softened somewhat. I will relate any historical points of interest we discover while we refurb and repurpose Gros Puy, suffice to say, we want to retain as many original features as possible and not undermine the integrity of the place, with its roots firmly embedded in the culture of the region.

Every inch of floorboard, every granite stone and every fireplace has its own story to tell and we feel that responsibility keenly as we refurbish the place. If I unearth that hidden treasure of priceless historical artefacts, you can be sure that I will be keeping that very much to myself.

When Johan turns up to work at Gros Puy, he poetically talks about the château giving him a hug when he walks in, which I can only concur with.

It was far too much work for one man and he brought in extra help in the shape of Bart, a real character with a strong Bristol accent.

Bart burst into our lives with what we'd learn to be his usual enthusiastic manner, chattering away in his booming voice dispensing advice on everything and anything to anyone who was willing to listen. We have come to know him as a man with a heart as big as his character.

Following in his sizeable wake came a spirited, equally enthusiastic French man called Louis. He looked as fit as a fiddle for a man in his seventies, despite having various illnesses including lung cancer (twice), diabetes and several broken bones. His voice had the same gravelly growl as Monsieur de truffe and his dog, but his was evidently due to a tracheostomy. His voice was so raspy, he could have filed down metal with it.

Bart himself had survived a near fatal motorbike accident on his Harley a few years earlier when he skidded on gravel laid by road-workers who had failed to steam-roller it down. His wife, Jenny, who we would meet later on, was riding pillion and both spent a considerable time in hospital. Bart has shown us the scars and there's no doubt it was a hell of a scrape.

Despite their dalliances with death, Bart and Louis formed a dynamic duo capable of tackling any job grande or petit.

The arrangement is for Bart to help Louis with his English and for Louis to teach Bart some French. This hilariously involves Bart shouting at Louis in slow deliberate sentences at the top of his voice, shifting from English to French explaining what he wants him to do. 'I WANT VOUS TO CONNECT LE DRAINAGE PIPES FROM LE SALLE DE BAIN DOWN THROUGH LE KITCHEN S'IL VOUS PLAIT, LOUIS, COMPRENDEZ VOUS?' He would boom in his West Country accent.

These conversations in Franglais and pidgin French have

echoed through the château while Johan puts on his classic rock on an English radio station to be heard above whatever piece of hard-core machinery he has whirring away at any given time. It's been the soundtrack to life at the château for months on end.

Bart is a salt of the earth kind of guy. His humour may not be totally PC, but he will go above and beyond to help anyone he knows who's in need. He too has acted as taxicab for runs to and from the airport and when we have had an exhausting day of decorating, he's had us and the family round to his place about 2km away for drinks and something to eat with Jenny.

Jenny makes a mean banana cake and we've made short work of a few of them and several cocktails on their terrace, but have politely declined when Bart has invited us to join him in his Jacuzzi. He likes to go starkers and that might be a bridge too far for the ladies and I've seen all the scars I want to see thanks, Bart.

'I got nothing to be ashamed of,' he declares and his neighbours, no doubt, agree with his cock-sure statement.

I'm sure Tom would have been perfectly willing to go straight in wearing only his birthday suit, if Yazmin hadn't kicked him hard under the table. Tom's streaking is the stuff of legend having once got naked onto a stage at Glastonbury, and who else do you know who went butt naked at their own wedding reception?

I'm sure I'd leave a horrifying film of scum on any Jacuzzi surface after the jobs I've been doing. Refurbing means rolling up your sleeves and mucking in, with muck being the operative word here.

One of my many jobs was to sand the floorboards of the kitchen before the units were fitted and clear the living room to do those as well. These are ancient floorboards with deep grain and they were coated with a thick veneer of old paint and ground in grime. This required a visit to Leroy Merlin (a renowned French DIY chain akin to Homebase in the UK) where we picked up a heavy-duty sander that weighed more than me.

After a quick demonstration and being flung a load of sanding pads, we were on our own. I had an all in one white paper suit which when I squeezed into it and pulled up the hood, made me look like I had donned a condom. Well I do like to practise safe sanding.

With mask and goggles secured and looking like an NHS frontline worker in full PPE, I got the plate rotating to the right speed before lowering it onto the planks. I'm not sure at this point whether I was operating the sander or vice versa.

It was like having a wrestling match with the Rock and it would go off on its merry way, with me fighting a losing battle to keep it going in the direction I'd set it on.

There was a hessian sack strapped onto a big metallic pipe on the back that was supposed to collect all the sawdust. Guess what, it didn't and before long I was in a thick fog that resembled a wartime pea-souper.

That stuff got into every nook and cranny and the mask was about as much use as a chocolate fireguard. Getting through decades of grime was also getting through sanding pads at a rate of knots and several passes were needed to make any progress at all.

The sanding pads were looped and had to be fitted over rubber rollers. These slipped off and shredded as I tried to manoeuvre this hulking big machine and with my white paper suit tearing in all the wrong places as I struggled to grapple with this monster, I began to resemble the Incredible Hulk.

I should have warned the sander not to make me angry, but I was going full Bruce Banner and my rag was well and truly lost.

As we had the machine of misery for a limited time only, I had to power on for a whole day and into the night. I finished the vast combined square footage of the kitchen and living room, with the help of Zak who realised I was flagging at times and then we had to go around the edges with a hand-held sander to complete the job.

At the end of a battle that would be a match in ferocity to any that Richard Coeur de Lion had waged, I was, to use the cockney rhyming slang, cream-crackered and to coin another endearing phrase, totally Hank Marvin.

Every night on many of our excursions, we'd end up eating saucisson washed down with red wine and crashing out on a fold down sofa. This particular trip was in February and it was so cold, we slept without removing our layers of clothes inside sleeping bags with a paraffin heater going all night to prevent us from freezing. I hasten to add, I did remove the remnants of the shredded white condom suit before heading to the land of nod.

This was when we realised why the previous owners had a wood burner in the middle of the room with an aluminium pipe shoved up the chimney breast like a snorkel and we somewhat regretted not buying it off them. We did set a fire going in the grate of the open fire, but the chimneystack wasn't sealed above and we smoked out the bedrooms upstairs, not that there was anything in them at the time.

It also smoked out a few lodgers in the château, our resident mouse population that Zak had a real aversion to. I remember sitting on a sofa trying to thaw out as a mouse sat on one of the granite protrusions in the fireplace looking at me as if to ask 'What are you doing in my Maison, monsieur?'

I decided not to inform Zak as she sat reading on the other sofa swathed in a big woollen throw beside me. I couldn't bear to be rallied into action to get rid of the charming little fella that reminded me of one of the mice in Cinderella. Gus, the daft fat one.

We eventually had to move the bergères into the kitchen and light the open fire in the evenings. We would sit inches from it, swathed in blankets, throwing logs onto the fire with our socked feet virtually in the grate.

That visit was one where I had decided to go despite having man-flu and I laid on the drop-down sofa covered with every item of clothing we could muster to keep me from expiring overnight. I mounted a quite amazing recovery in the circumstances, because now was no time for slackers. We found that the best way to thaw out our extremities was to take extreme measures.

With no real destination in mind, we would drive around and around in the car with the heater on full blast. I think it actually saved our lives, even if not saving us any petrol money.

Besides the resident mouse population, the château and grounds were teeming with other wildlife, which was one thing us towny folk had to get used to. This is the countryside and we had mice, bats, lizards, wasps, mosquitos and flies and the occasional snake living inside and around us.

The bats in particular would hang around in the turret and it took us a while to work out that they were the culprits of heaps of guano we had to sweep from the steps every time we entered the château. I have pondered the question of whether when they poop, being upside down, does it roll down their bodies and over their heads? Gravity dictates that it must do, I suppose.

Having left the château empty for any length of time, Zak would push me through the door first to ward off any occupants that had moved in while we'd been away. Bats were up in the loft, down in the cave and hanging off the shutters when we opened them. The ear-piercing scream that greeted a little pipistrelle bat flying around the room was enough to shatter the windows before I opened them to let the critter fly out.

There was a tap outside under a manhole cover in the front garden to turn the mains water on and off and once, while doing just that, I found a mouse staring incredulously at me. It was one of those types that had beady eyes and big ears and unlike the scruffy type that scurries around on the London tube, this was brown, well-groomed and very cute. Probably a wood mouse.

Even Zak has met Monsieur Souris as she turned on the tap on arriving at the château and he leapt onto her hand. So charmed was she by the little fellah, she didn't even scream. One can almost imagine it speaking in the same voice as Pepé Le Pew, kissing the back of her hand and attempting to sweep her off her feet. 'Ah, mon Chérie, you are, "ow you say, so beautiful, I want to kiss you all over.'

Thankfully it didn't speak or I really would have assumed I was losing my marbles. I am not particularly perturbed by these lodgers, but Zak is determined to entice a local feral cat to patrol our fortress and keep them at bay.

The mice had infiltrated one of our drawers in a bedroom and made a nest in a duvet cover, so impenetrable chests and cases were purchased to seal and protect everything inside throughout the building.

Snakes haven't been found inside, but we've had our run-ins, or slither-ins with some mean looking black ones that we've been told could be vipers, but this is rare and fleeting and they are far more timid than the mice and disappear very quickly. Apparently they are good at keeping the mice populations down, so Zak should get on well with them, although probably wouldn't let one curl up on her lap like she would a moggy.

We don't have any internal birdlife, apart from the brave robins that hop in for any stray crumbs, but outside, buzzards circle overhead regularly, owls hoot in nearby trees and the distinctive call of golden orioles can be heard most evenings and they will respond to my crude imitation of their warbling whistles.

The golden orioles are canary yellow, but an extremely elusive bird to catch sight of. It seemed everybody but me had seen them, which made me green with envy. Yaz and Tom taunted me about this, knowing how keen I was to get a full view of this migratory bird and they like to call it the golden oracle. 'Dad, you've just missed the golden oracle again,' Yaz would shout from the terrace as I ran full pelt to get there, but always moments too late. One day, I will see this bird in all its glory and I will treat it as though I have been granted an audience with the golden oracle to impart its knowledge to me in its mystical song.

Woodpeckers are also much in evidence drumming their heads against trees, herons are a common visitor in this water wonderland, Angus has filmed a pheasant in our back garden and there are regular visits by hoopoe birds with their tufted heads and hooked beaks.

During this February visit, I heard a mysterious noise that grabbed my attention. I was outside getting something from the car and looked up to see thousands of birds flying in v-formations heading north. Wave after wave of them were flying overhead in platoons and we were later to learn these are grue, a type of crane, all heading to the arctic circle for the spring and summer months. Looking at their migratory routes, we could see it took them directly over the Dordogne and their collective calls made the most distinctive and entrancing sound.

The far noisier and less harmonious winged beasts that fly overhead on a regular basis are the French Air Force. It appears that their jet fighters use the château as a target point and roar overhead with only feet to spare. Thankfully they don't open fire on us, but travelling at hundreds of miles per hour, it's not until they are upon you that you hear their thunderous noise. If you happen to be holding anything in your hand, like the obligatory glass of red wine while wearing a white shirt, the inevitable is bound to happen. I am thinking of billing the French Air Force for my laundry and claiming back expenses for soiled underpants.

In the garden, we have yet to see any evidence of wild boar, but they are around and we often see wild deer roaming through the donkey field as we lounge on the terrace. They have to be fleet of foot in our region, as the French huntsmen congregate in large gatherings to flush them out and shoot them in hunting season. These guys have a menacing air about them driving in a fleet of vans with a lot of firepower on board and once we were surprised to see a moustachioed man in traditional costume galloping up and down the road on horseback. We shouldn't have laughed but he reminded us of Gaston from Beauty and the Beast.

Driving around the picturesque roads, especially at night, you have to always be on your guard in case any deer leap out of a hedgerow directly into your path. Toby speaks of one encounter in his Merc where he came to a screeching halt as an eagle owl stood imperiously in the middle of the road. It stared at him for a while before deciding to no longer enforce a route barrée and took off allowing him to recommence his journey.

Tom has had to slam on the anchors in our car to avoid a collision with a jaywalking deer and many of our friends can pay testament to the damage they do to the front of your car if you make contact. The only consolation is you can have fresh venison in your larder if you are prepared to do the butchery yourself.

In the forests we've seen beautiful foxes compared to the skanky urban ones we are used to in London and badgers litter the roadsides having not studied the French Highway Code. We are thankful that we have not seen rats or the loirs that, if they invade your loft space, will chew through all the wires and kick up a right din and our back garden is littered with mole mounds, although we haven't yet started cultivating lawns like billiard tables that would be ruined by the mini Mont Blancs of earth they push up.

Down by the pond, a strange squelching noise starts at around dusk. It starts a chorus that gets progressively louder and echoes around the valley. This is the distinctive noise of frogs that can get so loud in the Dordogne, there has recently been a court case where complainants insisted they move the amphibians out of the area and fill their pond in. I love hearing them at night as we sit out under the stars sharing the stories of the day.

Even though it's a small pond, there are always ducks that take flight whenever I appear. I have always been a bit of a twitcher, with a keen eye for birds and get excited when I see any of our feathered friends and point them out enthusiastically to the not so interested family.

My interest stems from my father who kept canaries, cockatiels and zebra finches in two aviaries in our back garden. For a hardened copper and ex-marine, he had a soft side when it came to tending these delicate winged creatures.

I grew up with him looking like one of the criminals he'd banged up, trapped inside a cage with exotic breeds flapping around him like the birdman of Alcatraz. His father before him kept birds including a bullfinch, which I still want to see in the wild, hopefully at Gros Puy.

I also try to identify birdcalls before I've seen the source of the song. The onomatopoeic sounds of Jackdaws seem to be saying jackdaw over and over again. I often wonder whether French birds have a different accent to their British counterparts.

Does a jackdaw called a choucas in French fly about cawing chou-cas I wonder? The cuckoo that I have heard making the unmistakable cuck-oo sounds in the Dordogne is known as a coucou. Not much difference there, apart from maybe a Gallic shrug thrown in as they're laying their eggs in a sparrow's nest.

Are chiffchaffs that definitely go chiff-chaff to my ear, heard singing 'pouillot véloce' in the cochlea of French people?

I have a very noisy robin outside my window here in Richmond, sounding much louder during lockdown now the planes aren't roaring into Heathrow on such a regular basis. It is a fact that urban birds sing louder to be heard above the traffic than their rural cousins and now without a series of A380's roaring overhead as competition, they've become positively deafening.

Robins are aggressive, greedy birds and their French name

of rouge gorge, does seem to suit them better than all that romanticised Christmas card nonsense we get in the UK.

I love the French word for birds and even one of our rooms at the château has been named chambre de oiseau to reflect their presence on the decorative wallpaper we've pasted up.

When I was sharing breakfast with Johan, getting our caffeine fixes and almond croissant sugar rushes to power us through the day, his knowledge of local bird life was excellent and he informed me that the little bird sitting on the end of my garden fork was a redstart.

Now talking of Johan, he has a son called Jon who we employed to get rid of the bamboo forest at the end of the garden. We decided he was a more practical choice than buying a panda called Chu-Chu. I had attempted to hack into it and dig up the roots, but decided it was too much for one man with rudimentary tools.

Anyone who knows bamboo knows it is one of the fastest growing plants on the planet and getting rid of it is technically known as being 'a right bastard'.

Jon borrowed Bart's digger and it took him a week and a lot of swearing to get all of the bamboo up and even then, there are roots that have sprouted again down by the pond.

I waded into that pond to try and pull them up and ended up covered from head to toe in thick mud as the wellies got filled to the rim in smelly bilge once they sank into the mire. In the summer months, that same pond attracts mosquitos and horseflies that leave you a pin-cushion of holes where they suck out your blood and no amount of repellent keeps them at bay.

I think they regard me as a fine claret and to be fair, I think while in France the red wine content in my veins probably rises by a good thirty-forty per cent.

These are the joys of château life they edit out of programmes like 'A New Life in the Sun' and 'Escape to the Chateau DIY' and if they had filmed me tackling the bamboo and bloodsuckers, the dialogue would have just been a series of bleeps from the stream of profanities.

We can test this out for real, as Zak has put us forward to appear on the show and they have interviewed us online to see if we are suitable candidates. They recorded us on a Zoom call and I was suitably grumpy as opposed to Zak and Yaz's polite repartee, which will either make them run a mile or think this is a volatile combo for on screen pyrotechnics. I might swear like a trooper on camera, which isn't far from reality, just to give the sound editor a lot of effing and jeffing to grapple with. They'll also have their work cut out with the inappropriate singing, non-pc ranting and unrelenting arse gags. Watch this space for updates.

Jon did a cracking job, but instead of a bamboo forest, we now have a bottom terrace full of dead bamboo and roots trying to re-grow again that'll take hours of backbreaking work to get to the déchetterie. I've started shifting them to the chemin with a wheelbarrow and the donkeys stand in the field watching me curiously as a beast of burden in human form. Their braying sounds like ridiculing laughter and I often bow to them for the appreciation of my performance. Yaz thinks I am a dead ringer for Dick van Dyke, nicknaming me Dick van Dad and this episode in my life always brings to mind him singing 'The Old Bamboo' in Chitty Chitty Bang Bang.

Lord only knows what horrors have happened in the time I've been in lockdown in the UK and spring is wreaking havoc with everything sprouting untended.

Methinks Jon will be called again to go for a second round

of digging and help me get rid of the old bamboo. I have plans to build landing stages beside the pond to put tables and chairs on and Tom has already erected some towel rails, but I do have enough bamboo to construct a small village.

Past summer months have been spent in the garden creating Zak's garden of Versailles, which includes four paths fanning out from a central circle with stone crescent benches and a fountain in the middle.

A circle of stones we had brought from the UK picks out north, south, east and west should I ever get disoriented in the garden without a GPS and urgently need accurate coordinates. This compass-like arrangement doesn't have any delusions of grandeur, as sitting on the centre stone is a small birdbath with a solar-powered fountain in the middle that spouts a few dribbles into the air when the sun comes out.

The birdbath itself is so shallow, this fountain just shoots the water into the air to be captured by the wind and empties out in about three minutes. The birds have to be quick if they want a drink on us before it's last orders at the fountain.

Taking inspiration from our Château Saint-Étienne experience, we have festooned the trees with lights and scattered luminous pebbles on the paths to bring a bit of night garden magic after dusk.

The digging out of the paths, the laying of the underlay to prevent weeds growing through and the spreading of the pebbles on the pathways has been tough enough. But doing this during the heat wave of 2019 was akin to punishment they meted out to chain gangs in the deep south.

Having no respect for my hard labour, the weeds break through the underlay and between the stones to ridicule my efforts. Moles? Don't talk to me about them. They are in collusion with weeds to try and wreck my very best efforts with mounds raising the paths I'd spent hours levelling out.

I spent five weeks alone at the château practising for Covid-19 isolation and during this time, I did start going stir crazy. I started to feel like Tom Hanks in Castaway and my appearance was the first thing to deteriorate.

When not needing to impress work mates, employers and fellow commuters with sartorial elegance and hygiene, I quickly descended into looking like a vagrant. A bedraggled white beard soon sprouted from my jawline, using a brush or comb seemed unnecessary for my bird's nest of hair and with a lack of conversation, I started listening to that berating voice in my head telling me what a useless failure I am.

I have a long history with mental health issues, mostly with depression and anxiety and this was probably the first time I'd spent alone for any length of time. My life has always been full of family, friends, work colleagues and a full and varied social life, so a prolonged period of solitude was new territory for me. The voices took no prisoners as they were given this open mic opportunity and didn't hold back in a one-sided roast battle.

In the château at night, any creak or bang was a homicidal axe-wielding lunatic who had escaped from an asylum and was looking to satisfy his bloodlust. Of course, an old building like this is always subject to wind whistling through gaps, expanding or contracting floorboards and maybe a critter or two out for a moonlit sojourn.

Imagination runs riot when you're all alone, but as we all know, a duvet pulled over your head makes you invisible and impervious from attack with any sharp or blunt instrument.

In this self-imposed isolation, the closest I got to communication was listening to birdcalls in the garden. One started to sound like it was saying 'so pleased to meet you' which was amusing at first with my retort being 'nice to meet you too', but after the 1,000th time of saying it I screamed out 'Okay, we've done the introductions, now ferme le beak!'

It was like the scene in Castaway, where Tom Hanks started having conversations with a punctured volleyball referring to it as Wilson. I'm sure the Wilson sports brand paid a lot of money for that product placement, but I wasn't getting a penny for speaking to my feathered friend who had a very limited vocabulary of sparkling repartee.

I did have Johan turning up for blessed relief and he must have lost several stones in the sauna inside as he reconfigured what was to be Yaz and Tom's bedroom, by shortening the central corridor and opening up the space to be much bigger. Eventually he had to start leaving at 4pm when the heat was reaching its peak.

In that time, he built a level platform on the sloping floor where now sits a blue clawed bath with golden feet, so you can look out of the window, immersed in hot soapy warm water, surveying the valley and forest.

He'd built a floor to ceiling pillar around an ugly metal support, to be in keeping with the huge oak beam that crosses the ceiling. These sturdy beams had been boxed in, which is one of those sins of the 70's that seem bemusing to us now.

A toilet and sink have also been installed in an en-suite room. There was a big metal bolt protruding from the floorboards that Zak didn't like the look of, so started to unscrew it with an adjustable spanner.

It was taking some shifting as it had some heft attached to it when Bart walked in and said, 'Don't undo that, it's keeping the chandelier up down in the living room.' It conjured visions of an Only Fools and Horses moment with Rodders and

Grandad on ladders, poised and ready with a safety blanket beneath a chandelier, as Delboy unscrewed the one next to it, which shattered to the floor with an almighty crash.

No doubt it would have been timed with comic perfection so I'd have been underneath it at the time, thinking I was getting away with a crafty bit of downtime with a beer or vin rouge. That bolt has been marked up and thankfully is out of the way now beneath the double bed.

Angus's room next door has also been rearranged to steal some space for a family bathroom with a level floor with a bath and shower going in there to cater for the other three bedrooms. The small narrow room the straw toilet had once graced was opened up to give more space with all the modern loo fittings you'd expect minus any trace of straw.

This gives Angus a corridor into his room, which is still a large double with its own fireplace and double aspect windows. Mackenzie's room has been largely left intact with cosmetic additions to hide pipes and boxes ripped out to reveal the original beam.

Zak tore that down and inside the old plaster was a mummified rodent that has been decreed a rat and not a loir.

Johan has placated Zak who was freaking out quite considerably by saying nobody has spotted a rat in the area for decades. For someone who is a rat in the Chinese horoscope, she has a fanatical dislike of a creature she is supposed to share certain traits with.

I might not be too bothered by the cute mice that scurry around the place, but even I'd draw a line at rats staring at me as I tried to relax in the living room. I think the Disney film Ratatouille tried its best to make a rat seem charming in some way, but didn't achieve it in the same way the mice in Cinderella came over as cute.

A rat named Remy under a toque hat somehow guiding the

chef in a kitchen to create gastronomic delights by pulling his hair? I think someone was smoking wacky-baccy that day in Walt's studio.

The bedroom, where some wooden cot beds and a ceramic wood burner had been left at our request, has been described as 'the child that died room' by Yaz. I think she has watched too many horror films and has an overactive imagination.

It is a perfectly charming room, but she has gone and permanently maligned it with this moniker that has stuck. I don't think we'll be putting that on a plaque to hang on the door, as it might not attract the sort of clientele we are looking to attract as a chambre d'hote.

We aren't looking to cater for haunted house fans and to date, none of us has actually had a paranormal experience. If we do have ghosts, they are very friendly benign ones. No old knights clanking their mace down the turret steps or headless damsels still in a state of distress wandering the corridors.

We were told by Xavier of an elderly woman who knocked on the door of the château one day and related a story about how as a young maid she slept at the top of the turret on the landing. She asked to go back up there to take a look and relive her childhood memories. Thankfully she hasn't returned again to haunt the place, unless that's her reincarnated as a bat.

Bart and Jenny have also been involved in the reconstruction of Gros Puy, with the re-channelling of plumbing to connect the bathroom pipes that drain out into the new fosse septique.

The installation of the septic tank system took a whole week of work with a troupe of builders who turned up daily, turning the east garden into something resembling the Somme.

They craned in a huge tank that looked like a green version of the Beatles yellow submarine before sinking it into the ground. The pit they had dug for it with a mechanical digger was filled with specific materials, which filter and purify the sewage before it soaks away.

Vents protrude out of the ground, no doubt to let gases escape. Hmm, what a lovely feature for any garden. I don't think a luxury yurt will be put up in that vicinity.

Of course, Bart pointed out they had put it in the wrong place, which involved him having to drill through four feet of solid granite wall to get the pipes out to it. Just the news we needed, but if they can build a tunnel under the English Channel, why not a hole through the hardest stone known to man?

Needless to say, that was all done with the right specialist drills and after the Spanc (Service Public d'Assainissement Non Collectiff) woman had given the work her seal of approval, we are now able to shower and bath and smell lovely and fragrant after a hard day decorating indoors or working up a sweat outside (even if resembling a desert-island Tom Hanks dragged through a hedge backwards).

Piping hot water is now available from the water tanks Bart has installed in the loft for the west wing and one in the utility room to supply the east wing. Bart even built an airing cupboard around that tank which also houses a washing machine and dryer. This is almost beginning to resemble modern-day civilisation with straw toilets a distant memory. I promise this is the last time I'll mention the straw toilet. Honestly.

What was once the games room is now my and Zak's bedroom with an en-suite wash and shower room that has been built into one corner with an east-facing window letting sunlight stream through in the morning.

To be honest, the bedroom is so vast, we could have got two bedrooms out of it, maybe even three, but we now have a living room area with two sofas facing each other across a Persian rug beside the fireplace and the sleigh bed fits snugly into the corner where the grain room has been ripped out and the bathroom wall erected.

Ornate wall lights bathe the alcove, which is painted a dark red, with a warm cosy glow. Once again, all the plaster boxes have been torn down to reveal the oak beams traversing the ceiling. The rafters must all have been hewn from one tree each as they are that chunky and robust.

How they got that tonnage of oak up onto a second floor to support a roof boggles the mind. My mind is constantly boggled by what they could achieve in those teen centuries without modern machinery. Ceilings and walls have been plastered ready to be painted and the rest of the bedroom, which has decorative wallpaper and walls painted a mocha colour are illuminated with decorative wall lights.

A peak up into the loft space above the bedroom at the summit of the staircase, opens up a complex network of wooden struts supporting the roof and the witch's hat that sits on top of the turret, which one day could be converted into living space.

We also secured the services of an electrician called Sam, a dyed in the wool Yorkshire man who had to rewire the whole property to incorporate the many new wall lights and chandeliers, not to mention new plugs throughout the building.

It took him months working around the rest of the crew, but bloody hell lad, he's done a smashing job. I must apologise to any readers from Yorkshire who are finding my repeated northern accent tiresome and clichéd. I worked with a lad from Rotherham for thirty years in advertising and his vernacular just spills out of me at the mere mention of the county of the white rose. It is all done with great fondness from a soft southern jessie.

Meanwhile, downstairs, the kitchen was being stripped bare and the fitted kitchen erected from the flat-packs delivered from Leroy Merlin. We even got a couple of chimney sweeps in to get decades of soot out of the chimneystacks.

Once again, I turned into Dick van Dad, doing my version of Chim Chim-er-ney, this time from Mary Poppins. Two strapping lads turned up and looked like a pair of small Oompa-Loompas in comparison to the fireplace's sheer size as they stood beneath the mantelpiece.

Brushes were connected and guided upwards, dislodging clumps of blackened dust and thankfully they'd put down plenty of tarpaulin to save it cascading all over the chapel. The same application was shown in cleaning the chimneys to the living room and bedroom above it and all the paperwork completed as a guarantee they'd done a thorough job.

This protects you from being culpable if your place goes up in smoke to prove your chimneys weren't the cause of the fire. Having clean and clear chimneystacks is a legal requirement in France and regular cleaning a prerequisite.

I of course shook hands with the sweeps hoping good luck would rub off in line with DVD's lyrics. I think with the magnitude of what we have taken on, I'm sure going to need it.

Things, however, were slowly but surely beginning to take shape and the next steps would require some decorating and no shortage of drama and confrontation. Much preparation had been done, but nothing was to prepare me for the differences of opinion that were yet to come.

Internal decorating and internal scrapping

As I have mentioned, I am a copywriter of many years' experience. That in no way has furnished me with the practical skills needed for DIY in a château.

I can knock you out a headline for a poster or press ad. I can write the copy with a call to action to make you part with your hard-earned cash.

I can even write a compelling script for a TV or radio commercial.

But show me a power drill and I don't know one end from the other. I can write something that'll sell one, but not be able to use one. The mishaps that occur with any DIY job is the sort of thing they tend not to edit out of the château renovation programmes, as it makes good telly when someone ends up looking like a prize pillock. They would have hours of footage of me making a pig's ear of virtually everything involving a ladder, a tool and simple reparation job.

In my time as a creative, I have worked on many campaigns, some of which you might know from the dim and distant past. I have been a creative director on hundreds of well-known brands, including Nike, Sony PlayStation, Kellogg's and McDonald's.

I have personally written famous commercials like Nike 'Parklife' where we put high profile players like Ian Wright, Eric Cantona, Robbie Fowler and David Seaman on the pitches of Hackney Marshes with Sunday League football teams to the strains of Blur's Parklife tune.

I've written an ode to McDonald's customers in a commercial with each line ending 'were just passing by'.

I recently wrote the end line 'we cross the T's dot the I's and put you in the middle' for the travel company TUI.

I've flogged Honda cars, Crunchy Nut Cornflakes, games consoles, pints of beer, bottles of spirits, bank and savings accounts, credit cards, sports gear, loaves of bread, airlines and dissuaded young men from drink driving and kids from being irresponsible on the road.

I've run departments full of moody creative types both in the UK and in the States, but have no idea how to motivate a team of builders apart from making mugs of tea you can stand your spoon up in.

Tradespeople terrify me at how easy they make things look and make me feel totally inept, but I'm sure they'd have a similar panic attack if I sat them down with an empty layout pad and asked them to write an advert to a brief from McDonald's for instance.

The big plus point about working in advertising for many years, is I've owned quite a few homes and earned enough money to fund the refurbing of a huge place in Brits' favourite region of France.

I'd also learnt the meaning of hard work and how to handle a roller and I don't mean the four-wheeled kind. This work ethic was, and still is, essential as you embark on a venture like owning a château. You have to roll up your sleeves daily and help with the decorating.

The physical fatigue is but nothing to the mental strain it brings. The never-ending to-do list can sometimes become all-consuming and while I had returned home to earn some much-needed money as a freelancer, I got an alarming phone call from my better half who was in the middle of a panic attack.

She was all alone going from the bank to the DIY store and the supermarket when she became overwhelmed by the scale of what we'd taken on. She has a form of dyslexia with numbers and had cocked up some dates for me to travel back out there and got some measurements wrong.

We all thought this was a subject matter for great hilarity, but it was seriously messing with her mind. The ongoing saga with rodents was getting to her also and she was stressing about the mounting list of tasks to be done.

She pulled into a car park and vomited. Thankfully she had the good sense to phone me as she got back into the car. Her heart was pounding and she had gripping chest pains so assumed she was having a heart attack.

I personally have suffered from depression and anxiety all of my life and recognised the symptoms immediately. I had to speak to her calmly and took her through some breathing exercises I'd learnt while practising yoga. Breathe in through the nose and exhale out more than you've breathed in. Hold at the bottom of the breath and inhale slowly again.

I was speaking as calmly as I could to help her relax her muscles and focus the mind on only the breathing.

It was pretty distressing from my end listening to her groaning in pain insisting she was having a cardiac arrest, but I knew she'd eventually bring down the levels of panic if she concentrated on the breathing and didn't fear the worst was happening to her.

Eventually, after about half an hour, she got herself back to an even keel and headed back to the château to sit down and relax.

This had taken me by surprise, as there are few more grounded and capable women than Zak. But it only went to prove what a mammoth task we had taken on and that we had to do it mindfully one step at a time and not expect it to be finished overnight.

We were going to have to learn to live in rubble, dust and disarray and accept we were just humble human beings with only so many hours in a day.

Entire rooms were stacked with paint tins, wallpaper rolls, paint stripper, tools and ladders, furniture and fittings, mattresses, rugs and curtains, baths, bogs and bric-a-brac and stayed that way for months.

The going was slow and stuff just wasn't getting done quickly enough. Tradespeople needed holidays and had family emergencies to deal with, ambitious plans require exceptional patience.

The decorating started in earnest in the living room. With the floorboards sanded, the wallpaper, although depicting pastoral scenes of Paris in days gone by, was yellowing and peeling away and had to go.

Stripping it would take time and the whole family got stuck in with scrapers, while tearing strips off of the wall and sometimes each other. We kept swathes of the wallpaper and have put them inside beautiful chrome frames that now adorn the walls either side of the fireplace.

What was left on the walls was a dappled patina that we have collectively decided to keep as it has a certain authenticity to it. Undoubtedly, that will change as the whole look unfolds and a new plan is hatched.

Sugar soap removed the sooty grime that had accumulated around and above the marble fireplace and mirror, which prepped it for painting. The skirting boards and cupboards were huge and they too would require gallons of undercoat to hide the eccentric purple colour scheme they'd been daubed in previously, before being ready for the Farrow and Ball we had brought over from the UK.

It's worth pointing out that most materials for decorating are far more expensive in France than the UK and of an inferior quality, so we brought loads of tins over in the car.

I know Farrow and Ball is at the higher end of the paint price scale, but we have found the choices of paint colours in France very limited if you're looking for something subtle with a strange name like Lark's Spleen or Badger's Scrotum.

So prep done, we set to work with the 'Strong White' and 'Blackened' bringing light back into the grand old room with the shades of white. The fire surround was finessed with flourishes of gold paint to the ornate architrave, bringing out its full character. Oh yes, we were going total Michelangelo here although the Sistine Chapel didn't have cause for concern that we might start stealing their tourist customer base.

Zak had decided to replicate two huge oil painted scenes of exotic birds, in a formal garden by getting a firm to print out decals with an adhesive backing. These were to be stuck to the walls either side of the doors leading out to the terrace and have a golden framework built around them.

Getting those aligned, even using a spirit level, was no mean feat, as anyone who owns a château will tell you, nothing inside or out is ever straight. You get one chance to stick those buggers down and using a ladder, peeling the back off and smoothing it down as you go, presents a real challenge when you're balancing on a small ledge several feet off the ground and somebody below is shouting 'up a bit, to your left, right-hand side higher' and other vague instructions.

We got those up to the best of our ability then delegated the task of getting the gold frames around them to Johan who had to use his considerable carpentry skills to make them work. We used gold spray cans on the beading and woodwork out in the garden and touched up bits once Johan had erected it on the walls. The clawed feet for the bath in Yaz and Tom's room were also sprayed gold and an elaborately framed mirror to hang above the bath was also painted gold. It looked like King Midas himself had been running amok touching everything he came across. From the look of my hands, we'd also done a couple of high fives.

When Yaz arrived to inspect the handiwork in the living room, she wasn't pleased. We hadn't followed her mood boards to the letter and she was spitting feathers. Her mum wasn't at the château when she arrived, but she took it upon herself to start painting over the Farrow and Ball with some cheapo blue paint we'd picked up from the bricolage, demanding more colour be brought in, even though we'd spent hours covering up the bold colours.

Now I know not to get caught in the crossfire between these two strongly opinionated women, but I did send a text to Zak explaining what was going on. World War Three broke out between them with me ducking for cover in the nearest trench I could find or dig.

Tom was also there and tactically withdrew from the field of conflict.

I was then subjected to the silent treatment, which consisted of hmmm's and huffs whenever I asked anything. I was in Gros Puy but was sent to Coventry.

I'd spent hours in her bedroom getting it ready for her and Tom to walk in and gasp at my hard work, but as I'd grassed her up I was in le Maison de chien.

Tom eventually acted as peacemaker, urging Yaz to concentrate on finessing their bedroom and a peace treaty was metaphorically signed and agreed to.

Their bedroom had a lovely frieze on the wall Zak and I had painstakingly added behind their metal-framed bed. Yaz had it delivered from Rockett St George and we had pasted it up onto the wall and made sure the eight separate pieces it came in, matched up perfectly. Guess what the theme was? That's right, a bamboo forest. Aaaaaaargh! It did look great though, beautifully painted in a Japanese style with herons wandering through the bamboo and leaves captured in shades of pink and white.

I'd spent hours on my hands and knees scraping black paint off of the floorboards with a wire brush and sugar soap and added two coats of clear satin varnish. Theatrical curtains and sashes had been sourced from a shop called Curtain Call in Richmond and I had hung them in the windows and stood back to admire my work. Zak had spent a small fortune on the heavy lined curtains, lengthy enough to go from floor to ceiling to cover every window in the château. These were of such intricate patterns, colours and textures, they required metres of sashes and tie-backs with ornate tasselled ends to do them justice.

The curtains weighed so much, it took me four visits to the shop on Richmond Hill to collect them all, my knees trembling under the weight as I brought them back to our flat and up three flights of stairs. The only way to transport them to the château was to pile them onto a roof rack on the car and secure them down with a maze of ratchet straps passed through the car's interior. I was at work the day Zak and Angus spent an entire day getting them on top of the 4x4.

When I got home from work, I'd never seen the arches as low over the wheels. The tyres needed a few more pounds of pressure pumped in to ensure they had enough puff to keep going. Zak's number dyslexia had us heading to Portsmouth an hour later than was printed on the tickets and when we got there, the ferry had already sailed.

We were fortunate enough to get a replacement ticket for the last ferry of the day, but no cabins were available, so we curled up on a reclining seat each to doze fitfully for the six-hour crossing, waking up with numb buttocks and stiff necks.

That was portentous of a very eventful journey all round, as we covered the 500 miles in high winds tearing at the plastic and making the straps hum and shred. Below the load, it was so loud in the car's fuselage, it sounded like we were piloting a Lancaster bomber plane.

At one stage, the curtains started to slip forward and obscure the front windshield. That would have been curtains for us if it had happened while on the motorway and veered into the central reservation. We stopped on several occasions to tighten the ratchets and ensure everything was tucked in and unable to fly free.

Having given the tyres a damn good thrashing back and forward from the UK, Bart pointed out that the tread was wearing dangerously thin and we had to have all four tyres replaced. I know that feeling of the stress of the château leading to premature baldness.

With the curtains hung over two windows and sashes added, the bed installed and mattress and bed linen added, pillows plumped and rugs laid, it looked like a boudoir suitable for my first-born princess.

Yaz, after she'd recovered from her living room meltdown, was of course delighted and spent the rest of her time painting the other walls, while Tom started building rustic benches, one with storage from reclaimed wood, that sat beneath the windows. When Zak did return to the château, we celebrated Tom's master craftsmanship with a bottle of champagne while sat in the window as the sun set in the background.

These outbursts of emotion and temper tantrums are rarely what they show on the château shows, preferring to edit them with a nice piece of musette featuring a romantic-sounding French accordion. Isn't life in the château a paradise of jaunty pottering, where everything just falls into place. Err no.

In Château Gros Puy, the dance of L'Apache, where a striped-shirted man in a neckerchief throws a woman around violently and drags her about the dance floor would paint a more accurate picture.

This is, however, interspersed with the stuff of Dordogne dreams, consisting of evening trips to restaurants, barbeques around lakes, lunches in the garden of cured meats, selections of cheeses and glasses of rosé wine. Nearby towns do like to throw a festival offering up spectacular buffets with beer and wine flowing, culminating in a firework show to illuminate the pitch-black skies.

Hours soaking up the sun in a hammock or a deck chair, smelling the waft of herbs and fresh-cut grass while building an impressive tan do occur in those idle moments in between jobs.

Nights on the terrace looking up at the stars and planets that are obscured in cities by light pollution reveal the Milky Way in its full glory and shooting stars that zip around the galaxy at lightning speed. Mackenzie downloaded an app which enables you to track where the International Space Station is in the night sky. On one occasion it was tracking right above the château and Mackenzie was pointing out which one of the bright lights it was.

This is when Zak said something that has been the topic of some light-hearted banter ever since. 'How come it doesn't bump into any of the stars?' she remarked.

Slack-jawed, Mackenzie and I stared at her incredulously for a while. It took us a moment before we could unscramble our brains enough to say anything, 'What?' Zak remarked as we stared at her before bursting into laughter. I was thinking she was just saying this for effect, but no, she was seriously asking us what she thought was a reasonable question.

Now Zak is a woman who can put her brain to many things, but anything to do with space and calculations seems to evade her on a regular basis. This is the same brain that sends messages to the mouth to ask such pressing questions as 'If the sun's a star why doesn't it come out at night?' and on being told the moon reflects the sun's rays said 'What, it doesn't emit its own light?'

There is an expression the family has all come to know well where Zak's face freezes in a vacant stare when a complex theory is mooted. Yaz has got it down to a tee as she impersonates it repeating the word 'processing' in a robotic voice and rolling her eyes. The only thing missing is a rotating buffering symbol in the middle of her forehead.

Thankfully, although measuring is a bit of an issue, this hasn't in any way curtailed her ability to get the château renovations organised and on track.

Once Yaz and Tom's room had taken shape, due to her own vision and careful planning, Mackenzie was suddenly not so pleased about her bedroom design and once again, a hissy fit ensued. I had worked tirelessly on sanding, painting and varnishing, but this was not enough for Mackenzie's demanding eye.

She was encouraged to make her own plans to personalise her space, which, with her strong artistic background, will no doubt bring an idiosyncratic style to her room. In my opinion, she has the best view of all the rooms with an unspoilt vista right across the valley with a huge expanse of sky to admire and be dwelt over.

Angus is not so fussy, but his room is now painted and wallpapered, with varnished floorboards and looking very chic. As a gamer, all he requires is wi-fi and a laptop and he's as happy as le cochon dans la merde. We will be renting out his room, so somebody will eventually get to see the hard work we've put in and admire the panels of green leafy wallpaper.

For our bedroom and the corridor in the west wing, more decorative wallpaper was added to the walls. A vivid red paint around our sleigh bed with a deep red golden latticed paper on the walls did worry me that we'd look like we'd inherited the log cabin in The Texas Chainsaw Massacre, but with two further walls painted a subtle shade of mocha and the stripped back oak beams it has all balanced out to look very luxurious and relaxing. The corridor had been dark and oppressive, but the light blue, latticed paper illuminated by two crystal chandeliers, has brought a grandeur and opulence that was sorely missing before.

We brought the big sander back in because of the surface area to be covered and once again, I girded my loins for a battle of wills.

We hired it from a different shop this time and it didn't seem to work with such brutal efficiency. The collection bag strapped onto the waste pipe at the back slipped off and split and I spent my time inhaling the wood dust and collecting it in my nasal passages, hair and ears. As the weather was hotter than it was during our first sanding, an all in one suit would have been far too suffocating, so it got into other nooks and crannies I dare not describe. Bogies were like wooden bullets.

This took me two days of solid sanding taking it right to the wire of allocated hire time doing the corridor, bedroom and en-suite bathroom with two coats of satin varnish. As I applied the very last rollers worth of the potent whiffing varnish without trapping myself in a corner, Zak was already revving the car to get us back to Caen in time. I did leave enough time to double check Zak's reading of the departure time on the tickets. Yes, we are leaving with enough time to get there without attracting the attention of le gendarme.

It is always with a heavy heart that we drag ourselves away from Gros Puy to return to London, but we all had to get back for work purposes and Mackenzie for school and university, but we always had progress from Johan, Bart, Sam and Louis to return to and that moment we first catch a glimpse of the turret roof and weather vane welcoming us back.

In February 2020, we returned and opened the kitchen door to see the kitchen units fully installed with the treated wood worktop creating the central island.

Instead of ordering it complete, Johan and Bart had sawn the wood to size, glued the boards together, sanded and oiled them to a smooth finish. The corners were rounded off and it looked stunning. A new sink had been put in with lavish new mixer taps and it looked like something Smallbone would be proud of. Stacks of slate tiles had been delivered to become splash backs and complete the look.

After a period of oohing and ahhing, we set to work painting this huge space of the kitchen including the ceiling. The fire surround that had been desecrated in a muddy green and orange paint job, had to be stripped back to its original wood finish. Mackenzie had started this process, but it needed hours of dedicated scraping with gallons of paint remover applied to make any inroads.

Up the ladder I went again, realising just how high this room is by having to stretch to get my scraper in between the highest grooves and carvings even on the very top rung.

It took hours of peeling away the sludge and gunk the acrid smelling remover turned the coats of paint into. It fell into my face and eyes and had to be removed quickly before it took a layer of skin off too.

There was no mirror in the space left vacant, but Zak had spotted a large sheet of mirrored glass in the loft that Tom and I were given the unenviable task of bringing down the turret stairs.

This was an enormous undertaking as the glass was a big heavy sheet about eight feet by six and we had to lay down blankets to slide it over the beams in the loft while balancing on planks of wood to not fall through the ceiling below. The mirrored paint on the glass was peeling off in flakes, which was probably a toxic hazard.

The whole way down the rotating granite steps, we were fearing that ominous cracking sound as we slid it over the blankets. If it gathered a momentum of its own and slipped through our hands, it would have got itself down to the bottom, but probably in a million pieces followed by a cascade of blood.

Delicate manoeuvring eventually got it from the loft, down the sixty or so feet of granite drop onto the kitchen level. Awash with sweat and relieved we still had all our limbs intact; the flaky mirrored sheet of glass was there to be fixed into place.

Now the walls and ceilings needed whitewashing and slate tiles adhered to the walls as splash backs before two further chandeliers were wired up from on high.

You know that punishment they use in the military where soldiers are made to hold their rifles above their heads for a length of time in a form of torture, well that's what I had to do with a roller strapped to a stick to get to the highest reaches of the walls and the ceiling. Not just once, but for two coats.

All I needed was the quintessential red-faced Sergeant Major, bellowing at me to keep going when my arm muscles were beginning to flag. Luckily for me, I had Zak to supply that form of motivation.

She and Yaz went to get new supplies and materials on a long trip to Périgueux with a stop off at le supermarché to replenish dwindling supplies in the fridge and freezer.

I remember a trip to the same location in a hire car, where Zak had parked precariously close to a bollard and forgotten her near proximity to it as she pulled out again turning the steering wheel before clearing the out of sight obstacle. I was outside of the car as I heard the crunching grinding sound as she ran it the length of the car. *F-F-F-F*-U-U-U-D-G-E!

As we usually only needed to hire cars for transit to and from Limoges Airport to the château on relatively empty roads, we rarely bothered with taking the extra insurance in case of an accident.

Seeing Zak sinking her head into her hands and letting out an almost primal cry, I didn't have the heart to add to her woes with further reprimands. Every penny counts in sticking to our budget and an expensive repair bill was not factored in. C'est la vie.

As Zak and Yaz headed to the car, do you think I would have said 'Look out for any bollards'? You can bet I did.

With them out of the frame for a while, I cranked up loud rock music from Spotify and rocked and rolled to help me get through the monotony of the task.

With virtually my last thrust of the stick, they returned

hours later telling me about their lovely lunch and little shopping spree. I didn't mind too much as the promise of a cold beer from the back of the car was just what I needed at that point.

Yaz and Zak got the slate tiles up which looked amazing and then came up with the idea of having a central strip of tiles down the middle of the central island and then drill through both those and the wood to feed through wires to a pair of very quaint central lamps.

The stools to surround this island had been delivered and Yaz busied herself trying to diligently follow the instructions for assembly with inevitable cussing when you realise you've got all the bolts in the wrong holes and the wrong way around. Their mixture of modern design with traditional materials, when completed, worked a treat. Madagascar was a dim memory and rustic chic had taken its place. All that is required now is the mirror fitted and a bit of snagging done.

The whole effect reminds me of our once favourite restaurant from our advertising days at Saatchi's called Chez Gerard on Charlotte Street in London with the ambient light from the central lights bouncing off the polished wood and grey slate.

Of course at landmark times like these, there's only one thing for it. Pink champagne so we can look at all of this through rose tinted and sparkly glasses.

Day-to-day living and future plans

Through the record-breaking temperatures of the summer in France, a swimming pool would have been a godsend.

Regulations say we can only do this if it is attached to the existing building. This would be quite an undertaking while we are trying to refurb the rest of the château and having had a swimming pool in Dubai, I know only too well the maintenance involved.

Throughout the summer, we filled up a sizeable paddling pool, which took all day to reach a dunkable level where at the end of the day we could leap in to cool down.

It did take a couple of days for the water to warm up to a temperature where a wimpy scream didn't emit from my lips when I lowered myself above groin level.

Within a week, the water developed a greenish tinge as there were no real chemicals added to keep mildew at bay. This made the bottom slippery and a bit unpleasant underfoot.

It was enough to make us rethink months of digging and building a full-sized swimming pool, not to mention the constant maintenance required.

In terms of priorities, it isn't top of our list to build a full-scale piscine, although a real ambition for the future to offer up to our discerning and probably demanding guests.

About fifteen minutes' drive away is a town called Saint Estèphe, where there is a large lake with a big beach where we can go if in need of a refreshing swim. It is surrounded by bars and restaurants and they lay on events in the evening where you bring your own baskets of food and wine and local farmers pitch up with fresh lamb, beef, pork and chicken to have a sizzling barbeque.

There is something no nonsense about the way French Farmers prepare their meat and serve it without all that health and safety shenanigans.

No kite marks offered up here, just some fat fingered guy in a blood-stained singlet hacking a hunk of meat while puffing on a cigarette hanging from his bottom lip.

Zak is the sort of diner who gets sneered at by some restaurant waiters when she asks for her steak to be served well done or 'bien cuit' in French.

Me, I'm happy for my beef to be virtually mooing and if I do eat lamb, which I'm not such an avid fan of, I'm happy for it to be pink and tender.

The vendors who turned up at this event were slapping big slabs of recently slaughtered meat onto a sizzling plate with onions and sliced tomatoes and the aromas wafted around prompting the gastric juices into full on mouth flooding action.

There was no dressing it up here, this was a carnival for carnivores where the meat had come direct from the fields where the luscious grass brought a flavour all of its own. No GM malarkey with fillers, antibiotics and battery farming. This was all free range and free from chemical additives, so very tasty if you're not the squeamish type.

Washed down with lashings of red from a nearby vineyard and accompanied with the freshest of salads and sauces, I was happy to be less city dweller and embrace the country life with a burger the size of Belgium.

We joined a table where Toby had already taken root on

one of the benches and introduced the Malcolm party to his mixed company of expats and local friends. There's something so convivial and unpretentious about this style of living, that any British reserve soon melts away with good food, good company and a good skinful of fine wine.

An evening walk around the perimeter of the lake tempted us into a bar for a bière and to listen to a very talented guitarist and singer and that all-pervasive joie de vivre soon permeated every cell in my body.

Paddling was the order of the day and a plan was settled on to install a plunge pool at the château, attached to the terrace which is elevated a good six or seven feet from the ground below.

Of course, this would have an element of grandeur attached to it that took it up a notch from a mere paddling pool. We wanted to make it feel part of the terrace raised up on granite stone above the cave, which incorporated sunken alcoves and a bread oven beneath it. Zak had already purchased ornate iron gates that opened up beneath a curved arch.

Revellers on the terrace are only protected from a steep drop by a wooden guard rail. This of course will not do for the château and so iron fencing reflecting a medieval pattern has been brought from the UK to replace what's already there.

This has to be effective in keeping people from going lemming like over the precipice, but not at the expense of blighting the incredible view over the valley.

The plunge pool is off to the side where a staircase and iron railings take you down to a gateway that has managed to survive within a crumbling wall held together with render and weeds.

The stairwell will form one side of the surround of the

plunge pool and a sweeping crescent of granite will attempt to emulate the curvature of the turret.

The furniture on the terrace has swapped and changed around since we've owned the château.

One evening, I was passing by Asgill House in Richmond beside the river that was built on the site of Richmond Palace where Henry I, Richard the Lionheart's great grandfather lived in 1125. The current owner had put a lot of garden furniture in the gateway inviting people to take it away and of course, I had the perfect place to take it. The place where Henry I's great grandson would stomp around engaging in pitched battles with the lords of Aquitaine.

The wood of the benches and chairs was a bit rotten in places, but it was of such a sturdy overall design, it was worthwhile doing a bit of upcycling.

That evening, I beat the scavengers by getting the car outside and via three separate journeys, transporting chairs and benches back home for a bit of refurbing and repainting. We already had a wooden table that was going to be relocated to Gros Puy, and I took hours in the garden filling, priming and painting everything the same colour to put out on the terrace for our grand lunches.

It was of course painted in a Farrow and Ball blue grey and taken on a crusade to claim its rightful place on the terrace of Château Gros Puy. It sounds ridiculously melodramatic, but life is full of coincidences that somehow connect up. In doing just that small bit of research on Asgill House and Kings Henry I and II, it appears the latter did business with King Malcolm of Scotland, but if I go down that wormhole, I might never come out of the internet for months.

Many of the lunches I have told you about were on that

table with the bench and seats the perfect perching places for our guests' derrieres.

Zak is also taking down twenty-three deck chairs sourced from a project Yaz worked on for Google. These chairs were used to seat the audience who were stargazing with the Google Pixel 4 that has the enhanced capability to offer astrophotography of the night sky. She'd even employed the help of Tim Peake, the British astronaut, to speak about his six months spent on the International Space Station and demonstrate the features of the product. Perhaps we can get him to explain to Zak how he managed to dodge around all those stars while he was on the ISS for that length of time.

The event stretched over two evenings, one in the Welsh village of Star and the other on the upper floors of the Shard in London where Yaz sought permission to have all the lights turned off for an even clearer view.

Each chair was emblazoned with the Google logo on the white canvas tacked over the wooden frames, perfect for laying back and gazing into the firmament. Following the success of the campaign, Yaz was given permission to take the deck chairs after they'd served their purpose and they were transported home to Richmond and reconfigured for more leisurely lazing in a French garden.

Zak has removed the Google emblazoned canvas and replaced it with designer fabrics that add a real je ne sais quoi to the iconic beach furniture. This involves poker-dot materials and tapestry scenes of old Paris, not unlike the designs on the living room wallpaper.

There are fabrics depicting birds and butterflies and a paisley design bringing a retro feel to the overall effect. We have looked at companies that offer this service online and

133

through a bit of luck and a little application have saved ourselves over £2,000 if we were to purchase this direct from the manufacturer.

Zak had to go to the building where they were stored, called Sea Containers on London's South Bank, where she had to drive the car into the loading bay in the basement. Security guards supplied her with a day-glo,hi-viz jacket to wear and this has led to a bit of a fetish she's carried into her daily life.

I'm not saying she has delusions of grandeur parading around in luminous green, but it definitely brings out that holier-than-thou officiousness about her. Yaz even bought her a gilet jaune of her own for Christmas, which she wore when we went for a walk in Richmond Park on December 25th and it was amazing how many people approached her asking for information.

'Excuse me, can you tell me where I can see the deer?' asked one person in a group, believing her to be a park ranger and Zak spent time explaining where they might be able to catch a glimpse of a herd, reminding them that they are wild deer and not confined to any given space in the park.

I was looking at her open-mouthed as she pointed, directed and acted like she owned the park, which is actually the property of her majesty the queen. Her Royal Highness Zak was only a visitor to this glorious nature reserve in southwest London, but in her hi-viz, I wasn't going to remind her of her far more humble position.

On our February visit, we had taken the ornate iron gates that will be a grand entrance into the plunge pool from the terrace when we eventually construct it. I removed a large wooden planter filled with about a ton of earth and mature shrubs that took up all the space where the leap off point through the opened iron gates will be.

The large oblong box was filled with huge rosemary bushes that when in bloom, seemed to attract every insect in the neighbourhood. They would dive bomb anything sweet during mealtimes, especially the bière and dessert.

To distract the wasps that would fly down in their hoards from the wasp's nest in the loft as we dined alfresco, we had to take action by wasting good beer, putting it into jars and placing it away from the table. It did make for quite good entertainment as the wasps dive bombed in and got drunk as skunks and staggered about getting their fellow wasps into headlocks and professing "you're my best mate". I of course exaggerate this, mixing up memories of how I behave after one too many pints, but the wasp problem was one we had to deal with to deter any stinging rebukes from our newfound friends.

On those hot balmy days of relaxation on the terrace, lizards would scurry around on the decking hopping from one foot to the other to avoid burning their feet. Angus, since childhood, had always been fascinated by lizards and on one beach holiday in Antigua, he'd entertained hotel guests around a pool by lassoing them with looped strands of grass and then lead them around like the lizard version of Crufts.

The rosemary bushes that attracted such a variety of insects, butterflies and moths was to be relocated down into the garden.

The digging out was done and hopefully they have survived the trauma of being moved into the garden amongst the other herbs and flowering bushes. There's nothing like the aroma of rosemary to soothe the soul and held under a running tap when filling the bath, they promote relaxation without having to fork out for a bottle of Radox.

The big wooden planter was then emptied of all the earth shovelled over the guard rails to form the flatbed of where the plunge pool would sit and the wooden box removed to open up the decking to the plunge pool entrance.

For the horticulturists, we have discovered many beautiful plants and trees in the garden and obviously somebody was once a keen gardener and had very green fingers. A Mimosa tree blooms in the summer that has the most beautiful blossoms that spread out to look like delicate pink sea urchins. Hibiscus flowers erupt from a bush in a vivid purple and Mackenzie, who often dyes her hair in a variety of hues, has been given a run for her money by the pink redbud tree flowers.

Winter roses have already exploded into a display of deep red flowers. Mature rose bushes produce huge heads of pink blooms, which Yaz has adopted as her own, dead-heading and weeding endlessly to keep them in tip-top condition.

An acer tree and rhododendron have been imported from the UK on the insistence of Madame Chatelaine, which hopefully will begin to take to the soil and flourish this season.

Wild strawberries and cherries grow in abundance with the masses of figs, berries, plums and peaches, while mint is never in short supply.

When the gin distillery is functional, we'll never have to outsource the botanicals and I plan to forage that garden for everything I can find. There are even the large land snails Helix Pomatia, Helix Aspersa and Helix Lucorum the French use to drench in garlic butter and serve up as Escargot. The frogs we hear at night around the lake at the bottom of the garden needn't fear we'll be rendering them legless, unless they join us for a few bevvies with the rest of our new-found friends.

The fertile garden once had a proliferation of vegetable

plots that have since gone to seed and have been overrun with brambles. These will be reinstated and raised to protect them and make harvesting less of a strain on the lumbar regions.

By missing the beginning of the growing season, we now have tray upon tray of beetroots, carrots, leeks, sprouts, spinach, hot peppers, parsnips, garlic, squash and swede at home. To join the rosemary and thyme already there, parsley is growing so I can annoy everyone with my rendition of Simon and Garfunkel's Scarborough Fair in a falsetto voice.

My back has been severely tested, trimming the box hedges and laurel bushes to be more ornamental and keeping the grass and weeds from reclaiming the grounds to nature.

When we moved in, Xavier gave us a box of powder saying it had to be diluted to spray on the box hedges to kill the moths that were decimating the box hedges to the west of the château. They are well over my height of six foot one (the bushes, not the moths) and I'd say a good 25 metres in length all together, so a lot of spraying and much strimming is required to make them look all regimental and box-like, not moth eaten and bedraggled.

For the grass, I would love to invest in a sit on mower, but the slope and terracing make that impossible and the granite boulders littering the garden would severely mangle rotor blades. A Honda mower you push with the help of a motor to power the rear wheels does a perfectly good job and I have spent so much time with it, Yaz swears she's going to bury it with me in an Egyptian style ceremony, when I finally keel over.

I have to admit that the first time I used it, I didn't know how to operate the belt driven back wheels, so I was knackered after the first sweep, getting through the overgrown grass before

Zak casually pointed out what the gear lever and red handlebar were for. Duh.

We have invested in a lot of other equipment from a rotavator to a chainsaw that I can't wait to get going with, but I don't want to be one of those gardeners with all the gear but no idea, which clearly I am. Instructions in French really don't help in my quest to look competent.

We have so many mature trees covered with mistletoe, that we feel the time has come to call in a tree surgeon to open up the spaces and the wider view. Yaz and Tom's tree surgeon friend has already expressed an interest in doing this service for us gratis, with costs covered with a bed, booze and brekkie thrown in for free.

Mistletoe is a parasite and if not dealt with will kill the trees leaving us with a garden full of dead wood. I'm not sure they observe the kissing under the mistletoe ritual in France, but if we get him in around December time, we could get a side business going and if Steve got the locals into conker-fighting, we can maybe get a yuletide snog-athon going in the car park, once coronavirus is under control and social distancing restrictions fully lifted.

We are also trying to tempt some workaway people to assist us with garden duties with the offer of bed and board keeping costs down to a manageable level. I love being in the garden on my own, as I am a solitary sort of person, but having some extra hands to speed up progress, even to keep going as I go about my other duties meted out by the slave driver, sorry, taskmaster, no, project manager Zak, will surely lighten the load.

Madame Malcolm, who is never short of a plan that needs realising, wants a far more spectacular entrance to the property than currently exists and the plan is to bring a path and granite steps from the car park, down through a gateway that will lead to the grand portal at the base of the turret.

I can see these things as she describes them to me, but on my own, they will take forever to achieve, so I hope the workaway's prove to be eminently capable.

Local history and Preparing to Open up Gros Puy to Guests

Gros Puy is a home away from home and being there is always very relaxing, even though there is a constant stream of things to do. When the family is all there, we are able to be together with plenty of space to do our own thing.

I of course am always in the garden, Tom, who runs a marketing company, mostly dealing with social media channels and experiential events, will occupy the living room tapping away on his laptop and having video conference calls.

Zak will either be organising our team of builders on what needs to be done next, travelling to pick up her newest acquisition from the local selling network, crashing and smashing her way through some DIY or preparing a lavish lunch.

Yaz will be rearranging furniture, painting walls, sourcing inspiration to facilitate her vision and creating plans for château events and new initiatives.

Angus is always given a job to do, like paint all the iron railings that will become the guard rail for the terrace, scrape off some old wallpaper or do some demolition work somewhere on site.

Mackenzie is up a ladder scraping down a fireplace or finishing off a mural or a painting.

Thankfully we have wi-fi and Sonos so music echoes out through the massive rooms and come the evenings, we have a large flat screen TV linked up to Netflix and British TV so we can watch a movie or series together as we flake out exhausted.

Every morning, everybody is tempted from their beds with the smell of eggs and fresh bread, bacon and saucisson and the aroma of freshly filtered coffee.

Just down the hill from us is a large lake that filters down through sluice gates into Xavier's smaller one some thirty feet lower down. This placid lac has a landing stage with a picnic table on it. In the summer months, we transport the petit dejeuner down to the lakeside and gather there to eat while admiring the tranquil surroundings.

When Cosmo has travelled with us, he can be tempted into the lake with a thrown stick and tentatively go in as a big dog with a thick coat of brown fur, to emerge as a skinny dog resembling a mop from a bucket of dirty water.

From the lake is a trail that takes you into a network of forest paths leading all the way back to the rear of the château past Xavier's lake. He keeps a small caravan down there, which no doubt he and Annette return to when the lure of Gros Puy weaves its magic spell.

They did knock on the door once while we were right in the middle of varnishing the wooden floor of the kitchen. We will always welcome them back, but their timing couldn't have been worse as we had to make them tiptoe across the floor on cardboard sheets and hurried them around an impromptu guided tour before politely bidding them adieu because we literally had only half an hour before leaving for the airport.

When we feel in a better position to lavish more time on them, we'll invite them in for a full tour where we'll treat them like visiting royalty and uncork another bottle of pink champagne. They'll probably think we drink nothing else. "And here is the clawed bath where we bathe in pink Champagne Xavier and Annette" I'll explain with tongue firmly in cheek.

Perhaps we will throw an opening party when the chapel is finished, as it feels like the one room we have paid least attention to, while it has doubled up as a storage unit.

Zak is designing a stained-glass window to go into the clear glass window that is there at the moment. She is putting in designs that represent different facets of Gros Puy and it will pay homage to the history and beauty of the area.

The history, as alluded to, has links to Dear Dickie whose ticker was compared to that of a big African cat. British Royalty was once intrinsically linked with the royal families dotted around Europe.

Although King of England, Richard was the son of Eleanor of Aquitaine, who also once ruled as Queen of England. Richard, although French, had the crest of three lions designated to him, the same ones every England fan wears next to their chest when also rampaging through Europe creating havoc and Zak has brought a large flag upon which they're emblazoned in yellow on a red background.

Her intention is to conceal the two satellite dishes that are a bit of an eyesore on the side of the château.

My Scottish relatives might have something to say about that and demand a blue and white saltire take its place to rekindle the auld alliance where Sassenachs were the common enemy.

We will also be assembling a pack of great local towns, castles and attractions to visit, with all the enchanting historical stories and rich heritage attached to them.

Local rumour has it that there is a rock in the Abjat area where Richard and Eleanor met to discuss his feuds with Barons in the Limousin region not long before his death.

As you roll into Abjat-sur-Bandiat, you are welcomed by a coat of arms featuring a yellow snake, an armoured arm holding a weapon, a bridge with red waves beneath it, under which is a bell.

This was inspired by the Battle of Fargeas that raged in this corner of the region in 1642. It transpires that the evil Lord Francis of Vaucocourt took a shine to a young belle in Fargeas and used his 'lordly rights' to secret her away from the hamlet she lived in. Just to clarify, Lord Voldemort, sorry, I mean Vaucocourt, is represented by the yellow slithering snake, not unlike he who shouldn't be named in the Harry Potter movies.

This caused villagers to rise up in arms to put Francis to the sword in a fierce battle that caused the river Bandiat to flow red with blood. The victorious rebels hastened to throw the lord's body under the bridge of the Charelle, just outside Abjat. Again, for clarification, dismembered arm with weapon represents the rebellious villagers, red waves equals the blood that was spilled in the conflict and the bridge is the one over the Charelle where Francis was so unceremoniously dumped and still hides as a yellow snake.

Now these actions had dire consequences for the villagers of Abjat-sur-Bandiat and the markets were prohibited, the village hall demolished and the church bells lowered from the steeple and removed as punishment.

In the legends peddled in local patois since those dark days of emancipation, it is said that the bells rolled into the bottom of an abyss at a place called Le Saut du Chalard, where they are still heard tolling every Friday. Needless to say, the last symbol on the shield beneath the bridge is one of the church bells.

Or to use the French word, La Cloche, which brings us

back to the restaurant beside the church where we first met our many new friends.

While sitting there on another occasion, we listened to the replacement bells tolling from an expert team of ringers and we peaked in through the door to see them enthusiastically tugging on the ropes in choreographed unison.

But what of the belle that the naughty Lord Vaucocourt tried to snaffle away for his own amorous purposes? She is still seen as a ghostly white lady appearing in the steeple of the church, although I suspect one too many at La Cloche may bear some responsibility for these apparitions.

There are also stories that are far darker. In the nearby town of Oradour-sur-Glane on June 6th, 1944, soldiers of the Der Fuhrer Regiment of the 2nd Waffen-SS Panzer Division, Das Reich, rolled into the village and killed 642 men, women and children, leaving only a few unintended survivors.

They then destroyed the entire village, which has been left in its ruinous state ever since as a memorial to those killed and a reminder of the brutality mankind is capable of. It is hard to fathom what possessed heavily armed men to enter a sleepy French village and slaughter innocent people and even today there is no universally accepted explanation.

There is a monument to the dead in what is now a martyred town, which bears the simple and single poignant message 'remember'.

On a lighter note, kayaking, adventure parks, swimming lakes, great restaurants, bars and cafes and a host of other activities will all have to be trialled and given the Malcolm star rating before anything is committed to the guide.

Hopefully that will also include vineyards and all their produce tasted by myself with my educated palate giving them an Appellation Controlle de Malcolm stamp of approval.

I'll try and avoid any descriptions like fruity high notes of gooseberry with lingering aftertones of nettles urinated upon by pine martens and barn owls.

Although an incredible area for the production of foie gras, that is a practise we can't possibly approve of, so will leave that to our guests' discretion.

At the time of writing this sentence, we have secured our place on a Brittany Ferry travelling on June 22nd, 2020.

We are praying nothing stops us crossing the Channel and travelling to the château as we have now secured paying guests who will arrive while we are there. We have all the official paperwork to prove we run an ongoing business concern in France and are more than happy to lock down for a fortnight in the château.

There is plenty to be doing to ensure their stay is as comfortable and restful as possible. Hopefully we can get the plunge pool installed and finished off and we now have purchased a spiral staircase that we will attach to the front of the terrace for even swifter and more ornate access to the garden.

Zak's eBay searches unearthed a wrought iron set of steps with a pole, but no spindles to run a banister from.

She weighed in with a bid that she thought would probably be bettered, but we got it. Not quite at 99 pence like the mini grand piano, but still a bargain for such a fine example of anti-clockwise iron steps to match the granite ones in the turret. I'm not expecting any sword fighting to take place from any rebellious villagers and I'm no yellow snake, so hopefully none of my activities in the Périgord Vert region will spiral out of control.

Having 'won the bid', which always strikes me as a weird

way of putting it, because you've paid for it in full, we had a nice day out travelling from Richmond to Ramsgate in Kent.

Having been isolated for two months, it felt strangely liberating to be able to travel the seventy odd miles to get there. The car had developed a veneer of dust and bird dropping that had to be cleared before we set off. I don't know what the birds had been eating, but I would venture they'd been scavenging out of someone's discarded Indian takeaway carton. A jalfrezi by the look of what was caked and dried onto our windscreen, which took some shifting believe me.

It was a super sunny day and we punched the coordinates into the sat nav, lowered the windows, opened the sunroof and got our motor running to head out on the highway. Oh yeah, we were feeling born to be wild with our first road trip in ages.

We pulled up outside our destination and were greeted by Pete who offered me an elbow to bump. He was a great guy and invited us in for a glass of water, which after a while escalated to a glass of draft stout that he'd got from the tiny pub across the road from him, in a litre milk carton filled straight from the keg. Well, it had to be better than just pouring it down the drain when it reached its sell by date.

We surveyed the goods and Pete was happy with our bid, despite the stairs being worth twice the amount we had paid for them. He had just purchased a villa in Spain and vowed to come and see his staircase in situation and stay overnight to break the monotony of the journey down to the Costa del Sol.

We loaded them all into the car and set off to the seafront to have a quick paddle then look for some fresh seafood. Ah the bliss of a tub of prawns and cockles sprinkled with pepper, with a couple of oysters doused in tabasco sauce and lemon juice to wash them down with.

We were pleasantly surprised at how picturesque Ramsgate is and from a nearby restaurant, where we bought some chips, saw that we were there just days before the anniversary of Dunkirk starting May 24th and ending on June 4th. Eighty-four vessels had left from the harbour there to pick the troops from the beaches with the flotilla of British boats.

The irony of us taking this large piece of iron across the Channel to France wasn't lost on me.

Of course, after this four-hour round trip around the bottom of London on the M25 into the depths of Kent, Zak decided this wasn't the right spiral staircase for her. There were no spindles or banisters. So back onto eBay went Zak to find spindles and of course she found some. Seventy of them.

These were in the Barnet area and when we reached the address, we found the owner had a lovely big house where his wife had attempted to build a spiral staircase, but wasn't happy with how it looked, so it was an expensive mistake and the spindles got rejected. He had them piled up in the corner of his garage and seemed relieved to be getting rid of them to free up his garage for something more appropriate like a car for instance.

With any property I have owned with a garage, the last thing that ever got put in there was a car. And even if we did, the car would be filled with surplus crap anyway. No matter what sort of company car I'd had down the years, with the family I have, they always ended up looking like a skip on wheels. I have resigned myself to never having a car that stays looking good for any length of time and my current car that looked so sparkly and new when I saw it in the showroom in Chicago, now looks a shadow of its former self as we bundle more random stuff into it to be transported hundreds of miles.

In Zak's defence however, we were the lucky recipients of three grand's worth of spindles for a couple of hundred pounds. I always feel guilty relieving people of expensive items for a pittance and this felt like the big spindle swindle, but the vendor seemed more than happy to wave them goodbye.

The banister would have to come later, perhaps shaped and fitted by a blacksmith we had made a connection with in Abjat.

So we had burned a lot of rubber to land our spiral staircase for Gros Puy, but the following day, Zak announced to me from behind the computer, 'This spiral staircase has its own spindles and banister and the bid ends in ten minutes and I'm going in at £300'.

'You what?' I retorted, 'after all the hassle we've been through to get what we're storing downstairs?' I asked.

But she'd already weighed in with the bid and justified her rash decision with the caveat 'Well, this probably won't win it." There we go with the winning word again. "Somebody else is bound to go higher than that" she added in that casually defeatist tone to placate me from saying "what the actual fuck?".

Minutes later she was punching the air shouting "oh my god, we've got it."

This is when I dropped the burning question "Where is this second spiral staircase of wonder?" "Clevedon near Bristol", Zak casually dropped into the conversation. It occurred to me we had gone from east to west of the south of England, with Barnet in between, to land ourselves the perfect spiral staircase.

All we had to do now was offload a spiral staircase and seventy spindles and take a second day trip out to the seaside. Yippee, more seafood, chips and ice cream.

As it happens, we have decided to keep the spindles to

make a fence for the front of the château and to get rid of the hideous white plastic fence Zak bought online in France.

If, by revealing Zak's addiction to online buying, I'm making her sound a little bit deranged, that is entirely my intention.

We still had a surplus spiral staircase stored in our flat, so Zak got onto eBay and put it on there for sale. Some 'winner' made a bid of more than we paid for it, which squared the circle in Zak's mind as she declared 'that's paid for the petrol money and the seafood, chips and ice cream at least."

The new spiral staircase is now in our possession after a trip to the West Country and compared to the first one, it is far more sturdy and in keeping with a medieval property. It has thirteen steps, which no doubt will be unlucky for me in tumbling from the top to the bottom as I'm delivering refreshments to the garden. It has thick dye-cast spindles and comes complete with its own curving banisters, which I have promised Zak I won't attempt to slide down.

Our only problem now is finding enough space in the car for this wrought iron escalier in kit form, as well as everything else we have to pack in, including Cosmo for what might be his last ever visit to Gros Puy. He'll be fifteen in August, which is 105 in dog years and it is entirely possible this trip will prove to be the end of him.

Of course Zak has sought to solve the problem by going online once again to buy a second trailer.

I am thinking of putting boxing gloves on her to prevent her tapping out anything else on the computer keyboard, only removing them when we are safely on the overnight ferry with all her new acquisitions in the back of the car.

The trailer will however buy a bit of space in the car to give an old man like Cosmo space to recline in, unless we strap him to the roof rack.

It will no doubt prove to be a comical situation as we load all of this up and strap it down and one I would prefer to do without an audience, but guess what? Zak, in her wisdom, decided to invite the camera crew from 'A New Life in The Sun' to capture the pandemonium.

As I mentioned earlier in the book, we were interviewed by one of the producers on Zoom to see if we would be suitable and I thought no more of it as it fizzled to nothing in the wake of lockdown.

But only two days ago from this moment of writing, they have come back, no doubt because they can see potential for many comedy moments with our family dynamic. With lockdown beginning to be lifted, they have decided to pick up where we left off and make us part of the show.

Now I am by nature a private and somewhat paranoid person. Now I am going to be followed back to Château Gros Puy with a camera crew in tow, as well as a rattling old spiral staircase on a trailer. Please God, help me!

Loosening of Lockdown

The first lockdown proved to be a challenging time for all of us. Zak had the distinct honour of having it called on her birthday, curtailing all the celebrations planned for the landmark occasion organised in Marrakech. It seems insensitive to moan in light of the sacrifices made by many of our heroic frontline workers and I am proud to count my nephew James as one of the doctors putting his life on the line to help save lives.

I cannot begin to compare my travails to the NHS staff dealing with the pandemic. Watching the daily briefings became painful as the death toll climbed and the infection rates increased.

But where PAYE workers were receiving furlough money to ease their own personal suffering, us limited company owners were left out in the cold with any financial support in sparse supply.

Thankfully, there were no travelling costs to get in and out of London for my freelance work, but unfortunately, there was no freelance work either. Good old George Michael had once penned the immortal lyrics, "give a wham, give a bam, but don't give a damn, coz the benefit boys are gonna pay." In my case, they were going to do no such thing.

From our first visit of the year in February, we returned to be struck down with Covid-19, which we self-diagnosed from the list of symptoms experienced. I was bedridden for four days with a long Covid, which included exhaustion and aching muscles for many weeks. Zak also had the muscle pains and exhaustion, so we might well have had the antibodies, although scientists still aren't fully sure how long immunity to Covid lasts for.

Restrictions in travel and movement, unless you happened to be an adviser to the prime minister with dodgy eyesight and a history of consummate lying, meant you were stuck inside with very little room for personal freedom.

The new normal was abnormally frustrating with rules changing by the day and the guidelines becoming less and less clear and concise.

I got out each day for an hours exercise with Cosmo and I am fortunate enough to have Richmond Park on my doorstep and let's be honest, where else would I have found the time to write this book?

From years of looking at Japanese tourists wearing face masks with mild amusement, we all became used to donning them on a daily basis in medical blue, a fetching pattern or a statement about who you supported as a footie club or how hilarious you are in the face of impending death.

Clapping our heroes on a Thursday night, donating to Captain Tom doing 100 laps of his garden before his 100th birthday and doing Zoom quizzes were all de rigueur in combating the unrelenting monotony of being confined to barracks.

Binge watching Netflix and baking also became the subjects of daily repartee, along with that staple of incredulous comment, can you believe what Trump has said or done now?

Small surprise that when given the opportunity to escape to our own particular château when travel corridors were opened, we leapt at the chance.

Midsummer's day arrived and with-it Father's Day. Instead of putting my feet up as is my right as a lazy dad to three brilliant kids, I spent it loading the trailer behind the car with a cast iron spiral staircase and other ephemera destined for the Dordogne.

A fellow father from Leeds called Peter turned up nice and early with his camera to film us turning the car and trailer for the first episode of 'A New Life in The Sun'. The central post of the staircase was so long, it straddled both the trailer and car and was secured to the roof rack with a mattress on top to soften any bouncing that would damage the car's bodywork. It was so long, it protruded over the bonnet of the car looking like a tank's gun turret.

I think he found it particularly amusing that we looked like we were about to invade France on what was just 15 days after the anniversary of the D-Day Landings.

I did manage to get to the Terrace on Richmond Hill to sink a few pints put together in a picnic constructed by Yazmin and Tom for me and his dad, David, which also included a selection of savoury nibbles.

Richmond Hill is a favoured spot of theirs where Tom proposed to Yaz with Cosmo in attendance who hilariously had his lipstick on display in the picture Zak took to mark the occasion. How romantic.

Because it was him and it's the epitome of what we've come to christen 'A Malcolm style situation' it has never been photoshopped out.

If you watch the popular daytime series, you'll be able to watch what the editor chooses to put on the screen, but Zak decided to direct operations from the ground as I relayed the tonnage to be towed from our second floor flat.

153

Mackenzie helped by throwing out non-fragile items from the dining room window to rain down with loud thuds on the garden path.

Interviews were held with the optimism of a successful forthcoming voyage hopefully captured, before everything was strapped down and a good night's sleep had before heading off in the early hours of the morning.

We rose with a feeling of trepidation of the lengthy journey ahead. The tyres on the trailer were carrying a lot of weight. Prior to us repurposing it to be a haulage carrier, it had been used to dispense crepes and drinks at outdoor events.

We weren't sure whether the tyres could handle the weight we had piled on to them and had to get to a garage to pump some air into them. We had to get from Richmond to Dover around the M25 and the last thing we needed was a flat tyre or a blowout.

Just before we joined the motorway, the tank rolled into a petrol station and drew up next to the air and water pump. I was totally paranoid that we'd end up letting all the air out without being able to pump any in. That would scupper any plans of making the ferry in time.

A hiss of air greeted the pump being attached to the nozzle and the PSI was particularly low. A loud hum took the pressure up, with a beep signalling when we got to the chosen 32 PSI.

The second tyre received the same treatment without any Malcolm style situations occurring and we were ready to hit the road.

Zak had taken the stop as time to re-look at the tickets and I shouldn't have been surprised by the next words that she uttered with that first word that alerted me all was not running as smoothly as I thought.

"Tone:, she said with her voice a little higher pitched than usual.

Gulp, here comes something that's going to soil my underpants.

"I've read the ticket wrong and we have to be there an hour earlier than I thought" she said, making my blood pressure go higher than the PSI we had just pumped into the tyre.

"What is it with you and numbers for Christ's sake? Are we going to miss another ferry now?" I replied with my voice going an octave higher than hers.

Going into one of her 'processing' moments, Zak looked like she'd frozen with the multi-coloured spinning wheels going around in her eyes that usually appear on your computer screen when it starts buffering.

"Hello" I said, trying to reboot her brain with a voice command.

"Can we still make it in time?" I demanded to know with a growing sense of urgency and rising panic.

"Yes, if I put my foot down, we'll get there just in time" she replied as the processing ended and her system got back up to speed with a sudden jolt.

We had planned to take it at a leisurely pace with the packed trailer, full car and loaded roof rack strapped down under a flapping tarpaulin.

Suddenly the proposed 50MPH limit was increased to 70MPH, which felt like warp factor speed with everything rattling and shuddering as Zak pressed the pedal to the metal trying to make good time.

The bottom end of The Road to Hell was, to our relief, reasonably empty and we progressed with haste, keeping an eye on the ETA display on the sat nav like hawks.

We slowed down to go through the port's checkpoints, including a new one where we were asked by a French voice for our attestation. We had filled these in with details of our final destination and reasons for travelling and printed them out on A4 paper.

"Zese are not right" the man declared as I held them out of the window for him to study. I looked at Zak who barked "Yes they are". The man looked again and changed his mind.

"Ah! yes they are, thank you" he said casually, not realising what trauma his original remark had caused a man who was already on the edge.

We fell into line with minutes to spare before the proposed time for arrival, which lessened the time we had to wait before being beckoned onto the parking deck with the vans, lorries and motorhomes to incorporate our increased headroom and extended length.

Cosmo was checked up on in the back and left a bowl of water and he looked very relaxed, unlike his frazzled owners.

We took our hastily assembled breakfasts of yoghurt and granola with a flask of hot coffee and went onto a deck with a big table where we could create our own socially distanced zone to eat with plenty of elbow room.

We considered going al fresco as the weather was good, but there was a fresh breeze blowing and beneath deck was an oasis of calm by comparison.

We were surprised to see how many passengers were totally ignoring the signs requesting people to wear masks throughout the voyage. Maybe the lifting of lockdown had lowered defences and in their minds, a return to normal was just a matter of time. Little did they know.

This daytime crossing seemed to be over in no time, with

the northern coast of France looming into view quicker than anticipated. The last time I had left Dover Harbour was in a Thames Clipper, rowing the Channel with a team of inexperienced dads from my daughter's school.

It had taken six hours of solid rowing in pretty rough conditions where we disembarked and dragged the boat called St George onto an empty beach upon arrival. I was absolutely shattered as the only member of the crew who didn't take a break on the tiller.

We returned the very same day in the pilot boat that had accompanied us over with Zak on board as the official photographer. She was frozen solid and had to massage my back for much of the journey home to prevent me seizing up.

This crossing was far less dramatic and we were off and running heading south on what was to turn out to be a ten-hour road trip, including a slow amble around the Périphérique of Paris where fellow drivers were stunned to see a tank entering their city.

One Parisian who drew up beside us looked in through the passenger window and laughed, prompting me to pretend I was firing a missile from the gun turret.

Le Gendarme might not have found that quite so amusing, as I do remember an incident in London where some terrorists mounted an attack on the Thameside MI5 building, using a similar pipe as a makeshift mortar launcher from the back of a van on Vauxhall Bridge.

Eventually, we escaped the gravitational pull of the Parisian orbital and headed out onto the toll roads that took us deeper into rural France.

The signs letting us know we could push on at 130KPH teased us as we set cruise control at a steady 80 KPH to avoid any potential damage to our cargo.

We often put on a French radio station to pass the time and try and understand what the DJ is saying. It is also interesting to hear what tunes are cutting the moutarde on the continent and one always emerges as the hit of the summer.

We also made three stops to let Cosmo stretch his four legs and relieve himself on the green spaces surrounding the services car parks. He's always been a good traveller having been transported on the six-hour journey to Cornwall where we spent many a summer holiday at the caravan.

Oh the irony that we bought him after the tsunami, pledging never to go abroad again and here we were on our way to our château in the Dordogne.

We reached our destination at around 10pm French time and started to unpack the essentials to be able to go to bed after a nightcap.

The initial inspection confirmed our worst fears that spring had sprung with a vengeance a month or so previously and Versailles now resembled a jungle of weeds and brambles.

Welcome to your next six months of backbreaking work Monsieur Malcolm they seemed to be challenging me. We will not give in without a fight.

The many weapons in my armoury would be pushed to their limit in the battle that was to ensue and of course, it was all to be broadcast on Channel 4 for everybody to watch blow by blow.

We would also be welcoming paying guests for the first time into Château Gros Puy, some delightful, some as prickly as the brambles including one unwanted occupant with a real sting in the tail. A good night's sleep was definitely required to help us prepare for what was to follow.

The Summer of 2020

We needed to get things into shape for the forthcoming season and things were off to a messy start.

As usual, the bat guano was all over the turret stairs and it didn't take long for one of our resident mice to reveal itself to Zak who greeted it with an ear-piercing scream and a loud exaltation of "TONE!"

I knew in the next room exactly what had happened and dragged myself into the kitchen to hear the news of what I already had guessed with my Sherlock Holmes-like intuition.

"A mouse ran from there to there" she said, fixing me with a wild stare and tracing a route between the fridge and the dog bowl with her index finger.

All I could helpfully ask was "what was its name? Jeff?"

Making light of this situation always met with a frosty reception and the inevitable question was once again asked. "How do they get in here?"

My stock answer of 'we're in the middle of the countryside' and 'they can get through even the smallest gap' did not meet with approval and I was sent to see how they'd got in from the cave below to plug all gaps with wire wool.

The same applied to a gap in the wall leading into the salon, where another of our furry friends had been spied on the premises. I was beginning to think we'd have to get the whole place hermetically sealed to keep out any unwanted interlopers.

Have I mentioned OCD, as once Zak has a bee in her

bonnet or a mouse under her fridge that becomes the main focus of her attention. The word mice and mouse will feature in every conversation even when discussing something totally unrelated.

"Nice weather today, Zak".

"Yes, about those mice".

She'd even installed motion detection cameras aimed under the fridge that sent a text alert to her mobile phone whenever a mouse dared to even twitch a whisker.

Extreme measures were rarely far from coming into the equation and before I knew it, we were to become the custodians of a cat Zak arranged to take part ownership of, that had an impeccable CV in mousing.

I'm never consulted on these decisions, even though I am asthmatic and allergic to cat fur.

Cosmo isn't consulted either, even though he is a dog, and as a canine beast, a sworn enemy of any member of the feline world.

Lulu came into our lives one day unannounced, brought by her owner who was returning to England and wanted somebody to look after her while she was dealing with personal issues in the UK. Ideally she didn't want to take her back to the concrete jungle of London, but leave her to patrol the granite-stoned enclaves of a residence in France to evict any unwanted rodents.

In a swift handing over ceremony, Lulu was given her own quarters with her bed put on a shelf in the boiler room.

She was to undergo a settling in period in her own quarantine, where all we saw for several days were two glowering eyes peering out from the boiler room darkness.

Bit by bit, she emerged to hiss at Cosmo, who'd learnt from his run-ins with our cats Teddy and Coco at home, not to mess with sharp claws that could strike out at a delicate brown nose.

She would also strike out with a paw or sink her razor-sharp teeth into any hand that reached out to pet her.

A brief stroke of the head seemed to be okay for a couple of seconds, but if you strayed down towards her back, boy, you were in for it.

Zak of course loved her, sharing very similar personality traits with her acerbic nature and standoffish character. It takes time to understand that underneath that crusty exterior, Zak is actually a real pussy cat.

Over weeks and months, Lulu, who became appropriately known as Loopy, installed herself as the château chat and would roam the property as if she was the rightful owner. I have been reliably informed that to pronounce the t at the end of the word chat takes you into territory that describes a private part of a ladies anatomy. Something I need to remember when speaking in French about stroking the cat.

Having previously put mousetraps around the fridge, we dispensed with them and left Lulu to supplement her biscuits and Felix cat food with whatever creature was foolhardy enough to cross her path.

Bart had been looking after the château admirably in our prolonged absence with Johan who had started the strimming back process so we at least could recognise some of what we had left behind in February.

When not trained on the mice, the motion-activated cameras had been strapped to a post aimed at the front door unbeknownst to Bart and he was bemused when his phone would go and Zak would know his exact whereabouts.

Bart now has knowledge of Zak's surveillance techniques and no longer thinks she is psychic when she phoned him whenever he approached the front door, but knowing him, he'll leave her something to look at that no eyes should ever be subjected to in future.

On his days working, he turns up at 8.20am sharp, as he's a stickler for time keeping. I subsequently haul my carcass out of my pit with Zak's mobile alarm of a dawn chorus waking me up at 7.30 am, to stagger down the granite stairs to put the coffee on and throw some frozen croissants in the oven at a low temperature.

Poor old Bart has been unfortunate enough to see me in my underpants of a morning when I've chosen to lay in for that half hour too long.

The boulangerie in Abjat does some beautiful pain au raisin and almond croissants and if we're lucky, Zak will leap into the car to go and get some for a bit of luxury to fuel us through a day of hard labour.

In summer, this daily ritual is taken onto the terrace where we drain the black coffees and chomp on the croissants while marvelling at the vista that stretches before us to the forest that surrounds the field. Misty clouds often rise out of the forest and spill over the field tinged with the pinks and oranges filtering through from the sunrise.

Like a general commanding an army, Zak will point out which jobs are her priority for that day. I have learnt through the years to not question orders, a skill that Bart has yet to master, having a very strong opinion of his own, based on years of experience that he's not reticent to share with others.

He has a very strong West Country accent, which Zak now imitates whenever she speaks to him. It starts off okay, but often strays around a bit to include Welsh, Irish, a bit of Scottish and unnervingly Indian.

These exchanges of views are often prolonged and noisy,

acting as my cue to take Cosmo on his morning walk through the forests surrounding our property.

The chosen route takes in two lakes, leafy tracks through fields, a right of way through Moulin Gros Puy and back to base via the road. En route, we are greeted by many feathered friends, escaped sheep, dogs from the local commune called La Grange that are noisy, but friendly and on rare occasions actual human beings, to be met with a friendly 'bonjour, ça va?' and a cursory smile before forging ahead.

Seeing as we were in French lockdown and isolating for the first fortnight, we couldn't have felt more isolated than this.

Before our return back to Blighty, this route was to change from verdant greens to parched browns and gold's and oranges beneath a selection of varying weather conditions. If applying insect repellent had been forgotten, you'd return looking like a victim of smallpox with the blood sucking mozzies that seemed particularly thirsty that summer.

Worse still for Cosmo were the blood sucking ticks picked up on the way that were often concealed in his fur. Horrible things that we'd learnt to pull out with tweezers in an anti-clockwise twist and dumped into alcohol. A nice way to go I reckon.

Bart would tell us of the one he'd picked up in his shower that he'd had to pluck out from his chest hair, which was always a delightful tale to listen to, especially over a meal.

On returning from the morning walk, the daily briefing was either in a Brexit negotiation standoff point, or some form of agreement had been reached subject to certain agreements still to be fully ratified.

Zak ultimately admires Bart for his can-do attitude and Bart respects Zak's determination to get stuff done. There were no to do lists, just whatever Zak had decided was the priority for that particular day, which could be revised at the drop of a hat.

The château needed to be in a condition to welcome guests in comfort and cleanliness and the garden needed to be transformed to be an Eden of relaxation and calm, for everyone but me.

We had plans to open up the garden for visitors to enjoy afternoon tea with scones and sandwiches and whatever else Zak felt like baking with her own fair hands.

For this she would commandeer the assistance of Jenny, Bart's wife, who was renowned for her banana cakes. Everyone who was to appear in front of the cameras for the Channel four camera people, had to sign a waiver form and after much deliberation, Bart and Jenny succumbed.

Needless to say, they, like us, are a bundle of nerves about how they will come across on screen.

Our only consolation is that the show isn't as sensational as a reality TV programme and it's not really in anyone's interest to make us look like fools, however hard we've tried to look like one.

Of course for the sake of drama, a bit of jeopardy will no doubt be factored in and I imagine there will be scenes and interviews that will allude to the fate of our chambre d'hôte business being in the balance.

I have to confess, I did play to the cameras a bit in that respect. Zak on the other hand just got weary of them shooting her vacuuming bedrooms and not being someone of a naturally bright and bubbly disposition regularly rolled her eyes and refused to speak, hoping they might leave her alone.

Our very first interview was done in blazing sunshine when temperatures were soaring to 40 degrees and we had sweat pouring down our faces. Makeup and foundation was running freely and we were getting progressively redder and redder.

There were days when we were moments from disaster, but came through by the skin of our teeth. Not everything went smoothly and we are sure those will make it into the edit, but what's done is done now and we will just have to accept the consequences.

We had three different camera people, each with their own style of shooting and asking questions. They spent so much time with us, we became firm friends, which might change on first viewing of the series.

It is true what they say about forgetting the cameras are there, so there are bound to be surprises in store for everyone. Zak cannot complain as she is the one that initiated the video casting session. As I write, leading up to Christmas 2020, we've been informed we'll be on air on January thirteenth, fourteenth and fifteenth 2021.

You'll find me hiding behind a sofa on those days or going totally incognito. Perhaps I'll take to wearing a disguise. We shall see.

Renovations Resume

When you rise from your bed at Gros Puy, you are never entirely sure what the day is going to bring. All I do is put on my working gear and see where the mood will take me, or more accurately, where Zak will point me.

I know it is never the priority, but I like to head into the garden to attempt to restore Versailles to its former glory. A trip down to the cave of wonders is often required to drag out the tools of the trade. A wide selection of equipment is stored there over winter including the heavy-duty strimmer, lawn mower and rotavator.

Zak had bought a wheelbarrow for 5 euros on the local network selling site and it wasn't the sort with the one wheel at the front, but a two-wheeled affair on a central axle, which never balanced out properly and tipped out anything you filled it with.

There was a technique to filling it that I mastered and after that, I wouldn't hear any criticism of it when others commented on how dysfunctional it was. Perhaps I understand that lack of technique and adeptness, but appreciate the effort if guided properly.

It does amuse me that in the French language, where inanimate objects are given a sex, a wheelbarrow is female. I won't relay this to Zak but I am having a relationship with this particular lady that regularly ends up hot, sweaty and very dirty. As a female, the wheelbarrow reserves the right to be temperamental at times and demands delicate handling.

To me, the garden is a jewel in the Gros Puy crown and although there is great grandeur inside the 13th century pile, in summer, you spend more time looking at the great view and admiring the flora and fauna in the garden.

Zak had started to grow vegetables from seed in the UK, which we had cultivated on the roof garden at home in tubs.

The shoots that had thrived in the warmest spring on record in the UK had been transported with us and now needed to be planted into the fertile soil of the Limousin forest.

I rotavated a small patch of earth to get us started and to turn the ground over to remove the abundance of weeds.

We'd planted indigenous tomatoes down on the bottom terrace before and they'd given us a wonderful yield of juicy, big toms bursting with flavour.

I had aspirations of being the Monty Don of the Dordogne as I lined up the plants in neat rows with wooden sticks with their names written on them. I'm not talking of their Latin names, just what we might be expecting to harvest if our labours bore fruit, or veg.

One of Zak's pressing demands was to have a drying area for all the sheets and pillow cases she'd be washing on a regular basis and a spot was chosen for where this would be located to not be seen directly from the terrace.

She did, however, want it to look in keeping with the rest of the garden, so it needed to be done to her exacting standards. This was to be my first foray into laying melange and gravel, surrounded by a semi-circular granite stone wall.

I was being mentored by Bart who, possibly through sympathy of who my boss was, offered encouragement whenever I did a good job.

Bart is the owner of a mechanical digger with a swinging arm and a selection of earth-moving buckets. What you can do in a day with that marvellous piece of machinery saved me weeks of hard shovelling.

Digging out the chosen area left us with several hills of topsoil but a beautiful flat amphitheatre, which needed a sheltering curved stone wall at the northern end to hold back the bank of earth behind it.

A gleaming orange concrete mixer had also been purchased for me to grapple with, which would also be a learning curve for me to mix concrete in large quantities. Another French female I would get to know intimately.

The wall and drying circus became a point of pride for me. I was the apprentice and felt like this was my first step into becoming a master concrete mixer extraordinaire.

I also got my first experience of using a wacker plate, a big vibrating machine that glides over pebbles, embedding them into the melange and making everything look smooth and orderly.

Where had this been all of my life? There are fewer things more satisfying than starting it up and just guiding it where you want to bed in a path, drying area or pétanque court.

Oh yes, the bottom terrace was to become the site for sporting endeavours for active guests who fancied a game of boules or a go at archery, so it needed clearing of the tons of the old bamboo (a quick chorus please Dick) to flatten it out as level as possible.

The west side of the garden was virtually impenetrable and was the only way for vehicle access from the chemin, so Bart waded into it with the digger, pulling up saplings, digging out old tree stumps and creating new pathways. With military efficiency, he clanked and clunked onto the bottom terrace and shunted all the bamboo into what was once a punting lake beneath it. From old photographs, we've seen a bridge that was once there, but can find no evidence of it now.

Bart then set to work clearing the required 12 metre by five metre area to be constructed into the boules court. It's always a joy watching the concentration on Bart's face as he manoeuvres this hulking great machine to perform tasks with great delicacy. I'm sure he could pick individual daisies with it if asked to. A mountain of melange and gravier would be required to finish this off after a lot of raking and wacker-plating from yours truly. The idea of delegating this job was very tempting, but to keep an eye on the coffers, the responsibility lay squarely on my weary shoulders.

Bart did bring in extra muscle on a number of occasions to spare mine. A lifetime of sitting in offices doing a sedentary job had kept my hands beautifully soft and uncalloused. You can always tell a builder from a handshake. They feel like they're coated in coarse sandpaper and often crush every bone and digit in your right hand. I would be glad that the practice was off limits in lockdown and a bump of elbows became the preferred method of greeting.

Two Harry's and Jon were drafted in to mix cement and lay stones on four other garden projects that needed some attention. The first was to create a room that the plunge pool was to sit on. The second was to create a second terrace below the top one, where a barbeque and other garden dining experiences could be enjoyed. The third was a pathway down from the car park to make it the new entrance, leading to the big turret door to add a wow factor when arriving. The fourth was to build a suitable granite stone stairway up to the big wooden door to match the grandeur of the turret exterior.

The nearby quarry just outside Abjat was the supplier of granite stones, along with gravel and pebbles that cost a fortune if you buy them from DIY stores. Bart's tipper van ferried heap after heap of materials that were unceremoniously dumped to make the outside area look like a building site. It will take months, maybe years to return these areas back to their picturesque best, but for the time being, the front of the château looks like a run-down council house garden.

Through the heat of summer, these four projects have taken shape and lots of water kept the chaps irrigated as they slaved topless in the sweltering heat. I myself was out there most days when I wasn't required to work a three-day week remotely indoors, sitting at the laptop writing scripts and headlines on freelancer projects.

Some of the guys, when working shirtless, were a treat for the ladies of the château, invoking the scene and music from that famous diet coke commercial. Bart and I, being in our late fifties, were enough to induce projectile vomiting.

In this period of preparation, the family were to visit and stay for the summer months. The château became a hive of activity and there was a real buzz about the place. Yaz and Tom brought Mackenzie with them and their new puppy, Whisky.

They even invited their friends Colin and Marianne to stay on their tour of Europe in a camper van and all were required to pitch in and help. These were great days of remote working mixed with pleasurable day trips and dining on the terrace. My son Angus even joined us for a week when he could get time off of work and we would drive to Limoges Airport to pick him up and bring him home to the madness that was brewing at Gros Puy.

Tom runs his own company that provides digital and social media solutions to alcoholic drink companies, Yaz works in events management and was at the time, working with Time Out. Colin was organising a South African start up business and Marianne, as a therapist, was conducting online video sessions with her own clientele.

We had to remember we also needed holiday time and visited nearby lakes, restaurants and regularly visited vide-grenier and other organised events. Lockdown seemed a distant memory as we mingled with and met lots of people in the region including friends and Tom's half-sister and nephew.

With two dogs and a cat chasing each other around, ongoing construction, indoor renovations in full flow, painting and partying, video and phone calls, cooking and baking, coffee and gin brewing and thirsty workmen trudging through the kitchen for water, it became a delightful mayhem.

All this was happening as the bookings started to mount up and we had days to go before our first paying guests arrived. Would we be ready? A flurry of buying tables and chairs, constructing garden furniture, laying out deckchairs, getting the garden ready, creating a bar area, sweeping and cleaning, fighting and arguing ensued into the run up to our guests ringing on the door to herald their arrival.

The bell is something Zak acquired that had Titanic 1912 carved into it. I was starting to have my own sinking feeling about all of this, as I was several leagues outside of my comfort zone and was hoping the ship's name wasn't going to be prophetic of our own impending disaster.

To be honest, I was petrified about what was to come. And to add to the stress and worry, the camera crews were on their way to commence filming for *A New Life in The Sun*. So much for the quiet life I was expecting in France.

Lights, Camera, Action

Natalia arrived one morning with her forms and thermometers and ensured we were all adhering to strict Covid rules. Thankfully she aimed the thermometer at our foreheads and didn't require us to lower our undergarments to get an anal reading.

The camera was to be lifted onto her shoulder after we'd gone through the formalities and introduced ourselves to her. We were expecting a small team, but she was a one-woman crew who was operator, interviewer, director and producer.

She also brought her own packed lunch, so she was catering as well.

Many was the time we would offer her a coffee, lunch, piece of cake and at one stage a glass of red when Suzy and Ken popped in after visiting the Épicerie across the road, but she was not allowed to partake of any of our hospitality. We couldn't even offer her a bedroom to sleep in and she would stay nearby to adhere to strict rules of not accepting accommodation with the people she was shooting with.

Despite all of this, we all became friends from the many visits she paid to meet up with us. She was French, but had been brought up in Dorset in the UK and had gone to university in Bristol, so her English, as well as her French, was impeccable.

Zak would use her as interpreter on the many messages received from incoming guests and on one occasion when the gendarmerie turned up on our doorstep, she was able to let us know they were there enquiring about our neighbour and his errant dog, Bruno, who'd forced a passing kid to fall from their bike.

She was also very helpful in making sure our menus, signs and messages were all accurate in French.

Zak had spent an entire week going back and forth to Périgueux to do courses that made her understand her responsibilities in running a chambre d'hote and be fully compliant with the rules and regulations that entails.

I was a regular spectator in a war of wills between Natalia and Zak about what was going to be shot. Zak would often question what would make good viewing for the general public and Natalia was the guardian of what she was tasked to capture that found favour with fans of the show.

'Oh, you're not going to show me making beds and hoovering again,' Zak would moan and Natalia would re-iterate this is what they want to see in running an ongoing French business.

But it wasn't just us who were being interviewed. Guests who stayed with us overnight, or for a few days would give their feedback on how we'd performed as host and hostess with the mostess, or was that leastest?

English was often the language of choice and we'd earwig in on their replies to see if we'd come up to scratch. Others replied in French and Natalia was interrogated afterwards to spill the cassoulet on what they thought of their stay.

We were soon to discover that the small things made a huge difference to what our French guests expected and the biggest bone of contention was the coffee and bread.

Zak had taken a course at Richmond College and did her best to speak to French guests in French, but some took exception to the fact we weren't fluent. We get this and have made that clear on our website that our French is rudimentary, which will improve with time, but I don't think we were prepared for how much guests expect to engage in conversation with us.

Some are happy to be shown the ropes of the château to enjoy the rooms and facilities and others use it as a B&B, choosing it as an overnight stopping point to get out and enjoy the delights of the surrounding area, while others expect a more immersive experience.

We have to take on board that we run a château with a fascinating history that has deep roots into French culture and people are expecting an experience that reflects that.

Although I believed my role in this was as groundsman and caretaker, it soon transpired I was to entertain guests with tales of yore, leaving them open-mouthed in wonderment and delight about where they had chosen to stay.

I grew to quite like being a raconteur, usually spent on the terrace on balmy summer evenings with an Aperol Spritz or voice-lubricating vin rouge. Or two.

I had no intention of being a waiter, which Zak did with aplomb with the help of Yaz and Mackenzie in the first few weeks. Zak was keeping the menu as simple as possible for multiple orders, but creating dishes that delivered it terms of deliciousness. The many compliments she received showed she had got it right and any quibbles were tweaked and improved upon.

It was on one such evening with guests on the terrace that disaster struck. I was called in from the outside table with some urgency. I walked in to see we had an indoor waterfall that hadn't been a feature of the château thus far. Gallons of water were cascading down the wall above the kitchen sink and were running along the boxed-in rafters and pouring out from the chandelier's light fittings.

To add to the horror, the water was scalding hot. Steam was beginning to build the temperature in the room and condensation formed on the windows.

Years of built up crud and grime were being flushed out by the flow of H2O and there was a smell of damp plaster and decades of detritus filling the air.

Towels were thrown onto the beautiful wooden worktops to protect them and soak up the effluent. Shouts and screams were being stifled in an attempt to keep the histrionics away from the ears of the guests enjoying their dessert.

Zak strolled in during the pandemonium to cast an eye over the kitchen, then just grabbed her dessert and strolled nonchalantly back onto the terrace, closing the door behind her, acting as if nothing was happening. Tom, Yaz, Mackenzie and I were flabbergasted by her casual demeanour.

That Titanic bell seemed appropriate in this scenario and Zak was the equivalent of the band that kept playing on board to try and quell any panic from the guests.

We assembled in the chapel, not to pray, but to muster and formulate a plan. This is when bats started flying around our heads to add an almost comical element to the unfolding drama.

It became a recurring theme whenever a situation heralded impending doom, bats would appear right on cue as if ordered in by some b-movie horror film director.

We rushed around the château trying to find the appropriate tap to turn off. Tom found the source of the cascading rapids and started to tear wood up in the guests' shower room.

I had gone down into the cave and turned a series of taps on and off that had no bearing at all on stemming the tide.

Eventually, Zak sauntered back in, ascended the turret stairs into the loft space and turned off a tap beneath the boiler. Calm descended as she did the same on the granite stairs. The tsunami abated and everybody breathed a sigh of relief.

The amazing thing was that the guests were none the wiser about the carnage that had been happening mere yards away indoors, even though the family that lived in the château all looked red cheeked and a tad flustered when they decided to retire to their beds. All that is apart from Zak who hadn't even broken sweat.

I should take note from Zak's technique, that the best way to avoid a surge of adrenaline and angst in the face of a catastrophe, is to pretend it's not happening.

A young German couple, staying overnight, even took photos inside the salon room as they were looking for inspiration on how to decorate their own home. Their comments on the booking website were delightful and there was no mention of any disasters in the kitchen.

Our only problem now was how were the guests going to use the bathroom in the east wing when the hot water had been turned off.

To the tune of the Ghostbusters theme a question was asked. 'When there's something wrong with your waterworks, who you gonna call?' ... To which the answer is, in a chorus of me, Tom, Yaz and Mackenzie, *CALL BART*.

Bart had returned to the UK with the loosening of lockdown to attend to business back home, so was bemused to see Zak's number flash up on his mobile.

'What the fuck does she want?' would no doubt have been his response knowing he'd told Zak he'd be in the UK for a while.

Always willing to help as best he can, Bart spoke to Zak and phoned Louis to turn up at the château to see what he could do to get the plumbing back on tap and return life to normal.

In the meantime, we had re-directed anyone who wanted a hot shower into the east wing and our en-suite bathroom. Nobody seemed to take us up on the offer, choosing to wash and brush up with the cold water still flowing through the taps.

Thankfully the cameras hadn't been there to capture this Malcolm style situation, but when Louis did turn up, they were in evidence as he revealed the culprit as a junction where the pipe had dislodged under the water pressure, due to it being the wrong size.

Louis, being retired, didn't want to show his face on camera in case the French authorities had him up for continuing to work, but our second camera woman Ivy, did get footage of water running down the walls as he put in the working replacement and turned the water back on.

The paintwork I'd spent hours rollering was now a horrible brown stained patch that meant I'd have to do it all over again. Any warning I'd like to pass on to any aspiring château owners is, never assume a job is done. It won't be long before you'll be doing it again.

A scene that didn't go as well as expected was captured for posterity by the cameras. Natalia had been back and forth for a few days filming me wandering the grounds comparing myself to the Don with my garden exploits and showcasing my skills with a trowel and concrete mix.

Bart turned up in a bandana and wraparound shades for his star turn, looking like he was about to star in Easy Rider. I think I'd spent the whole of lockdown in shorts and t-shirt that was to be the de facto uniform for the next six months.

The distressed mirror brought down from the loft space was to be affixed to the kitchen wall. It was hard enough getting it down the turret, now it had to be hoisted onto the wall and as I mentioned earlier, it weighed a ton.

A frame made from the off-cuts of wood had been screwed into the wall, measured with great accuracy by Zak. Did I say accuracy? By Zak? Zak and her number dyslexia?

Here we go, this is going to turn Channel 4 into the Comedy Channel.

Sweat pouring from our faces, we lifted the heavy glass plate to fit into the frame. Muscles trembling with exertion and gaining the necessary elevation using metallic step-ups, we heaved it into what should have been a snug fit.

Surprise, surprise, it wasn't. The frame was too small by several centimetres. The editor will have their work cut out to eliminate the stream of profanities from me and Bart's foul mouths, unless they employ a bleeping machine to dub over the top.

The mirror had to be lowered again while Bart unscrewed the large bolts and refixed the side of the frame into its correct position. The mirror was raised again and this time we had a Cinderella moment shouting, "It fits, it fits."

By this time Natalia was in fits of laughter and Bart wished he'd never agreed to be shot, thinking this shoddy DIY debacle would be attributed to him.

This wasn't Bart's style at all. The off-cuts were rough and splintered, the gaps weren't closed and filled, the glass was flaky and discoloured and to anyone who prided themselves on a job well done, this was ramshackle to say the least.

Zak and I had coined a phrase that was to be our mantra for

all renovations at the château. 'Perfectly imperfect.'

Nothing was straight, nothing lined up and seeking geometric alignment was a futile waste of time. But to us it was art.

To save us having too many long-winded conversations about it, we brought it to a conclusion by standing back and saying 'That's art, Bart," before he had a chance to express his opinion.

We were thinking of pitching it as an idea for a programme to Channel 4, where we accompany Bart around contemporary art galleries. He would look at masterpieces from Hirst, Emin, Whiteread and the like and maybe describe Pollocks as bollocks, to which we'd respond, 'That's art, Bart'.

We floated the idea on A New Life in the Sun after the mirror was screwed into place, so watch this space to see if this innovative new series gets commissioned.

Before all this happened, Natalia wanted to set the scene of us turning up in the car at the château laden with all the new gear that was to be offloaded. It was supposed to have some continuity with where Peter had signed off with us fully loaded in the UK.

The trouble was, we had already unpacked much of it, so we hurriedly replicated the tank look that had rumbled through Paris down to the Dordogne and took the car around the block.

As we approached Gros Puy, we called Natalia on her phone to roll camera and we tried our best to not look contrived as we arrived. We proceeded to unpack the spiral staircase that we'd left till last in the trailer and I took the steps a pair at a time down the slope from the car park into the garden.

This sort of contrivance was to repeat itself on many occasions as we were often asked to go for a take two, three and four, with any spontaneity dying a horrible death as we attempted to repeat the first au naturelle version.

Natalia took her camera around the château, getting her first impression to be compared to any future improvements. None of this was going to be an overnight transformation, but perhaps in a few years' time, they might return to see something radical.

Now there are some meetings through history that have been ones of historical renown. Livingstone and Stanley, Lennon and McCartney, Moet and Chandon and when Harry met Sally for example. But none have been as tumultuous as when Natalia met Bart.

Both had lived in Bristol. Both were forthright in their opinions and you couldn't wish to meet two more polar opposite people if you searched from North to South Pole.

Yet through this most unlikely of pairings, a relationship struck up where neither were to give an inch to the other. I think Bart's opening gambit was "Are you one of those lefties?" being of a right-wing persuasion himself, Natalia countered with "Oh you're one of those people are you?"

This battle of wills from their two schools of thinking rang out throughout the building and gardens as they debated the rights and wrongs of the world from their different perspectives.

It was often followed by bellowing laughs and snorts of derision from either side of the chasm, but nobody ever took major offence and nobody was ever declared the winner.

Zak and I were just mere spectators like two attendees at the Wimbledon tennis finals, whipping our necks from side to side as slam after slam was hammered over the net on Centre Court.

In between verbal volleys, Natalia managed to capture

some of the other works that were in progress at the château.

Bart with his digger clearing the space for the boules pitch, for instance and the area that was to make the second terrace.

This proved to be more challenging than it sounds, with a huge stump that was once a massive pine tree that stood bang in the middle of the outlook from the terrace obscuring the view. Once again, we knew this to be the case from photos found on the internet when the terrace was first constructed.

Zak had a plan to create a wooden table out of the stump to protrude from the terrace, but levelling out the earth required removing the network of roots, so the digger won that particular argument.

The stump was dumped into the east garden, which the caterpillar tracks of the digger had churned into a quagmire. There is also a young olive tree that we've kept to protrude from the terrace and hopefully offer shade in the future. Being an olive lover, capable of eating a large jar in one sitting of the green variety when pitted and stuffed with pimento, we are hoping for a big yield in the near future.

The first Harry was brought in to help Bart dig the trenches and lay the breeze blocks to create the foundations for the terrace and the new poolroom. The cement mixer was on a constant rotation as barrow after barrow of the grey sludge was ferried in to build up the external framework.

Obviously, breeze block didn't quite match the medieval exterior look we are aiming for, so render would be required with a granite stone fascia applied.

I took Natalia on a tour of the grounds talking absolute drivel about construction and gardening, trying to sound like I had some level of knowledge about what I was doing. From years of busking it in advertising, I had developed a wide vocabulary of bullshit, bluster and balderdash.

I do remember coming up with a sound bite along the lines of 'if you don't get on top of nature, nature will get on top of you' and while feeling pleased with my improvised words of wisdom, I now realise how toe-curlingly cringey they might sound played out on national TV.

Natalia was also there to catch some of the events that Zak was to put together, like afternoon teas, but not before there was a rehearsal, with scones, cakes and other titbits prepared and cooked in the kitchen with Jenny assisting.

I was working in the garden as they busied themselves in the kitchen, creating cakes and scones and assembling a selection of sandwiches filled with egg mayonnaise, cheese, ham and soft cheese and cucumber.

There is no such thing as clotted cream in the region, however similar the topography is to Cornwall, so an experimental 36% fat cream used for gateaux in France was whipped up into an aerated cloud to be applied with the homemade jam and washed down with a choice of Earl Grey or English breakfast tea.

Jenny had made a 'here's one I made earlier' lemon drizzle cake, as she had never used our oven before, so wanted to ensure no disasters were caught on camera.

During the excavation for the lower terrace, we had unearthed what we thought were horseradish roots and as Zak considered whether we could use this in any way, Jenny recounted a storyline on the TV series Heartbeat where several people were struck down with food poisoning from making a similar culinary mistake.

That was something we wanted to avoid, having guests writhing in agony clutching their abdomens in the garden, so that plan was abandoned and the original menu adhered to.

At the end of the day, I swanned up onto the top terrace and replicating the sort of gastronomic expertise displayed by the food critics on MasterChef, I waxed lyrical about the fayre I was presented with to comment on. I've got to admit, the cream left much to be desired, but overall, I rolled out words like delicious, delightful and unctuous. What a pretentious knob of a food critic I made, even though still wearing my gardening clobber and looking decidedly grubby.

Still, everything takes on a more exclusive and luxurious allure when consumed in the open air on a terrace, elevated above rolling fields and a verdant forest, not to mention being plied with a few glasses of Prosecco.

Natalia had been in there for quite a few hours following the Zak and Jenny show, which I doubt will make a show to rival the Great British Bake Off or have Nigella quaking in her boots and from the mess left behind, it won't resemble the kitchen practices of Michel Roux JR.

Zak wasn't happy afterwards, getting a pastry recipe all mixed up, adding water instead of egg and proclaiming the whole look of the stacked cake stands 'too beige' but this was the first stab and there was time for tweaks and improvements before it was to be laid before paying punters on one of the garden table and chairs bought at a vide-grenier by Zak.

Once again, this was to be tried and tested on friends and neighbours invited to be guinea pigs for the new and improved menu and returning for more footage, the cameras were there to get their genuine feedback. They were invited to pig out, but not a guinea would change hands, so maybe the free part of this deal would make them go easy on the criticism.

Zak had fiddled and twiddled with various dough

formulations and times spent in the oven to get the perfect rise and make scones that came out moist and less crumbly like hunks of chalk.

A Brit friend who has lived in Perpignan for a couple of decades suggested a powder called Chantifix which thickened up the cream to be more Cornwall clotted and less like you'd expect on a château gateau.

This event followed one of the most eventful nights of the summer months when most of the family and friends were occupying the bedrooms.

They had just spent a glorious day out and about, discovering the delights of the Dordogne in the sweltering summer heat, while Zak beavered away in the kitchen and I spent hours preparing the garden for the influx of hungry invitees.

This included erecting a sail-like triangle of material to shade the guests in the unrelenting heat of a typical Dordogne summer afternoon.

We'd be strapping it between the cherry and mimosa trees and erecting a post with a hook screwed in to form the perfect triangulation to cast the maximum shadow over the table come three o'clock in the afternoon.

Zak with her skills on the sewing machine, had cut out and stitched the sail with its ornate pattern of butterflies, edged with a bunting of triangular flags. It took us a while to stretch it so it didn't sag in the middle, well not too much, and people could fit beneath it without garrotting themselves as they moved in to sit down.

That evening, we were waiting for the family and friends to return from their day out. They had taken a two-hour drive to the medieval town of Sarlat, where canoes and kayaks can be hired to paddle along a stretch of the Dordogne valley amidst the châteaux perched on cliffs above the snaking river route.

Tom was driving the Beamer, followed by Colin in his camper van. I think they'd underestimated the amount of driving involved to get to the Périgord Noir region and back. A long day of canoeing, swimming, picnicking and walking was made more fatiguing by hundreds of kilometres covered with a Cavapoo puppy in tow.

It was nearing midnight by the time they arrived in pitch-blackness back at the château. Weary and tired they headed for their beds for a much-needed sleep. As parents, we never went to sleep before offspring were back and safely ensconced at home. We were ready to hit the hay ourselves, but an unwelcome guest was buzzing about the bedroom.

A very persistent hornet that droned around the bedroom sounding like a Chinook helicopter at that time of night. We were pretty sure there was a nest somewhere in the vicinity, as several had got in through open windows to be a proper pain in the arse. Little did I know how much of a pain in the arse they could really be.

There was no way we could sleep with it making such a din in the bedroom, so we decided to usher it out of the window as best we could, trying to flick it out with towels. With one violent swish, the buzzing stopped. I thought it might have dropped stunned to the ground and both Zak and I searched with torchlight around and under the bed to no avail.

Maybe it went out of the window, we optimistically assumed, as we were too tired to search any longer.

We climbed under the sheets of the bed and turned off lights to hopefully head directly to the land of nod, without any more interruptions from Monsieur Frelon, as we were to learn was French for hornet.

'What the fuck was that," I shouted as a hot poker of pain jabbed into my right ankle. I leapt like a gazelle from the bed as Zak wearily turned on a light to see what the fuss was all about.

It was extremely painful and my ankle started to swell immediately. I had no real concerns at this moment, thinking it would just be a dull throbbing pain that might cause me discomfort as I went back to sleep, but things started to escalate quite rapidly from that moment on. The pain started creeping like a forest fire spreading in high winds, climbing first up my right leg and then the left. My heart started beating much faster and I was beginning to see blue speckles before my eyes.

A horrible blotchy rash rose to the surface of my skin and I looked like I'd contracted chicken pox. This rash went straight up and attacked my tender parts and shot up my rectum. That hornet, as I said, was a real pain in the arse, inflicting agony I hadn't felt before and hope never to experience again.

It was like I'd been sprayed in sulphuric acid and the only action I wanted to take was to tear my underpants and t-shirt off and head to the shower to cool myself down with powerful jets of cold water.

Things became a bit hazy to me after this as my tongue and lips had swollen up making me look like a botched cosmetic surgery procedure victim and my head was swimming, as I felt faint and nauseous.

I think at this stage, Zak had alerted everyone in the château and all I remember is emerging from the en-suite bathroom to find Yaz and Mackenzie staring at me in terror.

Apparently my skin had taken on a pallid complexion with my eyes red and unfocussed. I was speaking largely incoherently and all I wanted to do was lay down and be swathed in cold damp towels.

As with previous experiences, Zak decided to get back into bed, following the school of thought that if you ignore a crisis, it won't actually be happening.

Right on cue, to add the necessary Hammer House of Horrors element, bats entered the room and started flying around in circles. Do they have an in-built sense of when to enter a room to step up the alert status to 'everything's going batshit crazy?'

As I decided to roll on the floor like a person on fire trying to extinguish the flames, a plan of action was formed. This bloke needs to go to hospital. I was in the grip of an anaphylactic shock and my body was being attacked by histamine that required urgent attention.

With the help of my increasingly terrified family, I got back into my underpants, had a t-shirt hastily pulled over my head and was helped by Tom to descend the turret staircase, that's difficult enough to traverse when fully clothed without your body being bombarded with what felt like internal napalm.

I slipped on flip flops and Zak, now dressed and fully alert, took the wheel of the car, as Tom leapt into the backseat for moral support and navigation purposes.

I was drifting in and out of consciousness and Zak decided the best location to head for was the hospital in nearby Nontron. I was aware that Zak's driving was more in keeping with how Lewis Hamilton might tear around a formula one track and I could tell Tom was fearful for all our lives, let alone mine.

Tom had been talking to me constantly to ensure I was compus mentis at all times, while googling the French translation to say, 'I've been stung by a hornet,' which is how we discovered it was 'frelon'.

Back at the château, Yaz and Mackenzie were exacting revenge with furious anger and extreme violence, by pummelling the aforementioned frelon into a pulp on the floor with the heel of one of their shoes. Take note anyone who ever wants to cross the Malcolm family in future.

Circling the hospital at Nontron, it soon became apparent it was occupied by geriatrics and didn't have an A&E department. Technically, as a fifty-nine-year-old, I might have met the criteria for being admitted, but probably not for my particular ailment.

Further research from Tom discovered that the first port of call, when confronted with such an emergency is to call the fire brigade, or Pompier. I would have welcomed them pumping hundreds of gallons of cold water right up my backside at that particular time.

Zak phoned them and explained the situation and where we were. The person on the switchboard had very good English to save time on translation and they informed us the nearest emergency hospital was an hour away in Périgueux.

The phone was on speaker so we could all hear the responses and as Zak floored the accelerator, the last words we heard were 'good luck'.

In normal circumstances, that would have been an hour drive, but on empty roads in the early hours of the morning, Zak covered the distance in about forty minutes. In between prayers for his mortal soul, Tom kept speaking to me to see how I was doing. My reply of 'my arse is on fire' triggered a chorus from The Kings of Lyon 'Sex on Fire' with Tom changing the words to "wo-oh, my arse is on fire", bringing some light relief to an increasingly heavy situation.

When we arrived at Périgueux hospital, I was in a

sorrowful state and Tom escorted me to the A&E entrance to accompany me inside and explain what had happened. I wasn't in any fit condition to give an explanation in English, let alone French and due to Covid-19 restrictions, only one person was allowed into reception at any given time.

I staggered in like a drunk entering a western saloon after a long journey in the saddle and after establishing some sort of explanation, while they held out a cardboard vessel in case I vomited, was motioned to head in the direction of the waiting room with a piece of paper with a number on.

They had given me a form to fill in while I leant heavily on the front desk, once again like a drunk propping up the bar of that western saloon to prevent himself falling over. The form asked for my address, mobile, passport and EHIC card numbers. I have no idea what I wrote, but they were looking at me with concerned expressions and accepted whatever hieroglyphics I scrawled down.

I was feeling very vulnerable and disoriented in the waiting room, fearing this might be my final moments on this planet, hair damp and dishevelled, lips swollen with sunken eyes, my legs covered in blotches and dressed in nothing but my underpants, t-shirt and flip flops in this halogen lit hell-hole.

One other unfortunate lady in that same disinfectant-reeking, soulless place was doing her best not to make eye contact with me, or maybe averting her gaze from my ill thought through attire for a night out in the city.

Eventually, my number came up on the digital screen and I was ushered into a room, put onto a bed and attended to by nurses. Mercifully, they covered me with a flimsy sheet and told me to await the doctor. It took them a while to source one that could speak English, as he hadn't yet come on shift.

The relief when he eventually appeared around the curtain was immense. After establishing what had happened, I was wired up to heart monitors, put onto a drip and had my veins pumped with cortisol.

I was to be kept overnight for observation and I explained that my wife was outside and unaware of what was happening with me.

That lovely doctor went outside and brought her in to look at the patient and explain what was happening. I was to be assessed at 8am in the morning to see if I was in any condition to be released and I urged Zak to go home and return the following day.

I was then wheeled out of triage and given a room to recover in. The beeping of the heart monitor lulled me into a deep sleep and I enveloped myself in a cocoon within the thin veneer of the hospital sheet. Goodnight, God bless, see you in the morning as we used to say to our parents before bedtime in a Von Trapp children style ceremony.

I slept soundly and awoke to the nurse and doctor checking the monitors, giving me the once over and then offering me a drink of water. I was surprised to see Zak there at such an early time in the morning. My remarkable powers of observation noticed she was wearing the same clothes and knowing the importance of how her hair appears in public, noticed it hadn't been ironed through her GHD's. Not a good hair day for sure.

Hardly surprising as she had spent the night in the car park with Tom in the back seat and her in the front of the Beamer. Tom had even opened the rear windows so his feet could stick out and he could go full length.

It's a shame I'd taken the mattress off the roof rack.

The doctor handed us an envelope without really telling us

what it was for, but we assumed it was to do with the necessary bureaucracy we would have to go through to claim back the money through EHIC when the medical bill came through the post.

We thanked them, said our au revoirs and then I had to do the walk of shame through the waiting room in my underpants. In broad daylight and with more people buzzing around shooting me a curious glance or two, I felt even more exposed than I had done entering the hospital under the cover of darkness. Must've been a good evening for that couple, I imagined people assuming.

The fact was, I was in no fit state to give two hoots what people thought the night before, but now, I was much more alert and self aware, as the cortisol had brought down the rash, the swelling and the light headedness.

After such an eventful night where I had gone through a near death experience and Zak and Tom had slept rough, I suggested to Zak that maybe the afternoon tea party should be postponed.

I was surprised at the vehemence of her reply that immediately put me back in my place. "NO!" she stated indignantly. "I've worked hard to prepare for it and it will go ahead," she made abundantly clear.

Ooh, that's me told and I wasn't going to argue with some wild-eyed, sleep-deprived, crazy-haired woman who was behind the steering wheel on our way back home. We also had our second camera person, Ivy, turning up to record this afternoon tea run-through and get the reactions of the guests as to the quality of the culinary offerings. With Zak in her fatigued state, I don't think anyone dared give a negative response for fear of her pouring some piping hot Darjeeling straight into their tender areas, missing the cups with an insincere 'Oops, sorry'.

Just outside of Périgueux, we stopped to fill the car with petrol and refuel ourselves with some machine coffee, which pumped caffeine into our veins to keep us firing on whatever cylinders were still in operation. It wasn't a great café au lait, but it did the job and after what we'd been through the night before, it would have been a cruel irony if Zak had careered off the road after falling asleep at the wheel.

As soon as we arrived back at the château, everyone emerged bleary eyed to check out the walking wounded and get a lowdown of our nocturnal adventures.

After an abridged version of events, we all headed to our beds to catch up on lost sleep, but Zak just power-napped, before showering, ironing that crazy hair into a frizz free straightness, applying some makeup to conceal the exhaustion and going back into the kitchen to ensure her afternoon tea went down a storm with her carefully chosen guests.

Ivy was a good friend of Natalia, but with a more laid-back style. She was less likely to ask for retakes and certainly didn't enjoy the same tit-for-tat confrontational verbal battles with Bart. Everyone with a speaking part was fitted with a small microphone, apart from Bart whose voice was like it was rigged up to a megaphone already.

I remained in bed, as the cortisol was still in my system and I fell into a fitful slumber. I kept drifting in and out of consciousness as I heard the hubbub of jovial banter, clattering of cutlery and clinking of Limoges porcelain. Audibly at least, it sounded like it was going successfully.

Eventually, I felt able to rise from my pit and join everybody around the table. I still had the plasters that had secured the intravenous tubes hanging to my skin and the hospital admission bracelet on my wrist.

I apologised for my lateness and our friend Trisha insisted I was milking the attention with all the hospital paraphernalia I could've removed.

She was right, I'm a drama queen at heart and it was a good prop for the cameras to pick up on and after everyone had given their feedback on their afternoon tea experience, Ivy put me and Zak in front of their camera.

Keeping it light hearted, we spoke about how a near death experience wouldn't detract Zak from getting tea and cakes on a table and verified my lower standing in the pecking order of château priorities.

To the lyrics of Queen, belted out by Freddy Mercury, "The show must go on".

The following day I woke up with my eyes swollen and the rash once again appearing on my legs. I looked like an extra from Lock Stock and Two Smoking Barrels and considered sending a mug shot to Guy Ritchie to consider me for his next movie.

It turned out the envelope the doctor had handed us at the hospital was to be taken to the pharmacy that day, but we thought it was a get well soon card. No actually we thought it was for the insurance reasons and had just tucked it into the glove compartment of the car.

We went to see the local doctor in Piégut who was a genial older fellah with a decent smattering of English and took the envelope in with us. We explained the frelon frenzy and overnight hospital stay and I showed him the rash.

His eyes immediately widened and he said in a dramatic voice, "Zis is very dangerous. You must take this envelope to ze pharmacy at once". The cortisol at the hospital had worn off and I had to go through a course of pills and apply steroid cream. I was also equipped with two epi-pens because apparently anaphylactic shocks don't give you immunity, in fact they can worsen and if it happened again, I needed to jab my leg instantly to avoid croaking on the spot.

From talking to the doctor, I remembered from way back being stung by a wasp and having a skin reaction that a doctor had described as urticaria. This was urticaria full strength and now I have to be on my guard around stinging insects and keep an epi-pen with me at all times.

The cameras hadn't been around to record the actual events of that night, me rolling around naked covered in a red rash, the fainting, the race to the hospital, me insisting my arse was on fire and Tom and Zak sleeping in the car park, but had they been there, it would surely have made the cut.

Had the situation worsened though, they might have had to reconsider the title 'A New Life in the Sun'.

Ready for Guests

Before any mad hatter tea parties, bed and breakfast and bar parties were to commence, we had to be in complete readiness for the first guests.

The correct signage had to be put out, with booklets in each room about what to do in an emergency, something we'd forgotten to do ourselves in the blind panic of a frelon attack and of course clean everything to sparkling and launder all the linens.

Tom and Yaz with the help of Colin, Marianne and Mackenzie had reconfigured the chapel into a bar, moving a large bench we'd hauled down there into the fireplace to sit on. It fitted perfectly and opened up the space for the snooker cum pool table to be erected. A large union jack was tacked above the bench to ensure no debris fell from the chimney onto any patrons' heads.

The piano was moved to the wall with seats around it and what was once a bookcase in the salon was repurposed with a few alterations by Tom to become a bar. Zak had delved deep into the internet and found another fridge that was going for free. That was filled with Leffe blonde bière, bottles of Prosecco and white wine.

The shelves above it were filled with spirit bottles with a variety of gins, vodkas, scotches and brandy's including one called Bourgin that Yaz and Tom had bought from a distiller on a trip to Cognac.

They'd also brought an A1 poster that said 'Save Whisky. Drink Bourgoin Cognac'. With their Cavapoo called Whisky it sounded more like a threat than an invite.

A turntable was plugged into an amp and a collection of vinyls, that had survived through our many house moves, were dusted off and ready to rock the rafters of the room. As a headbanger in my earlier days there was a selection of rock classics in there including ACDC, Led Zeppelin and Motörhead. One French guest insisted on the former being played loud, cranking it up to 11 on the amp. Zak's Spotify playlist was more chill lounge to match the relaxed ambiance of the château, but this guy wanted to discover his inner Lemmy. Luckily he didn't emulate the drummer of Motörhead at the time who was called Philthy Animal Taylor or worse still Keith Moon, who was renowned for smashing up hotels and no doubt, French châteaux.

Mirrors and frames that had foundered on the floor were now put up on the wall and suddenly the chapel looked like a place for socialising and not just a dumping ground.

Zak had printed out a price list for drinks and we had to change our mindsets that serving up drinks was to be charged to a bill and not just us throwing a party and being generous hosts.

We first opened up the bar to guests who'd come from Belgium. The father was challenging his daughter to a snooker tournament. The mum was sitting in the fireplace, which admittedly sounds a bizarre statement.

We had walked across the road for an evening of music and drink at La Grange, a self-sufficient commune that was renovating a large old barn and the surrounding fields and forestry. Antoine, one of the collectives' five founders, had invited us. Zak, Tom, Yaz, Mackenzie, Cosmo and I had joined

Ken and Suzy to meet more locals and have a few wheat beers that were on draft.

There was a positive hippy vibe with some extraordinary haircuts and some equally extraordinary dancing in evidence. It was electronic music with a renowned violinist who was the furthest thing you can imagine from an orchestral virtuoso performer. It was trance, meets electro punk, meets synth, meets lord knows what else, but it was an eclectic sound that drew an equally eclectic crowd.

Xavier was there and we had one of our usual conversations where we eventually understood each other with sign language and our rudimentary grasp of each other's languages.

Suzy had studied French at university and could speak fluently, so we soon ascertained that he was moving his last two donkeys out of the field.

I, to be honest, was gutted. I'd become fond of them and how they watched me as a beast of burden in the garden often braying which sounded to my ear as laughter.

They were the nicest looking donkeys you could imagine, obviously spoilt and without being subject to any hard labour like the mad fool they used to observe curiously in the garden next door.

Perhaps the final straw had been when Coquette, the not so coquettish of the two donkeys, had escaped the field and gone walkabouts up the chemin. I had ushered her back to the field with a few loud commands of "allez". She seemed to comply until she took a detour into our garden where she proceeded to attack Cosmo with her front hooves.

Cosmo was lucky to survive letting out a yelp and managing to scurry to safety before being trampled. 'Death by

Donkey' doesn't make for a very elegant epitaph.

Suddenly at the gathering, a fight broke out.

No, it wasn't me after a few wheat beers losing the plot and getting a hippy into a headlock, it was the collection of dogs that wandered unleashed around the fields in the area. It was in complete contrast to the love and peace vibe our hippy neighbours exuded, but there was no messing about in pulling the dogs apart with boots flying in and scruffs getting yanked.

Cosmo was a shivering wreck, being as far from a fighting dog as you could imagine, or perhaps he was nervous he was going to be vomited on again. Zak decided at this point to take him back home and with the bar opening at 6pm, our guests might be getting thirsty.

The rest of us enjoyed a few more drinks and listened to the music, thinking some hallucinogenic drugs might improve the experience, but when Cosmo escaped and came looking for us, we decided to take him back home.

I invited Suzy and Ken back for a nightcap and we headed for the bar. I stepped into my new role as landlord and poured some wine for Suzy and Ken and opened a beer for myself. Ken pulled up the stool next to the piano and started belting out some boogie-woogie tunes that had the whole piano rocking on its three legs.

I was rocking on my two legs, but felt we had come a long way as I stood at my own bar as the proprietor where live music was playing and guests were playing a snooker tournament with their kids.

Tom offered our guests a beer, which they took us up on and we sat around having convivial conversation while the clack of snooker balls and laughter rang out. Zak, always keen to ensure our guests are having a great time, played a frame of snooker with the daughter. She would usually have wiped the table with her, but through gritted teeth, allowed her to win while the parents relaxed.

We learnt the lesson that evening to not offer our guests' drinks but to ask them if they'd like to purchase a drink and give them a bill. We had to also remember we weren't running a charity, but a business. The guests didn't pay for that evening, but that was our fault and we did have the rosy glow of the feedback that the kids said they wanted to do this every year.

Guests started coming thick and fast. The coronavirus had totally altered the sort of clients we were expecting. They were coming mostly from continental Europe, with few venturing across the Channel, probably choosing to take advantage of Boris's travel corridors to usual Brit hotspots where they could spread and catch Covid in the clubs and bars of beach resorts.

We ensured everything was in compliance, with masks and sanitiser in every room and every corner of the château. We had to remember the elbow bumps and a form called fiche de police for all guests to fill in, apart from French nationals.

Ice water was always on tap while people went through the formalities.

They were then shown to their rooms, given the keys and given the run of the château. Some stayed in their rooms, others took a deck chair in the garden or reclined in the hammock. Others took an ice-cold beer and admired the view from the terrace.

One guest was a motocross enthusiast and wanted to watch a grand prix race that had taken place earlier that day. I diligently searched it out on the TV and sat there with him as he gave me a running commentary of the riders, the bikes and the whole race history. Anything to keep our guests happy and he did leave a positive review, even though the bread didn't meet up to his French standards. He did say he'd come again but knew our prices would be going up as the renovations continued and the standards would improve even more so.

We had set the prices at very competitive and reasonable levels in line with other accommodation in the area. This was our inaugural summer and trial run after all.

Reviews became a magnet we were drawn to, even though we swore we'd take them with a pinch of salt. The majority were positive and we were getting some delightful comments.

Anything negative was replied to in the nicest possible way, even if totally unreasonable and unnecessarily caustic.

We had many fantastic guests who had a great time, some even playing the piano. It was spiritually uplifting to hear the château echoing to the strains of the theme tune to the film, Amelie.

We had a young couple that booked a room for a romantic weekend. The young lady turned up hours before her Romeo appeared and she asked me, ever so politely, if she could play the piano, which I of course agreed to. I was so delighted to hear the 99 pence worth sounding a million dollars and I wanted to capture this moment for posterity. I asked if I could video her tickling the ivories and half way through felt very self-conscious as an older man filming a young lady like some voyeuristic pervert.

I kept it short and disappeared to let her go through a repertoire of other French favourites. Later that evening she was joined by her beau and from Zak's enquiries, it turned out that they were two police officers from Périgueux. Obviously they were practising police procedure together and he was taking down her particulars.

"Do you have guns?" Zak asked with her trademark bluntness, delving into areas many of us would probably be thinking but consider a no-go area.

"Oui" was the disconcerting answer. We certainly weren't going to have a fall out with this pair. Most guests left the following day after their night's stay, these two asked if they could stay a bit longer and as we weren't receiving new guests that afternoon, agreed to let them stay on for a while.

Their romantic stay went well into the following evening and they were still doing what romantic French couples do together when offered a free bedroom and clawed bath for the day. The sun was setting when they came down and we were hoping this was them coming to say au revoir, but no. They were going to work on night shift and asked if they could use our washing machine and dryer.

Refusal might have got their itchy trigger fingers twitching and we didn't want to upset the gendarmerie, so we agreed. We wanted to make their course of true love run smooth and our more paternal and maternal instincts took pity on them.

When they eventually left, we didn't ask for any more money, although Zak did expect something in return.

"If we get pulled up for any reason, we will mention your names and you will vouch for us as decent law-abiding people and insist on our release without any fines" Zak declared with a look in her eye that spanned the divide between jest and utter seriousness.

Another couple, Benoît and Margot arrived to stay for one night. They were great company and we sat on the terrace swapping stories and it turned out they lived in Fulham, place of Zak's birth and on a road leading to my beloved Fulham Football Club.

Benoît even brought a drone with him and launched it in the garden. It was a state-of-the-art drone with incredible lenses. The first I knew of it was as I got out of the showers and heard the high-pitched buzz outside. I was hoping it didn't creep round to the bathroom window to capture me in my birthday suit.

Nobody wants to take that home with them as a holiday memory as I bend down to dry between my toes. One aperture catching sight of another.

Benoît downloaded the footage onto a USB stick which we kept and it even gave us a view of the roof tiles, some of which need urgent replacement, which has been relayed to Johan for him to get up there with a cherry picker.

Benoît has also sent us an edited version set to music that looked glorious as the sun began to set. What a wonderful gesture and we have invited them back for a free stay next summer.

We did have some disgruntled guests who were kept awake at night by a party at La Grange that went on into the early hours of the morning. The business plan of Antoine was to invite people to come and work on the barn to learn traditional craft skills. This they paid for to fund the ongoing renovation. Why I didn't think of this genius plan irks me to this day because in our world, we pay tradesmen to do our renovations. La Grange did throw in a free holiday site I suppose, opening up their field for a whole selection of clapped out transit vans and caravans but I didn't fancy our garden becoming a pikey camp, especially when Zak had aspirations of Versailles.

While working throughout the summer, they were creating an Épicerie and every day they'd be scraping out and pointing between the granite stones, climbing the erected scaffolding and wheel barrowing in a constant stream of concrete and building materials to hit the opening date of September 12th. Walls that had been covered in brambles and ivy were all cleared back to the stone by a seven-nation army.

Volunteers would run the shop and all produce would be sourced from the local area. The shop was to be open 24/7 with an honesty box for people to pay when the till was unmanned, or unwomanned, just to ensure I'm being woke.

The builders were being worked, sorry, I mean taught, late into the evening before taking to their beds. The surrounding fields were filled with yurts and lean-tos made from reclaimed wood and materials which were the furthest thing from glamping. Run-down cars devoid of wheels were discarded down dirt tracks, no doubt acquired as projects that ran out of steam, or spare parts.

When Antoine's cunning plan had reached its conclusion, all the workers clambered onto the scaffolding for a portrait to celebrate their landmark achievement. I happened to walk out from the garden when all the men had decided to moon at the camera and Bart also witnessed this sight yelling out 'et la femme?' being totally unwoke.

After all their hard labour and financial contributions, the least Antoine could do was lay on a lavish party with the music pushing the volume needle up into the red zone, so it could be heard for kilometres around. The party we had gone to, wrapped up at 11pm which we thought was very considerate of them as neighbours, but this one seemed to have no 'chariots at midnight' on the invite.

Tom, who was in one of the bedrooms nearest to where the action was taking place, also had a disrupted night's sleep and at 6am went bleary eyed over the road to make his dissatisfaction clear as they were doing the conga to 'Rocking All Over the World'. Maybe it's his aversion to Status Quo that proved to be the final straw.

Our guests who had really enjoyed their stay until the mini Glastonbury had broken out next door made their feelings clear, even though in the most polite way, realising it was not our fault, as we had no prior knowledge of the event that was going to take place.

Zak was so incensed, she spoke to one of La Grange workers and demanded that Antoine come and see her immediately and texted Steve, the deputy mayor threatening to report their disruptive party to the police. We didn't really intend to do this as we like our neighbours who are usually very pleasant to us and we want to recommend their Épicerie to our guests in the future. From my own experiences incurring the wrath of Khan, Zak's maiden name, I wouldn't have wanted to be in Antoine's boots that particular morning.

Had they let us know this was going to happen, we wouldn't have booked out rooms that night, or they could have rented out the rooms for their guests for a well-earned sleep and a little slice of château luxury.

Even though it was a Sunday, Steve appeared in next to no time. He went over to La Grange and had a word with Antoine. He told him that we were very upset and also advised him that if we had reported them to the police, they'd have relished nicking the alternatives for not observing social distancing protocols.

I use the word 'alternatives' as it was the way locals described them and there had been trouble in the past where a festival in one of the fields got out of hand, when about 3,000 people turned up disrupting the fragile peace of village life.

Apparently in an outburst of French provincial retribution for their noise pollution, shotguns were brandished and windows of vans got smashed in.

Steve came back to us and expressed apologies on their behalf and said Antoine would be coming over in person.

In their defence, Steve said the French tend to 'go for it' on special occasions and party all night. This was Assumption Day in France and Antoine and his crew had made the assumption that we knew this. A knock on the door and a heads up would have sufficed to let us know and take evasive action from our guests being disturbed.

While our Belgian guests were enjoying an afternoon tea indoors, as it had started raining outside, Antoine sheepishly knocked on the door and I beckoned him in. He was carrying bottles of wheat beer as a peace offering, which I suggested he take into the salon where our guests, whose night he'd disrupted, were tucking into cakes, scones and lashings of tea. I wasn't sure whether his ashen face was the result of fear or a raging hangover.

As Antoine is also from Belgium, the conversation started in a quite hostile tonality, but tapered down to Belgian banter and friendly voices. They were a jovial lot, always laughing and determined to enjoy their experience and they'd been joined by local friends to celebrate our guest Elsa's birthday.

Antoine left with a flea in his ear, but his gesture was appreciated and all was forgiven and forgotten as he left with a cheerful wave and a relieved expression on his visage.

Zak gave him a withering stare, that I've seen bring grown men to their knees, begging for mercy and we now have an understanding of where a line will be drawn in the sand mixed with cement of course.

Work upon Work

As the season wore on and we became used to the procession of guests coming and going and the ever more successful tea parties that had obviously benefitted from local word of mouth, I received freelance work on a three-day basis.

This suited me down to the ground in three days on, four days off situation that allowed me to continue with renovations, while earning income to pay for them.

It was getting particularly hot at this stage and I was happy to be inside working on the laptop as Bart walked in and out on a regular basis trying to cool down with gallons of iced water.

The work I had taken on was for a well-known international motor company with a formidable global reputation and I was doing regular Microsoft team calls with my working partner Simon where we would conceptualise for hours, fuelled by endless cups of coffee, tea and biscuits.

Remote working was something we had to get used to as we usually worked in an office in Shoreditch, where we had a more personable passing of ideas in an open plan office buzzing with activity. We would catch up with the wider team in meeting rooms and exchange ideas and of course, socialise with the odd visit to the pub on a Friday lunchtime and a pint or two of real ale or a glass of vino. Advertising has always been a sociable business, but the boozy lunches of the 80's and 90s had fizzled out to a far more sober approach to producing ads as it rolled into the 2000's.

The agency did still have a Thursday evening gathering where free drinks were on offer as the agency heads gave the staff a heads up on news and progress. People there worked hard, often doing ridiculous hours, so it was well deserved and an excuse to let one's hair down a bit.

It was leading up to March when news of the coronavirus started to become increasingly concerning. I was travelling from Richmond to Old Street in packed trains and anyone who let out the slightest cough or sneeze was eyed suspiciously.

Rumbles of the office possibly closing were beginning to circulate the agency. I myself was struck down with symptoms that left me bedridden for four days, which I can only speculate was Covid 19 as I was displaying lots of the symptoms with the long tail of exhaustion and muscle aches that followed. I can remember really struggling to bend down and do my shoelaces up like a fully-fledged old codger. I didn't lose my sense of taste though, although anyone who's seen my wardrobe might categorically disagree.

I got back into the office leading up to March 23rd, when the announcement was made by Boris and the rest is history. I went home to sit on my burgeoning backside over three months and begin to write this book.

The three months did give me some rest time in preparation for the onslaught that awaited me when restrictions were lifted.

In France, I chose to sit in the kitchen with the grand mirror frame behind me on video conference calls. I had noticed most other people would sit with a bookcase behind them to show how learned and intellectual they were. My backdrop just screamed 'I own a château."

On all the presentations to our executive creative director, Brian, as well as the account team and strategy planner, I would often be quizzed about the daily routine of château life and always the weather. At one stage I took the laptop outside so they could look at the stunning view and the blazing sunshine.

The wi-fi from the château did stretch to the terrace, but sitting out there in the suntrap that pushed temperatures well into the high 30s and sometimes the low to mid-40s, was not conducive to straight thinking.

The clanking of the digger and the construction of the spiral staircase from the bottom terrace to the higher one, which revolved around the tank gun turret we had made in Isleworth and transported to the Dordogne, added more decibels than the buzz of the office back in London.

I spent hours in my granite workplace and as Bart walked in overheated, I was complaining of numb fingers and toes as it was actually freezing indoors. Every now and again I would go outside just to thaw out and feel my extremities again.

The UK was an hour behind us in France, which allowed me some morning time to walk Cosmo through the woods, where we would often see deer crashing through the undergrowth. Cosmo, now a fifteen-year-old dog was still very sprightly, but took no interest in chasing other animals anymore. In fact, he would actively avoid them if he picked up their scent in the air.

Deer littered the sides of the roads around much of our part of the Dordogne and forests of the Limousin, having been hit by cars. We ourselves had put on the brakes many times when seeing their eyes glowing in the treeline by the roadside. These beautiful creatures didn't get much of a break around our neck of the woods. When not being rammed by vehicles, they were being hunted by le chasse with their ever-zealous dogs and rifle-wielding drunken huntsmen.

These were a sight to behold when you saw them in their luminous gilets squatting by the road waiting to shoot the poor deer being flushed out by the dogs and their fellow blood-sport enthusiasts. Perhaps they share Zak's change of character when donning hi-viz and they get a sense of self-importance and bravado. The idea of Zak in that garb carrying a high velocity rifle makes my blood run cold.

There were numerous stories of people being shot by these rifle-toting lunatics and probably after lunch, they'd have had a vin rouge or two and were a lot more trigger happy. There were horror stories of one gunman shooting his son and even a motorist on a motorway being shot by a stray bullet.

The local website always had the latest posts of windows being shot out of their conservatories and dogs rampaging through their land. It was so worrying Zak bought me a luminous orange gilet to wear on walks with a matching bow to tie to Cosmo's collar. It did make me feel a bit camp strolling around with a labradoodle sporting matching colours, but it was better than someone popping a cap in my ass, or as they say in France, la balle dans le derrière.

After surviving a morning walk, I'd get back to the château for a catch up with Bart, a coffee and croissant and when guests were there, whatever they'd left from their buffet breakfast.

Zak laid on a tremendous spread, having sorted out the fresh bread situation with a trip to the boulangerie in Abjat for chocolate and almond croissants, pain au raisin, brioche and abacoise, a selection of ham, and cheeses, orange and apple juice, yoghurts, confiture and locally sourced honey, boiled eggs, a selection of cereals, fresh filter coffee and pots of tea.

Nobody leaves Château Gros Puy in the morning on an empty stomach.

Having discussed the day ahead, I logged on and spent the day indoors talking with Simon and the wider team while Tom and Yaz had business calls beside me and Bart would come and go, cursing the sweltering heat outside while I was on a conference call. Both the dogs would come in from outside panting and splay themselves out on the cold granite stones in the chapel.

Lulu, the loopy cat, had made her home on the green baize of the snooker table and we had to constantly sweep it down from all the fur she left there. She also left the remnants of some poor unfortunate rodents in and around the chapel, which was always my job to clear up and Yaz once watched in horror as she munched her way through a loir, otherwise known as an edible dormouse, leaving only its fluffy tail on the table top.

At one stage, Tom and Yaz had their first go at distilling their own gin in the kitchen with their mini copper still as I worked at distilling some ideas.

They served it up as a G&T after they'd gone through the whole process and it nearly blew my tête off. Well any gin that was to bear the Château Gros Puy name was going to have to be potent. Hic.

The other great way to cool down was in the paddling pool we had inflated and placed in the garden while the plunge pool was still in kit form in the salon awaiting completion of the platform that was going to support it.

It took hours to fill with mains water and I dread to think what our bill will be. The château had hitherto run off well water but been converted before we bought the place. We need to reinstate that for irrigating the large garden and keep an eye on those bills in future.

The sun warmed up the water and a quick wallow with an

ice-cold drink would definitely reduce your core temperature in minutes.

This was a temporary measure as Zak's plunge pool was dragged out and the task of following the complex instructions of self-assembly were passed on to Bart to figure out.

Yaz and Tom had been at the château for two months and left before the plunge pool reached completion. With heavy hearts, they packed up their convertible VW with Whisky and Mackenzie in the back and headed back on the ten-hour journey via the Eurotunnel.

Colin and Marianne had left earlier to continue their euro tour and the night before had treated us all to a vegetarian curry, which was delicious.

Yaz, Tom and Mackenzie had helped us out with guests and also helped get our social media and online booking sites up and running.

Zak's number dyslexia also extended to her use of a diary and one day, when Zak had disappeared for the day with her sister Safia for a day at St Estèphe for a wander and a swim, two unexpected guests turned up at the door.

We were all on our laptops and looked up with vacant expressions at these two men standing in the doorway.

"Bonjour, ça va?" we asked, wondering what they were doing there.

Tom had far better French than me and when they asked about their reservation, he replied, "Oh no, we are fully booked".

The two guys looked none-too-pleased with this response and demanded that they had booked to stay there for two nights.

"Ah of course" Tom exclaimed as if there was no oversight and asked them inside to enjoy a glass of water or something stronger. The bedroom they had booked had two single beds and hadn't been made up.

Two men, quite handsome and without female partners, we assumed might be a gay couple and offered them an upgrade to a room with a double bed.

This didn't sit well with them as they were on a hiking holiday and as two mates definitely wanted separate beds.

Safia and Lyndon, her partner, had been put in that bedroom and we suddenly had to run around to change the sheets, make the beds, replace water bottles and towels and shift Safia and Lyndon's cases and gear into Mackenzie's room. Mackenzie in turn was moved into our bedroom onto a drop-down sofa.

This was all done in a whirlwind of activity as we phoned Zak to get back tout de suite and welcome the guests she'd neglected to inform us about. We all had to stall on our remote working to get this done and luckily weren't in the middle of a Zoom call or something that couldn't be disturbed.

The two men who understandably looked disgruntled by our misunderstanding, turned out to be really friendly guys and when Zak returned and showed them to their hastily turned around room, they had a wonderful few days with us.

I was worried about how we would cope without Yaz, Tom and Mackenzie there to help out in a crisis, but things were never as bad as I imagined with just me and Zak left alone to cope.

We were getting used to running a chambre d'hote, while camera people hovered around and I was mixing remote working with physical working in and around the château. Bart was ever-present turning up to finish the plunge pool, which looked great and was christened by Zak taking the first dip, swiftly followed by me. I would have done a running bomb, but that probably would have ejected every last bit of water we'd taken ages to fill it with. Only one guest got to trial it out, he was a really nice guy from Australia who lived and worked in Paris. When singular guests turned up, usually on bikes, we invited them to join us to eat.

It always seemed wrong to leave a solo person at their own table as we sat at ours chatting away. One such biker was a delightful Dutch woman who turned up one day, swathed in leather, on a Royal Enfield motorbike. We all hit it off immediately, not least of all because she was on a classic British bike, but because we all had a similar sense of humour.

Another more elderly Dutch woman who lived in Nontron, about 20 miles from us, had cycled to the château because she wanted a change of scene and to try the food. She was fantastic company and said she'd heard about the château from her brother who was a nearby estate agent who'd had the château on his books. It had been an arduous uphill ride for her and we worked out the quickest and less hilly ride for her to get back from our own knowledge of the back road short cuts.

We had one last cameraman called Jack, who we were to meet at Brantôme, affectionately known as the Venice of Périgord, to capture us strolling through a market in the shadow of the great benedictine abbey beside the river Dronne. He was to cover us for two days wrapping up our season and heading into the autumn.

We met Jack outside by the main bridge and made our introductions. He was already doing his reconnaissance of the town and planning a shooting agenda. The idea was for us to stroll into the market and do a bit of shopping and bartering with the traders.

By this time, coronavirus deaths were increasing in France and social distancing and mask wearing was being even more strictly adhered to. Through the summer in such an isolated and sparsely populated region, we'd been lucky enough to live mostly mask free. Every time we entered a town to go shopping, masques obligataire signs were diligently observed. We'd been in the Gros Puy bubble for months and cases in the area were minimal to nil.

We crossed the Pont Coude and stopped to gaze into the river, where I immediately spotted the azure blur of a kingfisher flashing below us and shouted it out with ornithological excitement. There is a restaurant across the bridge here called Moulin de l'Abbey where diners can sit in a garden overlooking the weir that spans the river beneath the bridge. From here, boat trips can be taken to observe the beautiful countryside and sights from the gently flowing river.

The abbey itself is built into a cliff-face where there are many troglodyte caves that show evidence of occupation of monks since the 8th century. One grotte is known as 'The Cave of The Final Judgement' I think I'll avoid venturing in there for a while. Brantôme is a beautiful location full of charm, history, riverside restaurants and watering holes that we recommend to all our guests.

The only trouble with filming here was that everyone was wearing masks, which was being closely observed by two gendarmes once again, toting their guns.

Every stallholder had their bouches disguised beneath various designs of cloth, which, being muffled made their thick regional French accents even harder to understand.

But we pressed on trying to pretend everything was as normal as possible should Channel 4 wish to repeat the programme once Covid 19 had been banished as a virus like the many that have afflicted humanity in the past. I think this won't be the case for some time to come, but we were just following instructions going maskless when the camera was rolling.

Jack had asked us to haggle with the traders in that quintessentially French way that looks so evocative of the region on screen. We thought about what we actually needed that we could buy from a stallholder and as I'd been working so hard for so many months, I'd lost a few pounds and my shorts were in danger of falling down at any moment. That might well have got the gendarmes reaching for their pistols and shouting 'pull them up' as opposed to 'put them up'.

The first stall we approached was a guy selling belts of all different styles and materials. We looked at a few and settled on a thin leather brown one that looked like it would do a perfectly good job. I slid it through the belt loops and fastened it to see if it would fit and keep me from being arrested for exposure.

At this point, I realised Jack had crouched down and was aiming his camera at my waist and groin area. 'Are you sure this is the sort of imagery the viewers of A New Life in The Sun want to be looking at?' I asked Jack.

He immediately stood up realising what this must have looked like from an onlooker's perspective and stuttered "ah yes, I see your point."

I'm sure rolling hills and breathtaking vistas is what the archetypal daytime TV viewer wants to see and not rolls of fat and a hairy midriff.

With the new belt firmly in place, we walked past the abbey and onto a fruit and veg stall. As with all people who would appear on screen, Jack needed to get consent and the woman behind the stall had an expression like she was sucking one of the lemons she was attempting to sell under her mask.

As Zak attempted her best French in her faltering Fulham accent, the woman just scowled and the finger pointing technique took preference over any attempt to communicate via words.

With the bags thrust into her hand and the transaction complete, we walked across the bridge into the main throng of the action. A boulangerie stall was the next point of perusal with the camera rolling, as Zak chose some French sticks and half a dozen fresh baked croissants.

This proved to be more jovial and Jack might have got something the editor could use, but it was hard going. Maybe these marketeers were sick and tired of cameramen shoving a lens down their throats for this most clichéd of vignettes for programmes and tourists alike to capture. Maybe they were on the run from the authorities and preferred to remain incognito. Perhaps Covid 19 with all its restrictions and drawbacks was beginning to affect everybody's mood, so we headed for an outdoor café where we could just sit and enjoy a coffee.

The moody waiter pointed to a table that distanced us from the other patrons and we sat down, ordered and waited for the café and a few biscuits to arrive.

Jack was giving us directions in English to follow as we quaffed the café and attempted what looked like natural dialogue, discussing our purchases and swatting away the swarm of flies buzzing around our sugary treats.

In doing so, he drew the attention of a young English couple on a nearby table asking what he was filming for. After giving them the full background, they informed us how they had sold up everything in the UK to open a gallery in the area. The husband was the artist and was intending to run courses at their smallholding.

Jack gave them details of the production company as they expressed an interest in being on the show and Zak gave them our email address if he was interested in running a course from the château.

We could see in their eyes and their demeanour that they had put everything on the line to get this business up and running, so we were surprised that they didn't follow up on the conversation with an email. Perhaps they did approach True North and perhaps they will appear on the next season's show, but that was the last we saw or heard from them.

We headed back to the château with Jack following in his car and continued to go through the shot list he had compiled over the next couple of days. Bart was building a granite stone set of steps that led to the large wooden door at the foot of the turret. I was finishing off the pointing between the cracks and doing a running commentary about what I was doing and trying, possibly in a desperate diatribe of futility, to sound competent.

Things were beginning to come together after these many months on site, but running the chambre d'hote and the remote working had slowed us down considerably. The falling leaves were telling us that autumn was well and truly on its way, even though the sun was still managing to push the mercury past 30 degrees Fahrenheit.

As I used to bang on about the beautiful nature surrounding us, Jack joined me on the usual morning walk with Cosmo. Past the lakes and into fields, I pointed out the most picturesque views and waffled about anything else that entered my mind.

Jack shot the château from a lake that butted up to Xavier's field, to see the château from another angle. As we walked back across the field that led to it, Jack was very excited to see a large collection of what he informed me were Ceps. They looked like burger buns growing in large congregations and trusting Jack's judgement, having studied them for any green around the edges, he deemed them safe for a nibble.

Yep, they were mushroom. "Best way to know if they are edible or not, is to take them to your local pharmacy" he piped up as I was swallowing what was already in my mouth.

"Oh great," I replied, "I'll just hang tough to see what this does to my insides tonight" I added expecting a scene to resemble the one in Alien where Jon Hurt's stomach bursts open as the fledgling alien appears and then scuttles off with a squeal.

"You'll be fine" he reassured me. Jack did seem to have an awful lot of knowledge about all the nature we were walking amongst. He himself owned acres of land about a few hours' drive from us near Lyon and a few dogs.

He also owned an Aston Martin, one of which Bart owns as only a handful of the iconic and beautiful cars registered in France.

Bart had been a bike enthusiast riding a Harley Davidson with Jenny on pillion. This came to an abrupt halt one day when going at low speed, they lost traction on loose gravel and both he and Jenny ended up in hospital needing extensive surgery for their injuries.

They are both fine now, although bearing scars and long-term ailments from the damage caused, but Bart went from two wheels to four with his Vantage that is always polished to gleaming and kept in a garage at his property.

Once Bart and Jack started talking cars, Zak and I blanked over and left them to it. Both were classic car nuts and when valves and pistons became the topic of discussion, we peeled away silently and cracked on with the tasks still left to complete.

Jack did get a lot of footage of further renovation and overnight used a stop motion camera pointed at the turret to see the rotation of the stars above it, pending a clear cloudless night. More guests' feedback was recorded for posterity and more posed shots of Zak and I leading the idyllic château lifestyle.

As Jack was the last cameraman we were to see in 2020, he did a summing up of the season with me and Zak sat in the garden. We reminisced about how things had gone, the surprises and the dramas, the delights and the down moments.

Were our expectations met or dashed against the granite rocks that protrude all around the château?

Finally, he asked if we'd learnt anything about each other.

I waxed lyrical about how brilliantly Zak had managed everything, her devotion to guests, her delicious cooking, her overall brilliance in every aspect of being a chatelaine, almost wiping a tear from my eye.

The camera turned to Zak and the same question was asked of her. What had she discovered about me?

Zak turned and looked at me and the famous 'processing' expression crossed her face. "Not much really" came her considered reply. I was shocked. I'd worked my butt off for months, I'd been bringing in much-needed income to pay for the tons of materials being ferried back and forth from BricoMarche, the quarry and Leroy Merlin.

I'd entertained guests with my sparkling repartee, I'd done my best to shine in front of the cameras for a programme she wanted to do and then spent the majority of the time moaning about it.

I was devastated. Surely there was some redeeming feature

she could wrench from the depths of her memory banks that would paint me in a golden light?

"Oh I suppose he's been quite helpful" is about the most exuberant testimony she could muster to sum up the toil I had put in that virtually rendered me a broken man.

And that's a wrap.

No more cameras. No more camera people who we'd grown fond of and would miss. Less guests arriving, as the season wound down and less sunshine as storms started rolling in and our wardrobe changed from shorts, t-shirts and flip flops, to jeans, jumpers, waterproofs and wellies.

It had been a glorious and eventful summer for us, with minimum interference to our business from the pandemic. But that was to change and so was the rest of our stay before returning home.

Late Summer to Autumn

On my four days off, I really ramped up the lugging, digging, decorating and renovating. As Zak was working on the interior with the sound of the sewing machine rattling away, constant hammering and washing machine going, we muddled through together.

I got to work on ripping up the paths I had painstakingly laid the summer before, as the membrane I had laid beneath the gravel was no protection from the weeds that grew on the dust deposits that blew between the stones and the voracious weeds that tore through the sheets of underlay.

One thing you get used to when owning a château, is that there is always another job to be done, even the jobs you've already done need to be redone.

The path already dug out with all the removed earth piled up to the base of the turret and the lower terrace needed making into a rockery with a water feature sunk into it. The melange had been wacker plated, but the gravel chosen by Madame Chatelaine still had to be spread between the borders of granite stones that had been put in place by Jon.

My wobbly green wheelbarrow was spurred into action for the backbreaking work. As Zak's newly selected gravel was totally different from what had already been laid, I was going to have to relocate all that lighter gravier into the west garden that Bart's digger had laid waste to.

The mountain of gravel outside looked like south west

France's equivalent of the Alps, but I was to make a molehill out of the mountain in the next few days of shovelling, shifting and shaping.

The sundial in the centre of the garden all had to be put to one side and the birdbath disassembled to leave a whole lot of des oiseaux looking at me thirstily and angrily. Blimey, I'd really ruffled some feathers. A couple of collared doves floated in every day for a splash around in the shallow waters and they were livid.

From the air, I'd created three prongs of a cross and still had the southern facing stem to dig out. I would slave all day in the garden with the word Versailles, Versailles, Versailles echoing through my head.

My reward was a lovely lunch each day on the terrace beneath the large parasol. Meats, cheeses, French bread, salads and pickles were laid out on the table with decanters of ice-cold water to slake a thirst I had also built up.

The French take their lunchtimes very seriously and they often go on for two hours, involving red wine. Water? Don't be silly. It has to be fermented grape juice and probably a snooze afterwards.

I was lucky if I got twenty minutes and that suited me, as my muscles would seize up if I'd relax for too long and then rising from my seat became a job for the mechanical arm of Bart's digger or Zak's right foot.

The autumnal weather was surprisingly hot and I would work until sunset, which was arriving earlier and earlier by the day. At that stage, I'd down tools and head inside to shower and flake out in front of the TV to watch a Netflix series or catch up on the news on BBC. Boris, Brexit, coronavirus was what BBC stood for right then and Trump was never far from the headlines with his narcissistic and dangerous antics.

A bit of light-hearted relief was needed and we binged on The Crown, The Queen's Gambit, Designated Survivor and whatever else took our fancy.

When Zak's friend Emma and her two daughters Maddy and Josie arrived for a few days in their half term, The Great British Bake Off became the central theme of evening discussions. I was very happy for this passion from Josie to spill into the kitchen where she baked some delicious brownies.

During their stay, I was thankful to take a break from constant labouring to get out to some local tourist attractions and a shopping trip. Maybe the shopping trip with four women wasn't quite my cup of tea, but compared to hauling, heaving and huffing, it was far more palatable, even if I did still huff a bit in exasperation every now and again.

On our road trip, we decided to take an educational trip to Oradour-sur-Glane, which is a town that bore witness to a horrific atrocity at the hands of the Nazi's in World War Two.

A museum of the events that led up to the fateful day where the villagers were herded into a church, which was then set ablaze, and anyone attempting to escape was felled with machine gun fire, is chronicled in historical detail. It was very grim reading with black and white photographs painting a vivid picture of the events of 1944. It left me feeling bereft of hope for the fate of humanity if we are capable of such barbarity towards each other.

With the world divided by so many global issues, it served as a reminder of where this sort of hatred and extremism could lead and the consequences suffered by innocent victims.

From the museum, we walked along an alleyway that led directly into the village that had been left exactly as it was the day it came under attack.

Rusting old cars lined the streets. Signs told you which building you were looking at as they had been razed to the ground in many cases.

We passed them in silence, as words couldn't convey between us what must have occurred on that day. It was beyond comprehension. The road led to the church that was typical of the villages in the region, set in a picturesque corner surrounded by fields and squares.

Walking in felt disrespectful, but at the same time necessary to sear into our minds the final moments of horror the victims were subjected to. Only a few survived and we'd seen pictures of children wide-eyed in horror wandering the streets aimlessly. Who could imagine what they must have witnessed and how the rest of their lives will have been scarred?

We left, traumatised, but pleased that the younger generation had willingly participated in learning lessons that should never be removed from school curriculums or historical records.

A coffee in the new town was downed with cakes to fortify us for the shopping trip ahead in nearby Limoges.

We entered a shopping mall and this is where my mind went blank as I was led through fashionable shops to look at coats and clothes to be worn in the forthcoming winter. Zak acquired a white woolly coat that made her look Eskimo-like, a very glamorous Eskimo I might add, which would definitely come in handy in the month or so ahead.

I drew the line when Emma and her daughters went into a fashionable silk lingerie shop that I would have felt decidedly awkward browsing around.

We went back to the château and sat down to an evening

meal of boeuf bourguignon that Zak had made especially for our honoured guests.

These days of recreation and relaxation were few and far between with the rapid encroachment of autumn, as the yellow, oranges and browns crept into the leaves in the forest that made up our view from the château in a southerly direction.

One such day was a tour of the wine châteaux around the Bergerac region. As previously mentioned, Ken was a wine connoisseur and the time was ripe to go on a wine tasting tour and buy some reds and whites befitting of the discerning clientele we were attracting at Château Gros Puy.

Ken was the driver for the day with Suzy navigating, as they had done this trip on numerous occasions and turned up outside at 8am sharp with a toot of their horn.

It was a particularly gloomy day with drizzle falling constantly, but it didn't dampen our spirits as we made the two-hour journey south into the Périgord Pourpre or Purple Périgord, so named because of the colour the vine leaves turn come harvest time.

The landscape changed on our journey, as did the architecture, with the buildings made more from sandstone than granite. The capital of the region is Bergerac, which resides beside the lower stretch of the Dordogne river. After a short break for some of the rankest coffee I've ever tasted, served in a small bar a short hop from our first stop off point, we headed to Château de Tiregand that was along a particularly churned up muddy track. No delusions of grandeur here.

The château was charming though, although there had been some modifications with newly fitted double glazed windows that spoilt the overall authenticity. Not something we would ever consider doing to our petit château, but this was far grander and shortcuts were probably required on the property to concentrate on the wine the estate was producing.

Having been there previously, Ken and Suzy assured us it had moved on apace since their last visit, as the owner had inherited it and was in full on renovation mode to bring the place back to life and invigorate their wine growing capacity.

We walked in through the arched doorway into a large reception area with the wine cellars down some stairs to our left. A smartly dressed chap appeared like the shopkeeper in Mr Benn, as I had no idea where he popped up from.

Ken and Suzy's French is excellent and they engaged our guide in flowing français to talk us through the château's wines.

Glasses were proffered up to us as the first of the red wines flowed into the glass with an explanation of the year, the conditions the grapes grew in and how well it would keep, if stored in the right conditions. I followed Ken's lead as he swirled the wine around the glass holding it to the light to gauge the colour. He then buried his nose into the glass to inhale the bouquet and let it permeate into the membrane of his nostrils. I followed suit, closing my eyes as I lifted my head back like a seasoned sommelier. I thought it appropriate to let out a sigh that could be interpreted as questioning my own judgement. We then slurped it and rolled it over our palates, letting the tannins and nuances ignite different zones of our taste buds. Oh yes, I like this one, what do you think my fellow wine buffs?

I'm not sure our host was buying it, as my credentials are limited to what I read on the shelves of our local wine shop, or worst still, which label and price grabs my attention at Sainsbury.

My work partner Simon had recently interested me and Zak with his purchase of a breather, a device that aerates the wine through a filter as you pour it into the glass to replicate the effect of decanting. Zak mentioned this device and whether our host would recommend it or not.

The look on his face was as if somebody had let a real humdinger of a fart loose which nobody was admitting to and he wagged his head from side to side with an air of utter contempt for such crimes to wine.

Cover blown, we tried two other wines and compared the subtleties in difference using phrases like full-bodied, robust, fruity and smooth. We all agreed on the third choice that came at a higher price point and bought a case each.

Pécharmant was our house wine of choice and this truly was a step-up from the plonk we were used to. Two dozen bottles loaded into the boot and this was just the first of several other chateaux on our itinerary.

The country air mixed with the alcohol I had consumed before lunchtime and I was feeling quite lightheaded as we headed to Château de la Jaubertie. We entered through ornate ironwork gates and down an avenue of lime trees. This was a very aristocratic château. Some had fallen into good hands after the revolution where others had fallen into disrepair.

The roads were well maintained and led us through the sprawling grounds of fountains and forests with signs showing the way to the tasting rooms. Nobody else was around apart from a handful of staff and they looked at us like survivors looking for shelter after a zombie apocalypse.

The tasting room was much bigger than the first with rack upon rack of hundreds of bottles lining the wall. There was an oval counter in the middle that would accommodate groups of tasters en masse. There were just four of us, so we got a more personal experience from the attention lavished upon us from the female assistant pouring the wine.

All the usual rituals were observed, apart from expelling the liquid into a spittoon, which for me, would have been a total waste of a fine beverage. Maybe it's the Scottish tightness in me, where anything offered for free is not to be sniffed at, even after you've sniffed it.

As much as I paint myself and Zak as novices, we knew what we liked and our choices aligned with what found favour with Ken and Suzy. More red was stockpiled into the back of the car and we packed it out with picnic blankets to avoid too much rolling around and expensive breakages.

We had worked up quite an appetite and headed to Bergerac to find a place to eat and have a stroll around the city. We wandered through the cobbled streets, venturing into antique shops and the wine museum that had just undergone a major renovation taking us from a swish modern book and gift shop, up some stairs and into a medieval courtyard with vines climbing the walls to the colonnade up above.

As with the British Museum, this was a triumph of the antiquated being sympathetically combined with the modern, or maybe it was that I was half cut and just loving life with the eau de vivre.

Our sniggers at the statue of Cyrano de Bergerac with his sizeable proboscis confirmed that we were definitely 'merry' and photographs we took at the foot of the sculpture, when looked at later, showed broad grins and rosy cheeks prompted by vin rouge.

The nose of Cyrano really was something to behold and I wondered if he bothered drinking the famous wine from the region bearing his name or just inhaled it up his hooter as he checked out the aroma.

Social distancing and pandemic restrictions had minimised our options on places to eat, but we found a very cosy restaurant that served Argentinian food and we gorged on juicy steaks washed down with red wine chosen by Ken that he volunteered to pay for as it was the most expensive on the wine list.

We hadn't experienced the indigenous gastronomic delights of the area, but were more than satisfied with our choice and as Suzy and Ken had organised and chaperoned us through the grand tour, this was our shout and no arguments.

We headed out of Bergerac towards our next whistle stop to wet our whistles and climbed a hill heading towards Château Monbazillac perched on its summit. This had come highly recommended by Ken and Suzy as a highlight of the trip and looking at the château on our ascent, it was full of promise as a treat for the senses.

We arrived in the car park to see the entrance to the château had been barricaded with wire mesh fences. We walked up to see that you now had to pay a princely sum, just to walk around the grounds. 'This was free last time we came' Ken harrumphed and was clearly disappointed. The view from the rear of the château overlooked the vineyards that descended down the hillsides and was apparently spectacular, adding to the disappointment that we were being barred from free access to it. Others who weren't prepared to fork out an entrance fee, had found a car park just beneath the château and their camper vans were lined up there to drink in the stunning vista.

The tasting room had been moved from the château and into a supermarket style annexe near the front entrance. Boxes of wine had been stacked to create a snaking maze to the cash tills and the tasting room had been abandoned by anyone wishing to encourage us to purchase their vintage and therefore most expensive offering, by getting us royally hammered first.

The room did have access to an open-air balcony that overlooked the formal garden at the front of the picture-perfect château. I say this, because I took a picture and by my own estimation, it was indeed perfect.

We left empty handed and a tad disappointed, but forged ahead to the next destination, Château Corbiac.

This was a relatively small, but charming château with a tasting room and shop that, like Château de la Jaubertie, had racks and racks of wine lining the walls. Barrels were placed around the room as testing tables with the bar in the corner laden with tasting glasses waiting to welcome the fermented red grape juice into its depths, swirled around the tulip shaped confines and glugged from the narrow opening.

Or to sound less pretentious, slurped down sounding like a drain.

As a child, my parents called me 'The Drain' as I would walk around café tables after we'd finished our own order, draining all the dregs out of other people's teacups. To be honest, had we not been in such sophisticated company, I might well have done this with the remnants of wine in other people's glasses. That is known in today's parlance as minesweeping. I suppose that's when you pick up someone else's glass necking back the contents as if saying, this is mine.

More fine wines, more recognised rituals and more consensus on the most suitable one to grace our respective cellars. Our cellar was yet to be constructed, but that was just a minor oversight that was on the list of jobs to do.

We'd drunk a fair amount of and spent a fair amount on delicious red wine and with the boot full to overflowing, headed back to Périgord Vert, sharing some bonhomie as well as childish jokes.

The next we were to see of Ken and Suzy was to be on Suzy's birthday a week later and lunch with a selection of friends at a restaurant called Panivol and this time, Zak volunteered to be designated driver so Suzy and Ken could really let their hair down.

We picked them up from their delightful home about 3km away from us by car. We cleaned the car out as best we could, considering we'd been transporting building detritus back and forth to the déchetterie with any overflow from the trailer loaded into the back. Suzy had a lovely floral dress on and Zak and I looked at each other with dread when we saw Ken wearing white trousers. Oh dear, let's hope the muck doesn't transfer from the seams in the leather upholstery onto the material of his dazzling white strides. We both checked out his rear as he got out of the rear seat and there was some dust that had transferred from our seat to his.

'Go and smack him on the bum cheekily Zak to get it off and just give him a sly wink' I suggested, which met with a smirk and a stifled guffaw.

We'd made our orders in advance and realised why when we got to the farmhouse to see the fireplace being used as a cooker with the meat and vegetables bubbling on hotplates over the flames and pots of stew and vegetables simmering away under cast iron lids.

The smell was mouth-watering as we walked in and took our places around the table. There were faces we recognised and others that were new to us. Suzy and Ken were picking up the bill for all the booze and Ken was selecting the wine, which was always reassuring and it flowed like the River Dordogne itself. The rest of us were sharing the bill for the food.

Suzy got things started by opening the presents laid before her. She was delighted with the scarf Zak had bought her, which perfectly matched her dress. I think she'd picked it up during our shopping trip with Emma and her daughters and hadn't asked my opinion. Probably at that stage of the fashion frenzy, I had totally glazed over and gone into a self-imposed catatonic state for my own mental wellbeing.

All the dishes were ladled into ceramic pots and passed around the table for everyone to help themselves. There were some big lads around the table, including myself sitting between the more demure and dainty ladies, so it was every man and woman for themselves.

There was a real rustic flavour to the dishes and definitely to the presentation. I always find it amusing on shows like MasterChef, when they declare 'the presentation is a bit rustic' which translates to 'a heap of slop'.

Nobody was there for any fancy pants nouvelle cuisine and the food was devoured with gusto and the conversation was très jolie with the humour becoming more bawdy as the Bordeaux red took effect.

After desserts, we spilled out of the quaint farmhouse that was covered in ivy which was rapidly turning variegated shades of red brown and green and admired the view over the fields and filled our lungs with that heady mixture of autumnal fresh air and the alluring scent of dung heaps.

After dropping off Suzy and Ken and checking out his arse again, we were tempted in for more wine which had been bought during our wine tour, but Zak gave me that look that says 'only the one' as she was stone cold sober and there's nothing worse than listening to drunken drivel when you're as jober as a sudge.

We drove home as darkness descended and Cosmo was pleased to see our return. We had put his bed at the bottom of our bed and he had crept up the turret for some shut eye while we'd been away. He had turned fifteen while we'd been at the château and as he was still sprightly, we had to remind ourselves he was 105 in human years. Did he get a telegram from the queen's favourite corgi? Not a bit of it.

Le Terrace Terrible

Now the guests had dwindled down to a trickle, we decided to shut up shop for the winter and concentrate on making the terrace into something more befitting of a château.

The wooden decking was beginning to look tired and rotting in places. When it rained, it got slippery and we had to put out yellow triangles warning of potential accidents. Health and safety dictated we had such signs all around the château. Where was the one warning of demented hornet attacks I wondered.

I kept my epi-pens close by at all times after my experience, even though the hornet numbers had thinned down considerably as the autumn set in. The fig tree outside our bedroom window had grown out of all control since we'd bought the place and the hornets, or frelon, were drawn like a magnet to the ripening fruit.

They were plump, juicy and sweet I have to admit and Zak made a glorious fig infused cake out of them, which I buzzed around like an annoying insect.

We are pretty certain the fig tree was drawing the local hornet population and those from Asia and stray ones were getting into the bedroom, so we'd deal with that later.

As I'd been working my three-day week indoors, I was aware of the whirring of the cordless drill and the stacking of wood coming from outside. Zak had put the required bit on the end and was working her way through the hundreds of screws holding the planks down.

I remember that Johan had come around one morning with his dog Bella and she started scratching around wildly on the exposed surface underneath. She then started jumping about excitedly with what she had found, which was a discarded snakeskin. Zak had seen one slither away quickly once and this must have been residing, probably with a whole nest of family members in the cosy pied-à-terre the decking created.

I was glad they had been evicted as undesirable squatters.

The planks of wood started to stack up outside like you'd expect to see in a builder's yard and there were all sorts of sins to construction underneath that the wood had concealed.

Eventually from tapping on my keyboard, I was tapped up to remove the masses of wood to an out of the way place, which was next to the outbuilding which had previously been the outside loo.

We kept the wooden framework from underneath as intact as possible, as a plan had emerged where we would use the wood to rebuild a smokers' area with an awning so those hooked on nicotine could go outside in the pouring rain for a crafty ciggie without getting drenched.

Bart had taken well-earned vacancies in Spain with Jenny, thereby delegating me to be the tradesman of choice to construct this platform for the puffers.

Hauling all the half intact framework down the side staircase and along the path to its designated location in the rain, I looked like the lord himself dragging his own cross to Golgotha.

I thought it would be a job of an hour or two, but turned out to be an all-day job, levelling the ground, laying the framework and screwing the planks one by one with hundreds of screws.

The old planter was hauled into place and filled with soil to become a flowerbed, or more likely a place where butt ends would be discarded. It was filled with tulip bulbs and planted out with an azalea and about two dozen pansies. Some of the wood of the terrace was overhanging the edging of the granite stones, so a circular saw Zak had bought online was set to make its debut performance.

After a struggle to work out how it worked, it sparked into action and with a bit of muscle to push the blunt old saw through the wood, I managed to get through the twenty or so planks, managing to avoid Lulu the cat who had decided to roll about on the decking, right on the line the saw was inching along. As I said earlier, Loopy was a very apt moniker for this daredevil moggy. Perhaps she used to be part of a magician's act. We knew very little about her past and who knows what secrets lay in her history.

Soaked with rain, covered in mud, exhausted and hungry, my job here was done and Zak and I stood back to inspect and admire the craftsmanship involved. It was a bit wonky and makeshift, but once again to fall into line with the château's overall aesthetic, it was perfectly imperfect.

The bigger task was still to be undertaken and that would involve moving tons of melange, sand, stone slabs and mixed concrete.

We waited for Bart to return from Espana to really oversee this job. Zak wanted us to start it while Bart was away, having watched a YouTube tutorial on how to do it, but I wasn't keen, as this had to be perfectly level with drainage so it didn't become a slip hazard covered in puddles.

In the meantime, drama was unfolding back in the UK. Zak's beloved cat Teddy had developed a lump above his eye that the vet had diagnosed as a cancerous growth. Angus had been cat sitting with Teddy-Coco, who were known as a collective name like Brangelina and Kimye, although brothers, not lovers.

The vet had also said that it didn't look hopeful and knowing the costs involved suggested Teddy be put to sleep. Angus was doing his best to cope with the situation, but there was no way Zak was going to leave him to handle the situation alone, so booking an overnight ferry from Caen to Portsmouth, she planned to leave the following day. I waved her off trying not to make it difficult for her as she had a six-hour drive to the port ahead of her and she was returning under duress and in some distress. She later told me she cried the entire journey to Caen.

The paths by now had been re-laid with melange, wacker plated down and covered in new gravel that also got flattened down in an attempt to keep the weeds at bay. The only problem was keeping the pesky moles from digging through them, leaving their own version of the Himalayas in our formal garden.

I actually admired the tenacity of the moles that worked night and day to turn Versailles into a very informal garden. They served their purpose in cultivating the soil which eventually would produce more impressive blooms, juicier fruit and an abundance of vegetables and herbs. I even had a regular visitor to help me with lawn mowing and supplying fresh manure.

Folie was a female donkey from La Grange across the road who had free rein to wander around the area eating whatever took her fancy. Many was the time we would see her on our front path eating the sweet leaves of our bamboo like a ravenous panda. She also had a penchant for nettles and thankfully, I was no fan of either. The nettles seemed to be stronger than the ones in the UK, often numbing the stung area after a few screams of agony.

One time, I took a tumble into a large clump of them and had to race to the château to shower from head to toe. A dock leaf wouldn't have done the trick with a rub on all the painful, stung limbs, unless they too were stronger than those in the UK.

Folie didn't chew the heads off of flowers or interfere with rose bushes and low hanging fruit, so I didn't take exception when she clumped in without any regard to my privacy, even though we had recently put up red signs at every entrance saying 'Propriete privee defense d'entrer.'

They were there to serve as a reminder to nosy passers-by that strolling in for a look around wasn't acceptable, as we had experienced situations where we looked up to see strangers on the terrace and in our grounds as if we were a free for all tourist attraction.

We'd been informed they were totally in their right to do so unless the red signs were clearly displayed. This also applied to le chasse and their crazed dogs on the scent of an unfortunate deer, not that their dogs could read.

It was the owners to blame for their animals laissez faire attitude to cautionary signs and Folie's owner from The Grange did rush into my garden shouting 'pardon, pardon' flashing an apologetic smile and I didn't have the heart to say 'Attachez votre anes, s'il vous plait.'

Truth be told, I quite liked Folie and we had been informed she was thus-called as it translates as madness. No wonder I related to her on a cerebral level.

Meanwhile, Zak was keeping me abreast of her progress in

getting to Caen. At least she wasn't driving a tank this time and invading Paris. The journey was one we had done many times now and even though it involved six hours of driving, it was just a case of keeping yourself occupied and not getting flashed by speeding cameras.

After an overnight ferry crossing and the hour-long drive back to Richmond, Zak was back home and she joined Angus with Teddy at the vets. With all our animaux domestiques being much loved members of the family, Teddy received the VIP (very important pet) treatment.

No expense spared, he had all the tests done and received steroid injections. He hadn't been eating properly, but with his mum back nursing him, he rallied and was chowing down on tuna like the spoilt pet he was. I would often get onto FaceTime where he was laying on the bed with Zak under the covers, where she had cosied up as snug as a bug in a rug to spend quality time with Teddy.

As I shivered away in the dropping temperatures of rural Dordogneshire, I had to admit my envy at how warm and relaxed she looked. Teddy on the other hand didn't look his usual handsome self, but he seemed pretty chipper and his purring was testament that he was pleased his mummy was home.

Zak stayed there all week and I mean in bed. Teddy staged a remarkable recovery, so much so, Zak felt confident to jump back in the car and head back to the château.

Bart had returned from Espana and I, in my isolation, was pleased when things returned to normal again, to wake up each day with company, even though it usually involved having orders barked at me and meant doubling up on efforts to get stuff done.

Having started late in the season, I'd never had enough time to really hack back the overgrown garden. We had bought a brand-new chainsaw that had languished in the cave of wonders for some months and now was the ideal time to put it into action.

Bart had earlier in the summer ensured I'd put it together properly, with the chain facing the right direction and the right mixture of oil and petrol filling the tank.

I was filled with trepidation about using it, feeling sure I'd be removing an arm or leg as opposed to the limbs of any of our overgrown trees. Bart gave me a tutorial on how best to use it and I set to work on a tree that had fallen over the pond at the bottom of the garden and was too heavy to lift. Even the digger struggled to manoeuvre around it, so the next option was to go into lumberjack mode.

I equipped myself with a hard hat, goggles and noise cancelling ear defenders and Bart set the choke and pulled the starter motor chord to spark the chainsaw into life. The ear defenders were definitely needed from the high-pitched whining it produced.

Having shown me good technique, I took over sawing and it went through the trunk like a hot knife through butter. With the trunk now detached from the root system, the digger was able to pull the rest of the trunk clear and I was able to dissect it into several logs that could be used in our wood burner when dried out.

In the words of Spiderman's Uncle Ben, 'with great power, comes great responsibility' and I was aware the feeling of exhilaration I was experiencing could be dangerous if negligence crept in. I'd been sawing endlessly up until now and this felt so comfortably easy, I felt this uncontrollable desire to hack through every unwanted sapling and tree in the northern hemisphere.

Then the chain got trapped in a log I was tearing through, as gravity forced the gap to close in on the saw and jam it as the motor was running and kaput. The chain was, to use a technical term, fucked.

I tried to fix it, but in doing so, uncoiled the spring of the starter motor and ended up with bits and bobs all over the place when I tried to mend it. I am more lumbersome twat, than a lumberjack.

This was a job for someone with the right tools and a brain. I am often flabbergasted by what eludes me in a practical sense. Thankfully I found a course in life that afforded me a decent living without having to work with machinery.

I can string sentences together, but bolting, or screwing or assembling anything of use together in the real world, like pipes or wires or even flat-packs, renders me a gibbering wreck of a man.

Zak is far more practical than me and can wire up plugs, chandeliers and turn her hand to constructing things having watched a YouTube tutorial or often by trial and error. This requires me to be the hauler of large items and the tall bloke who can reach where her diminutive stature can't reach.

Both Bart and myself have christened her 'The Elf' as she stomps about in her wellies asking us to reach up to paint this or sand that or screw something in.

The chainsaw, however, was even beyond her capabilities and it was duly dispatched to Jon to see if he could mantle what I had dismantled.

In the meantime, I set about the garden with some heavy-duty cutters standing precariously on the top of stepladders to reach the uppermost branches.

With the fig tree, a saw was required to get through the larger boughs sprouting out in all directions and to be honest, it probably was for the best, as teetering on a ladder with a chainsaw would have been dangerous, if not suicidal knowing my luck.

While clambering up the branches like Tarzan without the loincloth, Loopy thought I was showing her my paternal cat qualities and followed my example. She got to several feet from the ground and sat there looking triumphant, seemingly grinning like the Cheshire cat in Alice in Wonderland at her achievement.

Loopy was far from slimline and would wolf her food down come her 4pm feed and we were hoping she was supplementing her diet with any unwanted guests who were dodging paying our B&B rates.

We also had a feral cat that seemed to get into the château via the cave and oft times would help itself to Loopy's food if she left any scraps. Scraps was the operative word here if the cat burglar was caught by Loopy wandering in under the cover of darkness and the ensuing commotion of a big fight would often wake us with a shock in the early hours.

I refused to get out from under the duvet to investigate as this cat arrangement was Zak's brainchild and she would go down the turret to see the damage. Fur was all over the place where they had locked claws and gnashed teeth and the feral cat was leaping like a gazelle at the kitchen door in an attempt to escape Zak's retribution from dragging her out of her cosy cocoon.

Zak has always been a cat person with her mum's adoration of Maggie May, a Burmese, Kubla a Siamese, Black, a big fat moggy who just walked into their life as a skinny stray and later on, Gypsy, a ginger and black cat with an attitude.

Claws hold no fear for her and her hands and arms were always a network of scratches from my recollections of knowing her since my late teens.

The more cats the merrier as far as she was concerned and another conscript to her army to repel the mouse hordes that were mounting daily sorties to enter our castle was always welcomed.

Feral cat was let out and henceforth encouraged to come in on an open invitation, even though Loopy seemed to come off second best in these feline fights, often cowering with eyes widening in terror whenever she sensed the interloper was on the premises.

Me, I've always been a dog person and me and Cosmo just left them to it, preferring to keep our heads down when there was trouble in paradise. He was happy to follow me out into the garden and find a shady spot as I manicured hedges and bushes and a huge laurel that cast far too much shade over the garden.

The resultant debris was all hauled down to the lower tier of the garden where we had built a fire pit to constrain the fire from getting out of hand when it had dried out long enough to be set ablaze.

Jon returned with the chainsaw all fixed and ready to fire up again. He refused payment, but Zak forced some bière money into his pocket and would hear no more of it.

Putting on all the proper protection of bright orange hardhat, ear protectors and goggles, I waded back into the garden and started pollarding and pruning with a vengeance.

Hitherto impenetrable thickets were thinned out to reclaim the view from the terrace. A row of hazel trees that had grown unchecked on the perimeter fence between the garden and Xavier's field were cut back to the stump.

Next time they grow back, I will be following the practise of intertwining them into hedgerows with the methods I've now learnt from Springwatch.

The thick branches were tossed into the fire pit along with the laurel. The excess built into a huge bonfire on top of the heaps of bamboo that had laid in the dried-up bottom lake all summer. What a blaze we were going to have when this was all tinder dry and highly flammable.

We topped the built pit with tarpaulin to keep the rain from dampening our excitement of the inferno we were going to ignite. This of course could wait for November 5th when, if the locals were nosy enough, we'd throw an effigy on the heap to freak them out with one of our favourite Anglo-Saxon rituals.

Zut alors, they are burning people. Let's not upset them again with our late-night partying.

With everything in the garden looking trimmed back and much smarter with the paths laid and grass cut, our attention turned to the upper terrace now cleared of the wooden decking and ready to receive the stone that had lay in waiting just outside the rear gate for weeks.

This had been Zak's latest focus of her OCD and Bart's ears had been virtually chewed off from her repeating time and again that this needed doing. Zak kept threatening to get me to do it on my own after she'd done her obligatory tutorial on line.

'It needs doing properly Zak,' Bart remonstrated, 'or you'll get puddles all over the terrace.'

Bart was the proud owner of a laser-measuring device that would ensure the slabs were laid level. We also had to ensure the shutters for the kitchen entrance and double doors into the living room could still close and there was a suitable gap for drainage beneath the steps.

From the violence of the storms that would unleash torrents of rain upon the terrace, we knew Bart was speaking sense.

His availability was limited at that particular time, as he had to go to Spain to help a friend going through bereavement.

We also were to receive news from the UK that demanded Zak's full attention. Perhaps Teddy the cat's remarkable recovery had instilled a false sense of security, but Angus had taken him back to the vet and the news was not good.

His tumour had worsened and the swelling above and behind his eye was causing him distress. This was not going to improve, even with steroid injections and once again, Zak decided that she needed to return as soon as she could. I wanted to go back with her, but she booked airline tickets immediately departing from Bordeaux.

I was going to drive her there and come back to the château, which was a four-hour round trip to be repeated on her return and this would push the limitations of the second lockdown that had been put into place by the French Government in the light of the increasing death toll nationally.

The police were coming down hard on anyone flouting the strict rules and on-the-spot fines were issued with impunity. I'd barely left the château for months with even an evening curfew starting at about 7pm.

Feeble excuses would not be tolerated with attestations required on your mobile phone to record your times of leaving home and reason for your journey.

Zak decided to book parking for her short term stay and this worked out far more economical in petrol money costs and the risks of hundreds of euros in potential fines.

She set off the following morning and once again, I watched her depart in the car without me on board.

My duties in her absence included feeding Loopy, Cosmo and feral cat, while moving the tonnage of slabs up to terrace level in readiness to be laid.

Beneath them would be a layer of melange, wacker plated down and then topped with soft sand. Daily routine was adhered to with Cosmo's walks through the forest, trying to avoid going via the road where I would be liable to be fined without doing a dog walk attestation. During one of these walks, Cosmo just stopped stock-still looking ahead in confusion. I assumed it was because he couldn't see with the rising sun shining in his eyes. He had cataracts, but this hadn't seemed to restrict his movements in the past.

I went back and put him on the lead to guide him along. A sighted guide human for a visually impaired dog.

Zak had successfully made the journey back to the UK and FaceTimed me to say that she had been with Teddy as he was put to sleep. I don't care what people say or think. Pets are members of the family and although we Brits are undoubtedly soppier about our four-legged friends than most, when they die, it is devastating. His twin brother is now an only child, although still answering to the collective name Teddy-Coco.

He is still with us as I write and calls out for his brother mournfully, looking for him in all the nooks and crannies of our Richmond flat.

His ashes are also tucked away in the flat, which Zak, still in mourning, hasn't been able to take to his designated scattering area.

Driven by her desire to see the terrace completed, Zak returned to the château within days of flying to Richmond to be by Teddy's side.

In that time, Cosmo's sudden faltering out on his walk had deteriorated into being very unsteady on his feet. I had to carry him up the turret stairs to put him into his bed.

By the time Zak arrived back, he was very wobbly and we weren't sure what was wrong with him. We thought it might just be a phase and he'd recover, but it worsened quite considerably so we decided to take him to the vet in Nontron.

I carried him into the waiting room and was invited into a room with the vet. He was laid out on a table and a blood sample was taken. The vet disappeared into the room with blood smeared between two slides. He reappeared seconds later and beckoned me in.

Looking through the telescopic viewfinder of his microscope, I could see the blood cells surrounded by wiggly entities that had penetrated the walls.

"These are parasites in his blood and his kidneys are failing" he explained.

The look on his face and body language was not painting a rosy picture. "We can treat this, but he is an old dog and there are no guarantees" he added.

There was no doubt in my mind that we would attempt the treatment, no matter how minuscule the chances of Cosmo coming through it. He had years left in him in my mind, as this set back had only happened over the space of days, before which he was in fine fettle.

We left him there overnight with tubes coming out of him as he lay in a cage with all the other dogs in there yapping away in their captivity. Poor old Cosmo. He was barely able to lift his head at this stage and it was heartbreaking to leave him alone for even one night.

We returned to the château and kept our minds occupied by forging ahead with laying the slabs for the terrace. Bart had done the preparation and now I was beginning to mix up the cement and wheelbarrow it through the château from the front garden. It was a meandering course through the chapel, going down boards, through doors and out through the living room double doors for Bart to lay and ensure all the combination of square and oblong slabs created the right pattern and were all on the level.

Bart wasn't hanging about with the laying, so I had to keep shovelling the sand and cement in the right ratio into the mixer and adding the right proportion of water, before doing the assault course through the chapel, kitchen and living room.

I returned to the mixing as Zak brought back the empty barrow to be replenished with the mix.

It was unrelenting and carried on all day long with short breaks in between. We were shattered emotionally and physically.

The following day, Zak went back to the vet as I carried on preparing for that day's onslaught. She returned with Cosmo in the back of the car and the news that the vet had said he wouldn't recover and to take him home to die. He wasn't in any pain, so we decided to let him live out the rest of his life with us.

The weather was unseasonably warm, so we let him lay in the sun as we completed the terrace. We kept him hydrated by bringing the water to his mouth and letting him lap out of our palms.

He slept at the château in the bedroom one last time and the following day he was out with us in the sun again.

We like to think he had one last day in the sun, but he was

twitching and fitting and it was very uncomfortable to watch. With no idea how much longer this would go on for, I took the soul-destroying decision to take him back to the vet and be humanely put to sleep.

We were given a time of 2pm the next day to take him to Nontron. This left us time to FaceTime all the kids so they could say their final goodbyes. I carried him around outside in floods of tears to show him the garden and surrounding fields one last time. As we reached the bottom terrace, his legs started moving frantically as though he was running. I had to put him on the ground to avoid dropping him. I like to think it was his last run in the garden before I scooped him up in my arms again and carried him to the car. I was inconsolable as we walked up the granite stairs, Tom and Yaz came onto a FaceTime call as I reached the birdbath circle and sat on the crescent shaped bench.

Everyone heaped their love onto this beautiful dog who'd been with us through our many ups and downs in life. Mackenzie also said her goodbyes, but we couldn't get through to Angus who was at work that afternoon.

We drove forlornly to the vet with Cosmo laying on his dog bed in the back. Parked up in their car park, we waited for the vet to be available. They asked if we were going to be taking him home with us and we confirmed we would be. The vet said she would carry out the procedure in the back of the car so he wouldn't be unnecessarily disturbed.

The vet was running behind time, which gave us the opportunity to FaceTime Angus after his work had finished. As he came through, Cosmo lifted his head, almost in recognition of his presence on hearing Angus's voice. It was a poignant moment and we left the call all feeling distraught about what was about to happen.

I never left Cosmo's side, stroking his head and speaking softly to him as the vet administered the first injection to sedate him. "You are such a loved dog, we will never forget you, you have always been a good boy" I repeated over and over with tears streaming down my face.

"He is asleep now" the vet assured me and I felt his little heart beating in his chest.

She administered the second injection, his heart ceased to beat any more and she pronounced "he has gone now. He is in doggy heaven".

He looked like he was asleep in his dog bed and we covered him in his favourite blanket and lowered the tailgate.

There was relief that he was no longer suffering, but that empty realisation he was gone forever.

We got home and had already decided where we were going to lay him to rest. We carried him down to the middle terrace. A distinctive sound from overhead drew my attention and the Grue that had migrated north in waves of v-formations were now heading back south for the winter. It was like a fly-past of honour and a reminder that we are all part of nature just doing its thing like it has done for billions of years.

In a corner of the garden, was the perfect place to lay Cosmo to rest, beneath the laurel tree I had pruned back and beside a stone wall with overhanging fir branches.

It overlooked the fields where he would run and frolic with his family and Whisky.

I got to work digging the grave and knowing how much wildlife would come into the garden, dug it as deep as I possibly could to deter them from exhuming him.

I was up to my shoulders in the hole when Zak declared it

would be deep enough and I clambered out just in case she felt like drawing a crossbow, finishing me off Richard the Lionheart style and shovelling the earth I'd dug over my twitching body.

The day was drawing to a close as we lifted Cosmo in his bed and lowered him in, still covered with his favourite blanket. Of course I knew this day would finally come as inevitably as night follows day, but nothing prepares you for the devastation of putting a beloved pet and all the memories they carry with them into a dark hole in the ground.

There was no ceremony, no hymns or prayers, just a ritual as old as time of committing a body to the soil and covering it up.

I have been to many funerals of family and friends through the years, even holding my father's hand as he passed away in an ICU ward in West Middlesex Hospital. My brother passed away so suddenly at an early age and I knew what was about to come.

Yes, this was a pet that had lived a full life, but I wasn't ready and prepared. I immediately started to descend into the familiar dark tunnel that is depression. Hello darkness my old foe.

The sun was setting as we lay a mound of granite stones on the site. Zak and I bowed to the king in deep reverence and then walked slowly back to the château in silence.

We had lost two of our life companions in the space of a week and we were to mourn in our own separate worlds of pain and suffering.

Teddy had been devoted to Zak sleeping on her chest every night. Cosmo had been a constant in my life as a running partner and was the reason I would get up early in the mornings to ensure both of us got our daily exercise.

It was to become a recurring comment of people asking "Are you going to get a new dog?" almost like a quick replacement would cure all ills.

It struck me that it is like saying to a divorcee, soon after the papers had been signed, "Are you going to get a new partner?"

I no doubt will be tempted by the allure of another puppy when my guard is lowered and the mental suffering has subsided, but for now, I'm still letting his loss settle on me, as Yaz suggested when I was clearly struggling.

The Big Clear Up

One of my biggest tasks was to clear out all the debris of the garden, the dried branches and leaves that were strewn all over the place. I dragged them in heaps down to the fire pit and loaded them in to be set ablaze.

Bart grabbed a canister of red diesel and doused the bonfire with the pungent smelling liquid. Petrol would just have caused an explosion, so this was less dangerous in the circumstances.

It took a while for the flames to get going, but once they did, it was as hot as an incinerator, turning the wood to ash in no time at all.

I was loading on branch after branch and heaping on the bamboo that had been drying for months on end and became highly flammable with the natural oils it contained.

The Prodigy's 'Firestarter' was on a loop in my brain and I was certainly feeling pretty twisted by that point, with my face grubby from ashes and a wild look in my eyes. Perhaps that was enhanced by my eyebrows being singed off by the inferno-like heat.

My eyebrows always turn a brittle hay-like texture after a long spell in the sun and resemble two shredded wheat sitting above my eye sockets. They went up as willingly as the bamboo canes.

The only problem was that the firepit was far too small to get through the tonnage of bamboo that had been pushed into the trough below that the pond had once occupied.

Feeling empowered by my arsonist exploits until now, I figured the fire wouldn't spread too far if lit in situ as the heaps of bamboo were contained within the granite banks away from overhanging branches.

Brandishing a large green container of paraffin that we used to fire up the heaters inside, I threw a few litres around with maniacal abandon and, with a hose run down the garden, in case it all got out of hand, lit the bamboo with something approaching devil may care insanity.

Boy, did it go up.

I had saved the igniting ceremony until the cover of darkness. I stood like an athlete who had just ignited the Olympic torch. The flames rose high into the night sky, illuminating the fields behind the perimeter fence.

It looked more like a scene from Apocalypse Now when the jet fighters laid waste to enemy territory by unleashing a payload of napalm into the jungle.

We never even considered a cremation for Cosmo, but there was something primal and ritualistic about watching the flames licking the blackness of the night sky. I stood transfixed by the mesmerising fire, its heat forcing me to eventually take steps backwards. I went inside and showed Zak the glow emanating from the bottom of the garden. We took pictures of me against the wall of flames that ended up looking like the front cover of an Andy McNab book called Operation Bamboo. I held up a cane to make my silhouette look like I was carrying a Kalashnikov, but I just looked like me carrying a bamboo cane. I'll avoid another Dick van Dyke reference here.

That fire roared through the night, blitzing much of the bamboo into a pile of smouldering ashes and to my relief, not creating a scene from A Game of Thrones where the dragon blitzed the defenceless King's Landing.

This had been a bonfire night in November that Guido Fawkes himself would have been proud of and thankfully, like his plot, it didn't succeed in creating unprecedented havoc.

What a shame the Channel 4 cameras hadn't been at Château Gros Puy to capture such a dramatic conclusion to our 2020 season.

It was to be another two months before we would be able to see what the editors had deemed suitable for their viewers and paranoia was creeping in about how ridiculous they would make us look.

Half way through the shooting schedule, we had been so inundated with guests from mainland Europe, the idea of using this as a tool for self-promotion had become obsolete.

We could barely cope with the demand as it was from online booking sites and Zak, especially, was running out of patience with having a camera in her face wherever she turned.

This of course had no bearing on Natalia, Ivy and Jack who were trying to do their jobs in as professional a manner as possible and just responding to orders from TrueNorth, the production company.

The storyline would be contrived by people we hadn't even met and whatever they gave the voice over artist Beverley Rudd to say about our journey during lockdown, making everything so much more unpredictable than anyone could ever have predicted.

Now that the terrace was finally nearing completion, we decided it was time to pack up and plan on heading back to Richmond. We had a cabin booked on Brittany Ferries and were utterly exhausted from mental as well as physical fatigue.

The weather had definitely turned and we were now

constantly frozen in the château, struggling to keep our extremities from being constantly numb. Another storm had rolled in taking down remaining autumnal leaves and dead branches and the wind was so fearsome, it had smashed out one of the windows in the turret.

The granite walls muted the sound of the gale force winds pummelling the outside of the château, but the shattering of glass and wood alerted us to the severity of what was hitting us from outside.

We went to inspect the damage and there was glass all over the stairwell and horizontal rain was penetrating our defences and soaking everything inside. A piece of wood was cut to shape and nailed into position as a makeshift replacement, but this just added another job to the to do list that never ends. Make frame and put a pane of glass in. A pain in the arse in other words.

It had been six months since I'd seen the motherland and I yearned to be back in our cosy little flat in the lead up to Christmas and find some form of festive spirit in my soul following the bereavement and ensuing mental strain.

Before we left, we decided to mark Cosmo's grave properly.

The following day after his burial, the sun, as promised by the spectacular sunset the evening before, was a proper shepherd's delight.

Using another piece of the oak remnant from the island in the kitchen, Zak sat outside with a workmate, chiselling Cosmo's name into a flat side of the wood.

The engraved letters were then painted white before coats of stain and varnish were added to protect the wood from the elements.

Perfectly imperfect in its simple crucifix configuration, it was embedded into the soil and heaped with granite stones at the head of the grave and once again, we bowed our heads as we stood back to admire Zak's handiwork.

We committed to salute every time we passed the site as a mark of respect to a loyal and noble beast who'd been loyal to the family for a decade and a half.

A chance happening lifted my spirits when the next-door neighbour's german shepherd puppy called Freya came for a quick sniff around in the garden. My eyes were diverted from whatever task I was in the middle of by a furry flash. Is it a dog, donkey or Dordogne sign dodger coming for a nose around. Realising it was the former, I called out her name in that high-pitched voice we reserve for animals in a stream of name repetitions. 'Freya' I bellowed in one breath making her ears prick up.

I descended down the granite staircase from the terrace and she came over, crouching down in that submissive way that let me know she was conceding superiority to me in the pack order. On giving her a rigorous rubbing, she leapt up at me enthusiastically as though extremely pleased to see me.

Zak was in the west garden, securing one of the white fences across the entrance from the chemin to ensure no animals could venture in to destroy our garden while we were absent.

Freya's timing couldn't have been better to prove that no matter the precautions taken, these beasts would go to Paul Newman-like lengths to leap the barricades to get in. Not that I'm suggesting Freya's Great Escape from our neighbour had involved her riding at full pelt on a motorbike. Hopefully the fencing is proving more effective against crazy donkeys.

Freya then headed directly to where Cosmo had been

buried as though paying her respects. I called Zak and she joined us there and took pictures as Freya sat by his graveside like a guardian statue.

I'm not sure why, but it lifted the cloak of depression for a brief moment and let some light in. In a Lion King way, it inspired a few verses of 'it's the circle of life, it's a wheel of fortune'. A vivacious young pup, full of life at the foot of the burial ground where an older dog rested, his journey through this life over.

Freya's owner came searching for her, realising she had escaped and I led her back by her collar, grateful that she had paid us a visit that particular morning.

Our only other outstanding piece of animaux business was what to do with the loopy cat we had fostered as resident pest controller.

She had over the months we'd been her custodians, worked her way into our affections.

After her triumph of getting up the fig tree to perch on a junction of two sawn off boughs, she felt brave enough to take on the much bigger fir tree that flanked the car park.

We hadn't seen her the evening before and were concerned for her wellbeing when she didn't rush in for her food, before feral cat wolfed it down. It was only as I was out in the garden tidying up the following day, that I was aware of a faint meowing floating on the breeze.

I was struggling to locate the source of the pitiful bleating.

I looked around and about, in the vicinity of where the sound emanated from, but not until I looked up into the tree, did I spot the big fat furball looking down on me like the Cheshire cat from Alice in Wonderland.

Standing at the foot of the tree urging her to jump, she was not in a suicidal mood and just stared back, challenging me to come and get her.

This was the clichéd fire brigade moment, but we didn't want to engage le Pompiers before attempting to coax her down ourselves.

A stepladder got us to touching distance, but she remained frustratingly out of grabbing distance.

We resorted to drastic measures and started to push her out of the tree with a large stick with the intention of catching her at the base. As a goalkeeper from previous years, I was confident in my ability to collect her in my arms, as long as I didn't then automatically attempt to kick her upfield for a breakaway attack.

Clinging on for dear life, we had no luck and if anything, drove her higher up the tree.

We started to use a long plank as a ramp for her to climb down, combined with a tempting bowl of cat food that we felt sure would tempt her back to solid ground. She had been up there overnight after all and would no doubt have been starving.

Even a passing couple were drawn to our attempts and they joined us, offering advice and guidance to no avail.

Even wearing gardening gloves and trying to get a handful of her scruff ended up with her sharp teeth being sunk through the material and breaking the skin of my hand to draw blood.

We left her to walk the plank on her own volition down to that alluring cat cuisine, but we overestimated her courage, her hunger and probably her self-survival instinct.

As dusk drew in, Zak decided to take matters into her own hands and taking no more nonsense, dragged her paws onto the ramp we'd erected, to save her from spending a second night up the tree.

We weren't sure how many lives she'd used up with her previous owner, but Zak had prevented her using one more of what remained from her allotted nine, without her showing any outward sign of gratitude.

'She didn't take my eyes out,' Zak observed, which was some consolation I suppose.

Loopy did pay us back in her own way. She had worked up the courage to enter our bedroom and sat on Zak's feet at night to warm up the two glacial icebergs that formed there before she went to bed.

As with all cats, she seemed to be sensitive to my suffering at the loss of Cosmo and took to resting on my chest, purring away like a mini generator, which did offer some comfort in my hours of need.

I would wake up to find myself nose-to-nose with her and knowing what those teeth and claws were capable of, didn't make any attempt to unseat her.

Zak took photos of the amusing scenario and sent them to her owner, who professed how much she missed her feline companion with her quirky ways.

Zak arranged a meet up for us to hand Lulu back to her rightful owner in the UK and a cat container roomy enough for her to be transported during the drive and overnight ferry journey to the UK was bought in preparation.

I could tell Zak was itching to keep hold of her and take her back to Richmond, but I felt sure Coco would turn all territorial and fur would fly if we attempted to relocate her to our flat.

'Shall we…?' 'No.' 'Can we…?' 'No,' was a perpetual question that I didn't allow Zak to finish with my negative answer.

The day before departure arrived, we went into a flurry of

activity to put duvets and sheets into mouse resistant boxes and tidy away all garden equipment back into the cave.

I used the opportunity to use up all the excess sand and stones piled in heaps outside to build a solid pathway up to the front double door. It was a hard task to finish in a single day, but I worked until darkness fell to get it completed, wacker plated down and a path transpired that could be trodden without running the gauntlet of slippery stones, dodgy dips and dangerous divots. It was the final act of the play that had been a comedy, drama, tragedy and thriller, all wrapped up into one six-month singular saga.

The pandemic has turned 2020 into a year that many will always want to forget. Many will have lost loved ones and had their personal freedom limited. Restrictions on movement and accessing loved ones and friends will be the abiding memory for the majority.

For me and Zak it had been very eventful, but we had at least spent the majority of it in the blissful heat and inherent beauty of the Dordogne. We would be returning to a third lockdown in the UK and the prospect of ten days of self-isolation.

That was fine by me, I thought. I'll spend all of that time in a warm bed resting my weary bones and thawing out.

It was December 11th when Zak got a surprise call from Lulu's mum. She had been trying to find a new owner in France without success, but at the eleventh hour on the eleventh day of the twelfth month, somebody had come forward and was willing to take her.

This was a man living just an hour away from us and he would be with us the following morning before we departed to take Lulu off our hands. I had mixed emotions about seeing her go. Losing three animals in such short succession was a hard pill to swallow, but at least she was going to a new home and not off to meet her maker.

Departure Day dawned and we rose to the tasks left we still had to complete.

Bart turned up with his usual promptness to receive his final orders from Madame Chatelaine. The obligatory coffee was brewed and ready and we quaffed the final cupfuls around the worktop.

After overcoming another navigational drama, a man called Cliff arrived to trudge down my new path and came in for a briefing over a cuppa on what to expect from his new housemate.

Bart gave his honest assessment of what he'd encountered with this strange beast. Lulu was magnetically drawn to him when he turned up, but when he attempted to pet her for any length of time, she'd strike out like a viper, sinking her fangs into his hand.

'Ooh you little bastard' was how he'd retort to receiving such an unwarranted response to his gesture of peace.

We at one stage were considering asking him to take her in, but that put the kibosh on that as a viable possibility.

Zak gave her interpretation of how best to treat this fickle feline who would need delicate handling if you wished to be welcomed into her circle of trust.

After what sounded like a final hissy fit as she was bundled unceremoniously into her cat carrier by Zak, we bid her au revoir with a final stroke and away she went.

Cliff seemed a genuinely nice guy and he was the owner of a farmhouse, which was ideal territory for Lulu to scavenge around, just as long as the trees weren't too tall and she had an abundance of vermin to devour.

It made sense for Loopy to stay in a rural idyll and not cooped up in an urban apartment, so we were happy she'd found a new home from home, from home and no more tears were shed as she disappeared up the road.

With her disappearing over the horizon and Bart receiving a verbal checklist of things to complete over the colder months, we locked all doors and closed the shutters.

It just didn't feel right to be returning without Cosmo and one last visit to his graveside did prompt Zak to further tears as she apologised for leaving him behind. "Don't start me off again" I begged her, stifling my own sobs from starting yet again.

"He'll be here when we get back. You keep guard, Cosmo"was my final command to my faithful hound before we headed for the car and the open road.

Returning to the UK

I decided to drive Zak bonkers by singing Chris Rea's 'Driving Home for Christmas' on repeat for hours on end.

Contrary to the theme of that song, I was feeling anything but festive.

After a false start where we'd travelled 8kms before Zak did her usual "damn, I've forgotten something" often involving a U turn at the nearest opportunity, we retraced our route back to Gros Puy to pick up her iPad, so she could watch a movie on the ferry crossing or read her current book.

"One day, she'll be able to read all about this very journey" I mused to myself and by the time you read this, she will have done so to correct all my mistakes and take out all the inappropriate gags that are either a) not funny or b) too rude and crass to go to print.

We had at least factored in enough wriggle room to account for any such oversights.

This was one ferry we didn't want to miss due to an error in reading the time or getting caught out by some unforeseen road incident.

In the height of the season, we'd been reduced to a crawl for hours by a roadside fire, attended by le Pompiers blocking the carriageway.

Big cities like Poitiers always proved challenging where roads merged and the traffic intensified.

Breaks have to be taken for full bladders and empty

stomachs and we've even had to stop for forty winks with seats reclined and naps taken.

We have received a fair amount of speeding fines down the years and now stick diligently to the speed restrictions. 130kph in fair weather and 110kph in foul.

Zak has this quaint habit of driving on cruise control, using the paddles beside the steering and putting her feet on the floor. This always puts me ill at ease when we are approaching slowing cars and she is lowering speed without the use of the brake pedal.

ZAAAAAAAAAAAAAAKKKKK!

"What?" she'll reply just inches from the bumper of the vehicle in front.

"Nothing" I'll say with my heart in my mouth not wishing to be seen questioning her driving ability.

I've learnt to hold my tongue now even in the face of what I consider a life endangering situation. I'll be going over a cliff one day wishing I'd said something beforehand, but just pleased I'm plunging to my doom without upsetting Zak in the process.

Today, with lockdown still in force, the roads were relatively empty and we made good progress towards Caen.

Service stations or Aires as they are called in France were all shut, so we'd made our own sandwiches, coffee and stashed choc-bars and sweets to chomp on in transit.

On one petrol stop, we were able to sample some machine café, which, had it come from a barista, would have been cause to employ a barrister to prove calling it coffee was an infringement of the trades description act.

I started telling Zak what time it was and looking at the ETA on the sat nav, announcing how many hours and minutes were left.

"Please shut up, I don't want to know" came the charming riposte to this talking clock service I was providing free of charge.

"Why don't you practice mindfulness" she suggested. "Look at the trees and the sky and the birds" she added.

I did so and averted my eyes from being magnetically drawn to the ETA. Maybe I'll crack out another verse of 'Driving Home for Christmas' to amuse myself and infuriate Zak.

Zak had invested in an automated tollgate gadget that lifted the barriers so you don't have to stop and use a card or coins. It beeped as we approached and meant we could glide through without pausing, although slowing down was something Zak would have to observe in case the barrier decided to take its own precious time.

We joined the queue in Caen with time to spare and Zak put the iPad on the dashboard so we could watch some downloaded film while chomping through whatever was left from our tuck box.

Security were walking up and down with sniffer dogs, shining torches through our windows to see if any refugees had managed to scramble into our back seats while we weren't watching, but none were in evidence this time.

Other security guards were opening the backs of trailers and studying the undersides of vehicles with higher ground clearance, by laying on their backs and beaming torchlight into any hidden cavities.

After what seemed an age, we were beckoned on board and headed for our designated cabins while social distancing and wearing our masks. No visit to the bar this time for a nightcap or to listen to the warbling's of a wannabe cruise entertainer.

We bunked down, covered ourselves with a sheet and looked forward to that delightfully incessant music to wake us from our slumber in the early hours.

England here we come. Lockdown, here we come. Isolation here we come and pared back Christmas here we come. The clunking of the engines and the rattling of the metal cell we were detained in, lulled us to sleep. A departure from France to a radical departure from what we had left on June 22nd at home.

Look, We're on the Telly

Christmas came and went.

Mackenzie came and stayed.

She'd undergone the necessary tests to be deemed able to travel and headed home from university.

We'd been visited by the police to ensure we'd adhered to the 10 days of isolation and received random calls to ensure we were compliant.

Angus and Zak were able to return to work with Angus doing shifts at M&S, which, because it offered food, was able to stay open unlike many other high street retailers.

Zak returned after months on furlough to her roles at Sky and the BBC, with news and sport ploughing on regardless with the ever reliable, or unreliable, Mr Trump keeping the autocue turning with his antics and Premier League football carrying on regardless to get through the backlog of the season's fixtures.

We'd managed a quite jolly Christmas Day with the family and Tom and Yaz on a Zoom call, with presents being opened amongst the decorations and piles of nicely wrapped packages bundled under our bejewelled and bedazzling Christmas tree.

Champers and bagels with smoked salmon and cream cheese was a tradition we kept going and a roast joint of beef with all the trimmings was being prepared for later on in the day.

Tom and Yaz had been to Richmond earlier in the week where a doorstep handover of gifts took place in masks with appropriate social distancing observed. The traditional snowballs were passed around going heavy on the Advocaat ratio to lemonade and a huge box Zak had wrapped for their present, only just about fitted in the convertible VW with the convertible roof folded down.

Yaz has always been a huge fan of Christmas Day morning, racing into our bedroom and leaping on the bed with her boundless enthusiasm.

Even now in her thirties it is a ritual she continues, the last time being when she used our bed as a trampoline, breaking the wooden struts that supported the mattress.

Going one after the other, we were unwrapping bottles of booze, items of clothes, lotions and potions, perfumes and aftershaves and books and jewellery. Yaz tore into the big box and discovered two gold painted candleholders, which were in the shapes of palm trees.

Yaz and Tom were planning on moving out of their London flat to a house in Whitstable and these were to be the first of many objet d'art that would no doubt be filling their new residence in a style they both loved.

Of course, Whisky the Cavapoo wasn't neglected, receiving a replacement pig for the one he'd chewed to pieces given to him at a picnic we'd had in Victoria Park earlier in the year. This pig is repulsive with a horrible grunt. The first one scared Whisky half to death, but now as a bigger pup, he attacked it without fear of the hideous hog.

The living room was a tip afterwards, so we tidied up and headed to Richmond Park for our traditional stroll and to wear off breakfast in time for the feast to come. I was pleased to see Zak had left her Day-Glo gilet at home this time to spare us all her misplaced delusions of authority in answering fellow amblers' questions about deer and giving directions.

We returned in time for the Queen's speech, praising the indomitable spirit of us Brits in what had been a collective annus horribilis.

We then devoured the Christmas dinner in a stripped back way within our bubble of me, Zak, Mackenzie and Angus, pulled crackers and told the painful jokes contained within.

We had planned to spend Christmas at the château at some point and in years to come, we will all be gathering in the chapel next to a roaring log fire for Christmas dinner and telling crap jokes in French.

I awoke feeling a bit hungover on Boxing Day, which always takes me back to the day sixteen years previously, where I chose not to run along the beach in Sri Lanka due to a pounding headache. We always remember the many who died that day in the Tsunami and I pulled on my running gear and headed to the park for a brisk five or six miles to ruminate over the trauma we had experienced in 2004.

The endorphins always help me find some equilibrium in my brain and the feelgood afterglow lasts well into the day ahead.

It was nice to be back in Richmond and the days ahead were relaxing and unfussy. But something wasn't right with me. I couldn't sleep from the dark thoughts that were haunting my every hour. I knew from experience what was to come if I didn't deal with this with some urgency.

I had a phone consultation with the doctor explaining my symptoms, detailing the morbid thoughts triggered by bereavement. I'd been dealing with depression drug free for several years now, but this was the time for antidepressants to help me through.

Once upon a time, the stigma of mental health issues led people to suffer in silence, feeling ashamed to admit to a weakness.

Recognition of the conditions and treatments are now commonplace in the workplace and beyond. The multiple challenges thrown up by lockdown have seen cases spiking to pandemic levels in its own right.

Knowing that it takes two weeks for the depleted serotonin levels to balance out and return me to feeling normal, even when dealing with a new normal, I was keen to start taking them immediately.

The doctor was hugely understanding and compassionate and sent a prescription of 50mg of Sertraline to the local chemist for me to pick up that day.

I'm happy to say that I am now feeling much more optimistic about the future going forwards and mixing up my treatment with continued running and a steady stream of incoming work.

I hope by sharing what some might consider personal issues, fellow sufferers might feel empowered to seek help and not feel they are alone in the world. Previously I had written another book called 'Saint Antony, Self-Proclaimed Saint of Mental Wellbeing'. It offers a light-hearted look into the many aspects of mental health, even though it is a subject I take very seriously. Through all the travails life has thrown my way, maintaining a keen sense of humour has always helped me through the darkest times.

I also needed to build up some fortitude for viewing 'A New Life in The Sun' which was looming on the horizon with our appearance scheduled for January thirteenth.

How would they portray us? What parts of the bits they'd

filmed will make the edit? How fat will we look? How stupid will we sound? Will the château look good? Will the guests say nice things about us? These and many more paranoid thoughts would prey on our minds until our segments were aired.

We would be watching from behind the sofa from 4pm–5pm.

A New Life in the Sun Premieres

We received notification from the production company about when we'd be on. They pre-warned us that they had no control about what people may post on social media, but were there if we needed support.

In the lead up to the first episode, they started putting out Facebook posts about the upcoming series. On the first post there was a snippet of Zak and Mackenzie outside our Richmond flat looking at the staircase pole on top of the car, as Mackenzie says "You haven't thought this through have you?"to which Zak replies with a concerned expression "No". They then cut to me loading the middle stanchion pole for the spiral staircase onto the roof to make the BMW look like a tank.

It was ten seconds at most, but it was our first glimpse of what was to come.

I shared this trailer on Facebook to my friends and had a lot of replies that they'd set their boxes to record and would be watching avidly. I questioned my wisdom of doing this, knowing that the sort of friends I've got would make fun of me mercilessly, but I could take it on the chin from people I know.

As the trailers continued, one showed me and Zak loading the steps for the spiral staircase into the trailer and as I do so, Zak says "Take four steps back" to which I reply, "I thought you were talking about social distancing" followed by us both laughing.

Two more were spliced together, one with me outside the

château with the digger behind me saying "Will there ever be a time where I can relax now? I don't think so" in a jocular but resigned sounding way and another one in the same location with me bleating on saying "The ongoing mantra here at the château is lots to do, lots to do" as I roll my hand like a hamster wheel towards the camera.

We had been watching other intrepid Brits, as they called us on the programme, going through their trials and tribulations in setting up their businesses abroad. They had people in Portugal and Italy to add to their roster this year, having only concentrated on France and Spain in previous series'.

We were a bit shocked by the footage standards, with everyone looking a vibrant shade of red and the places they were renovating looking somewhat bleak. This wasn't painting the romantic picture we thought they'd be going for. In fact in these first few programmes they were concentrating mainly on the difficulties involved and representing their participants as being hapless.

Oh dear, we were beginning to dread how we'd be perceived in our first episodes.

Yaz sent us a picture of me and Zak announcing that evening's episode on the Radio Times website. It wasn't the worst picture I'd ever see of us and at least we were smiling. This same picture was to be on our catch-up recordings and also on the Channel 4 website.

I'm afraid to say that curiosity got the better of me and I started looking at the comments posted on the Facebook fan site and also on Twitter.

There seemed to be a community of trolls who took the opportunity to slate everybody on the programme, obviously feeling we were fair game as we'd volunteered to be on the programme.

Some of the things they were saying were highly personal and vile, but Mackenzie found them hilarious and decided to start commenting back.

On the day of first airing, Zak was at work, but asked me to text how things were going. She was able to see the programme where she was working, but not have the sound up.

Our episodes were to last over three days and it started off with us at the château. I was waxing lyrical about nature, open skies and tranquillity, which I couldn't remember and Zak was talking about the challenges ahead and observations about what we had bought.

Mackenzie was with us at this stage and they showed us taking a picnic hamper down to the larger lake and sitting at the picnic table on the landing stage drinking Aperol Spritz. Once again I was prattling on about what a difference it made from working in London being crammed onto a tube train compared to all this open space where you could hear nothing but the sound of birdsong, while Zak uncorked another bottle of Prosecco with a pop, prompting me to say "and the opening of bottles", to which we drunkenly laughed. Cosmo was splashing around in the lake and this was the first time I'd seen him since his passing, a loud "ahhhhhh, there he is" greeted his first appearance.

These were the early days in late June and the place looked a bit of a mess and the garden was beginning to look parched from the heat. They made a big drama about small things like Cosmo putting his paw prints in wet cement. I wish we hadn't covered them over now and left them there as a memorial to our beautiful dog.

They followed us around the château with us pointing out

plans for the decor and things to do. We had erected a day bed in the garden, inspired by a visit to Club 55 in San Tropez, which obviously fascinated the editor as it got a fair chunk of attention as we put up the muslin curtains around it.

Beverly Rudd was chipping in with her scripted observations and overall, it wasn't too bad. The outdoor filming of me and Zak in direct sunlight was shown, but what we were saying set up the modus operandi that Zak was the guv'nor and I did exactly what she told me.

At this stage, the dripping sweat and dark patches under the armpits hadn't managed to creep through too much, but that was something to look forward to in subsequent episodes.

From our first days at the château, they retrospectively went back to Richmond to show us loading the trailer for the long journey ahead. I was walking up and down stairs with the heavy cast iron steps and spindles while Zak directed operations from the back of the trailer.

At one stage, Zak said to Mackenzie, do you want to give your dad a hand, to which she answered "no". They both laughed as Zak pointed out "Poor old Tone is exhausted and today is Father's Day."

The saga of what to do with the pole was played out with us figuring out that it would be best for the mattress to be strapped over the top of the pole to prevent it from bouncing about. Concerns about how far it protruded over the bonnet were discussed and some more amusement about how tank-like the car looked. We were giving the trolls a field day, but we all seemed happy enough and were being self-deprecating enough not to be seen as taking ourselves too seriously.

Mackenzie helped by throwing sheets and pillow covers from the top window to the pathway some 40 feet below, which landed with a thud, narrowly missing my head. A removals technique, which saved her the journey up three flights of stairs. Zak, stating the bleeding obvious said, "Don't throw anything fragile."

We then cut back to us arriving at the château as if on the first day. It was in fact several days later with us hastily recreating the scene for the sake of the cameras. The steps and the pole were then offloaded and transported down to the garden and stacked against a wall.

Overall, we thought we'd got off lightly from being set up to fall flat on our faces and I texted Zak my relief at how we'd come across.

Mackenzie meanwhile was replying to a guy who'd commented on Twitter, 'Tony and Zak look a bit gash'. Neither Zak nor I knew what gash meant, but we were pretty certain it wasn't complimentary. 'Prick,' was Mackenzie's retort, a one-word response that made me burst out laughing.

"Aren't you getting any responses from your friends about this programme, Kenz?" I asked. "Oh no, they won't be watching a programme like this," she proclaimed and I felt daft for asking, knowing this sort of daytime show would be watched by people without better things to do than watch daytime viewing on Channel 4.

Well those and every person I'd informed that I knew on Facebook.

Messages were coming through thick and fast from people on text, messenger and WhatsApp being very kind with their feedback. Of course the tank got a fair few remarks, but it was funny as we watched it back from a viewer's perspective.

Zak got home that evening and we sat down and dissected our starring roles again. "I look terrible", "I look like I've got sunstroke", "why did I wear that?" and other criticisms were hurled at the television, but we breathed a sigh of relief about our debuts.

As some scenes we thought certain to be included had obviously hit the edit suite floor, we speculated what would be shown next.

Bart was dreading the mirror scene being shown as it had gone wrong due to Zak's measuring error and he didn't want to be seen as the perpetrator of such a glaring oversight.

Bart phoned from France as soon as the first episode was over saying 'that wasn't so bad', but he'd only played a cameo performance, not getting a speaking part on day one, but he knew it was just a brief reprieve for him.

Fast forward to 4pm the following day and we hoped we wouldn't get too much flak for our dodgy DIY.

We were to be disappointed, as we struggled with the heavy piece of glass we'd salvaged from the loft and looked like a comedy trio in a sitcom attempting to secure it to the wall.

I of course brought up my dear wife's measurement shortcomings, saying "I don't want to say Zak's measurements are out, but they're OUT".

Bart took command of the situation and overcame the problems by moving one side of the frame and repositioning it. A few whirs of his automatic screwdriver and we got the job done.

With a few additions of copper pots hanging from an attached pole, Zak stood back and admired her masterpiece saying "It's gorgeous. It's my idea of beauty." Perhaps my distressed appearance and rough around the edges demeanour was what first attracted Zak to me way back when.

Next up, the day after the flooding debacle, which was still being dealt with as more guests were arriving. I was seen running around pointing out where the hot water had flooded through the ceiling and light fittings. Bart had sorted Louis to drop everything and come to fix the problem.

The water was turned off, but as he removed the offending junction that had succumbed under heavy water pressure, the remaining water in the pipes flowed down the walls.

Meanwhile, Zak was welcoming our overnight guests at the door and as she showed them to their room, asked Louis to pipe down for a bit as she explained the situation.

Everything was in hand and being handled, but it suited the programmes format to make it seem like all hell was breaking loose. Our guests were unperturbed by the goings on and stood on the terrace heaping praise on where they'd chosen to stay.

This episode was definitely shining us in a less favourable light, but who wants to watch everything going smoothly? A bit of jeopardy with a few cliff hangers thrown in made for much more dramatic viewing.

We moved on to Zak's practice run for her cream tea offering, the day after I'd been hospitalised overnight following the anaphylactic shock caused by the hornet sting.

"Today Zak is having a practice run with her afternoon tea," our Bev chimed in as Zak assembled the food on the plates that looked delicious. "Tony is in bed following a bad reaction to a hornet sting" was all she added to explain my absence in offering Zak any help.

Perhaps the story of a near death experience and anaphylactic shock didn't suit their storyline. It just made me sound like I was skiving off. Trolls agreed with some choice comments. 'Tony is in bed following a bad reaction to 12 pints' and 'Tony is in bed following a bad reaction to doing any work.'

Admittedly, I did find those witticisms quite amusing.

I felt let down though, as I did put in an appearance and went on camera explaining the situation and Ivy, the camera person was very aware how touch and go it had been.

But we'd signed away any editorial control and we had to accept how they chose to portray us.

Zak was even more distressed as she had specifically asked to not be shot from behind and she was very unhappy with certain angles they showed of her in the dress she's chosen to wear.

'Tone, why didn't you tell me I looked terrible in that dress,' she demanded to know. Two reasons. One, I was in bed laid low by a hornet, possibly from Asia, and two, that would be an act akin to committing suicide.

The afternoon tea was a success with the pronunciation of scones being a hot topic of discussion followed by Zak being interviewed in the aftermath of the event.

As I said earlier, she had spent a night in a hospital car park and was clearly exhausted. No sympathy there from anyone as they pushed the camera in her face and demanded she answer their list of questions, like she was being interrogated at Guantanamo.

The only consolation was that the château was looking great and that was the idea of being on the show.

Mackenzie was still sticking up for her parents from the abuse on social media, but her sister Yaz told her to stop it, as from her PR experience, any attempt to defend yourself in these situations just provokes trolls to up the ante.

It is enough to know most of these comments were borne out of a deep dissatisfaction in their own lives and most probably, jealousy.

The next and final episode usually gave the participants a chance to comment on how the season had gone for them. But before that, there were a few loose ends to cover off.

We had two wonderful families arriving from Paris who were attending a nearby wedding. They were precisely the kind of guests we were trying to attract. They treated it like their home from home and loved the lived-in atmosphere of the place.

The summer was rolling to a close and the weather turned colder day-by-day. The weekend was sunnier for the wedding and that is always a blessing as it allowed us to set up the breakfast tables on the terrace. Shawls and sweaters were required to keep off the chill, but they really appreciated the breakfast and the views as they recovered from the wedding the night before.

Their positivity on camera reflected the majority of the guests who'd stayed with us and the same went for the groups that turned up after hearing great things about Zak's afternoon tea. A local group of ladies had chosen to try it out for themselves and were shown to the table under the shade in the back garden.

I was hurrying to finish off the pointing of the steps leading up to the turret door and as I worked the wet cement into the gaps, Loopy chose that moment to trot through without a single thought for my craftsmanship.

"Thank you for this" I commented as she slunk past without a by-your-leave.

The ladies turned up and took their places at the table. I can't remember saying what was on camera, but I promised them I'd do my best not to show any builder's bum as I finished the job.

Having reprimanded Lulu for traipsing over my handiwork, Zak chose the quickest route to the table that I really should have taped off with a 'route barrée' sign and she walked straight through the wet cement.

"Why didn't you come down the other way?" I asked what I thought was a perfectly reasonable question. "Too many stairs" came what I thought was a totally unreasonable answer.

Some interviews with the attendees followed with everything receiving glowing reports and a friendly au revoir as we waved everyone off through the chapel doors.

One of our busiest times of the entire season was captured with several other guests passing through and Zak putting out a breakfast that looked absolutely mouth-watering.

We had learnt an awful lot in a short period being at the sharp end of the hospitality industry and were beginning to take everything in our stride. We almost looked like we knew what we were doing.

To bookend the season, they decided to show the construction of the spiral staircase. Hilariously, they inferred it was my job to build the iron stairway with all its intricate parts and I brought in 'my' builders to help.

In reality, Bart had just called me over to give him and Harry a hand as it was a three-man job and I pitched in.

We didn't complete the job, but put it together with enough sturdiness for Zak to walk down from top to bottom commenting on how wobbly she felt. This was an open invitation for me and Bart to suggest it was because she'd obviously been to the pub.

On the way to her maiden descent down the stairwell, Zak gave a glowing reference to the time and effort Bart had dedicated to getting us to the stage we were in renovations.

"He's a diamond this one" she enthused. "We wouldn't have got anywhere near as much done without him" she concluded, with Bart looking suitably humble and a quick shot of me nodding my agreement.

She spoke for us both.

They had chosen a few more soundbites from our initial interview and sweat was visibly dripping from us and my armpits had two patches that were virtually joining in the middle of my chest. It was more like an advert I might have written for Sure anti-perspirant pour homme et pour femme.

All that was left to do was for me and Zak to sit down, this time in relative cool, to surmise how the season had gone.

Jack had been the cameraman for this part and we both felt relaxed in his company. How well we'd done in setting up a thriving business under testing circumstances made us look far more competent than we'd looked in earlier episodes.

My armpits looked positively arid in my faded denim shirt and Zak was looking très glamorous in a silken shawl.

No more moaning, no excuses and complaining about things, just bright and bubbly about how things had panned out in setting up our B&B and the beautiful ambiance of the château.

That was it for us and to be honest, we were relieved it was over.

It was filmed pre-Cosmo's and Teddy's demise, which saved us both dissolving into tears and we requested that they put a RIP Cosmo at the end of the show.

This didn't happen, but they had saved a beautiful shot of him standing in the garden, which is how we wish to remember him.

The Long Goodbye

Teddy's ashes were delivered from the vet and Zak still hasn't been able to face scattering them at this time of writing.

The start of this story was at the beginning of the first lockdown and here we are, a year later still in lockdown and the prospects of us being able to return to Gros Puy looking slim in the new future.

Of course that doesn't stop us progressing with plans with Zak cutting and painting the stained-glass window to be put into place in the turret.

It features Richard the Lionheart with a St George's cross on his tunic and broadsword in his right hand.

Zak has been back on the Lots Road Auction site and there are now a host of winged angels dotted around the flat made from plaster and daubed with random patches of gold leaf.

One is kneeling on one knee praying, another is holding a shallow vessel to its chest and another is cupping a bird in its hands. To give you some idea of the quality I am talking about, the bird looks like a fat penguin which in proportion, is bigger than the angel's head.

The sculptor has captured serene expressions on their faces, but with a whimsical smile that suggests they aren't taking their job too seriously. Certainly not holier-than-thou, which suits the all-pervasive atmosphere at the château.

Bart has been busy finishing off the spiral staircase and laying the final stones of the terrace and Johan has been briefed on putting a skim on the walls of the living room so new panelling can be affixed above and below the dado rail.

We have to be wary of how much we take over, as the new Brexit duties will apply, so large items like spiral staircases and pianos might not be joining us on our next trip. Who knows what new adventures and challenges lay in wait for us in the next chapters in history for our thirteenth century castle?

Now, as March approaches, we have had a suitably long period of rest and with daffodils beginning to raise their dainty yellow heads and croci breaking the soil and opening up their colourful array of petals, plans are afoot to return to the château.

Bart is back on-site putting uplighters into the terrace and spotlights to light the turret and giving us live updates on weather, which is beginning to move up into the teen degrees.

The countdown to unlocking lockdown has been announced in stages and we are feeling the call of Gros Puy tempting us back.

The prospect of hot sun on the face and back, the lure of big skies and ample space with that ever enticing thought of a velvety Bordeaux red slipping down the throat is making our feet itch.

Summer holidays are being booked and the idea of guests holds less fear for us now that we have found our stride. What wonderful wandering spirits will ring on the Titanic bell in 2021. Who will return to say bonjour again?

Aches and pains that we brought back with us have abated and a second wind for continued physical exertion has kicked in to ready us for the onslaught of further renovations.

Already, Zak is hatching more plans for projects both large and small. I'm not sure whether Bart is dreading or looking forward to her dulcet tones entering his ears.

French must be brushed up on. Shorts and t-shirts have to come out of mothballs, along with summer dresses. I do look good in a summer dress, it has to be said.

Feet will be exposed once again in sandals and flip flops, so a pumice stone might be scrubbing at that hard skin that has formed into calluses on toes and nails trimmed back from looking like claws.

Those tans that make the skin glow will be replenished to replace the pasty complexions that have turned us a whiter shade of pale this winter. I say this, even though Zak has been cheating with fake tan coverings that make her look like she's spent months in the Caribbean.

It really is no replacement for the real thing and the full dose of vitamin D it impregnates your body with.

High factor sun creams and after sun will fill an entire bag to see us through to that brown hue that in me is a shade of pine and in Zak, with her Asian heritage, more like Mahogany.

Those wonderful memories mustn't make us overlook the less pleasant ones like mosquito bites and dare I mention wasps and hornets. Repellents and relief sprays must also be bought.

Who knows what critters will await to welcome us back in through the door. A procession of mice forming an arch at the door. A fly-past of bats dropping guano onto us like confetti. A Mexican wave performed by snakes and a thousand ants formed into an impressive pyramid to greet us.

There will be the inevitable piles of dead cluster flies and spider webs to sweep and clear. The dust to hoover up and rooms to air by opening up the windows and shutters and taking a deep inhalation of clean country air.

Neighbours will pop in, gossip caught up on, the long winter months raked over with tales of woe and suffering.

Neglected friendships will be resurrected and gatherings put into diaries.

Fridges and bars will be stocked for the ensuing revelries that are sure to commence once the pandemic has been banished to the annals of history.

Family and passing friends driving south will drop in for a few days and catch up on their news and recollections from the past.

Finances will be studied to see whether we can afford to expand, introducing yurts or bell tents for glampers and land cleared to make way for them.

The outbuilding will be made into a shower room and have outside sinks for washing up and self-catering.

Day trips to the unexplored places and events will extend our knowledge of nearby attractions with lengthy lunches, picnics and dinners arranged.

The sights, the sounds, the aromas, tastes and touches are all beckoning us back with the multi-sensory temptations.

We will gather as a family around the site of Cosmo's burial mound and celebrate his life in a booze-fuelled ceremony where hopefully Zak won't vomit where he lays.

Will we be able to take the unsightly render off the facade and re-point the exterior?

Will Zak befriend the feral cat or will a new Loopy be discovered?

Will we complete the outside columns with laurel hedges planted in between?

Will Zak demand that mini Versailles begin to look more like the real Versailles?

Will the golden oriole land before me as an apparition of a shining golden oracle, its song translating into the ancient wisdom defining the meaning of life?

There's so much to ponder and prepare for, the head starts to spin in anticipation.

I enter my sixth decade on this planet this year and time seems shorter than ever to bring the château up to the standards we are aiming for in my lifetime.

Will I eventually decide that this is to be my forever home and move over lock stock and barrel to become a French citizen in my retirement?

Will I be buried there with my trusty lawnmower like Yaz predicted?

I don't know all the answers yet.

All I can assure you is it will be another unpredictable and hopefully exciting chapter in our lives and no doubt the sequel to Château Shenanigans with all the ups and downs will keep you informed of all these tantalising developments.

Until then, bonne chance, à bientôt et bonne santé.